LET EXPERIENCE AND EXPERTISE SHOW YOU HOW TO—

—Understand for whom you are writing and how that affects your writing

—Choose the appropriate form for your communication

—Control the tone of your communication to make it as persuasive, stern, informal or solicitous as you want

—Organize your report to make your main points immediately clear and accessible, so that the associate who pores over the details of your report and the boss who skims your conclusion for recommendations come away with the same message

At once a practical instruction book and an essential reference work, *Writing on the Job* covers every aspect of the writing process to insure your successful performance in business or government communication.

WRITING ON THE JOB

A Handbook for Business and Government

JOHN SCHELL and JOHN STRATTON are professors of English at the University of Arkansas at Little Rock. Both have taught extensively in the university's renowned writing program. John Stratton is co-author of *The Writer's Hotline Handbook* (Mentor).

WRITING ON THE JOB

A Handbook for
Business and Government

John Schell and John Stratton

A PLUME BOOK

NEW AMERICAN LIBRARY

NEW YORK AND SCARBOROUGH, ONTARIO

NAL BOOKS ARE AVAILABLE AT QUANTITY DISCOUNTS
WHEN USED TO PROMOTE PRODUCTS OR SERVICES.
FOR INFORMATION PLEASE WRITE TO PREMIUM MARKETING DIVISION,
NEW AMERICAN LIBRARY, 1633 BROADWAY,
NEW YORK, NEW YORK 10019.

PLUME TRADEMARK REG. U.S. PAT. OFF. AND FOREIGN COUNTRIES
REG. TRADEMARK—MARCA REGISTRADA
HECHO EN WESTFORD, MASS., U.S.A.

SIGNET, SIGNET CLASSIC, MENTOR, PLUME, MERIDIAN
and NAL BOOKS are published *in the United States* by
New American Library, 1633 Broadway, New York, New York, 10019
in Canada by The New American Library of Canada Limited,
81 Mack Avenue, Scarborough, Ontario M1L 1M8

Library of Congress Cataloging in Publication Data
Schell, John.
    Writing on the job.
    Bibliography: p. 395
    Includes index.
    1. Business report writing. 2. Commercial correspondence.
3. Memorandums. I. Stratton, John, 1944– . II. Title.
HF5719.S33   1984   808'.066651   83-24423
ISBN 0-452-25531-7 (pbk.)

First Printing, May, 1984

2 3 4 5 6 7 8 9

PRINTED IN THE UNITED STATES OF AMERICA

Not love, hate, passion, or fear
is stronger than one writer's need
to change another writer's copy.

—MIKE NIEDERQUELL

Acknowledgments

Thank you to the individuals and companies that allowed us to use their writing:

Petersen Publishers for the *'TEEN* magazine subscription renewal letter.

The Foundation Center for the sample entries from *The Foundation Directory,* 9th ed. (New York: The Foundation Center, 1983). Copyright by the publisher.

Carole Nolte for the report on flextime.

CompuSoft® Publishing for the page from David A. Lien, *Epson, MX Printer Manual, Graftrax PLUS* (San Diego, CompuSoft® Publishing, 1982). Copyright by the publisher.

John Chamberlin of Arkansas Systems, Inc., for the press release.

Thanks to the people who responded to our informal survey about writing on the job; many of whom supplied us with helpful materials: Vikki Axiaq, Marilyn Baldwin, Suzann Welty Barr, John Chamberlin, John Coffin, David Cole, Joel Garrison, David Goike, Gayle Jenkins, Jerry McRorie, Thomas J. Miller, Michael Niederquell, Susan O'Sullivan, Mark Reinhardt, Nancy Simpson-Banker, Jo Ann Talbert, H. Bradley Walker, Monna Wier, and Virginia Williams.

Thanks to Randal Owen for researching bibliographical questions.

Thank you to Joe Esposito and Dan Frank of New American Library for counsel, advice, and appropriate goading, and Arnold Dolin of New American Library for originally suggesting this project. Thank you to Bill Reynolds for a fine copy editing job.

Finally, thanks to Dotty, for reading copy in the late-night hours and putting up with things, and thanks to Catherine and Elaine— the Stratton kids—for letting Dad monopolize the computer.

Contents

Part Three: The Writer's Self-Help

You Can Write!

This is a book with a message: You can write.

You can write that report or letter, that proposal, grant, or press release you've been putting off. Not only can you write it, you can write it well.

Are you afraid of the next assignment or promotion because it may involve more writing? You can become a person others turn to for writing help.

How?

Writing on the Job shows you how to pay attention to your writing in specific ways.

It helps you understand

—whom you are really writing for and how that affects your writing.

—the many kinds of writing used on the job.

—the specifics of on-the-job writing so that you can always work like a pro.

—rewriting and editing so that your writing will be clear and effective while keeping the tone *you* want.

Writing on the Job is not elementary. It deals with the realities of today. It deals with the practical things that make a difference to writers and to readers.

Skim through the first two chapters; then look over some of your past writing. Immediately you will begin to see what went wrong and what was right, why one project was more successful than another.

Then keep this book where you can get to it quickly. When you begin a writing task, read the relevant section to help you understand how to tackle the problem.

Read the section again as you finish your first draft so that you can correct problems as they develop.

As you finish, read about style in Unit VIII. Consult the Bibliography. Find out how to get help and information so you can be correct. Find out how to control the tone of your writing.

Writing may never be easy for you, but you will know that you can do the job.

Let *Writing on the Job* help you do the best work you can. Good luck!

WRITING ON THE JOB

A Handbook for
Business and Government

PART ONE

The Theory

UNIT I

Writing in Organizations

1

You and Your Organization

THE GOALS, STRUCTURE, and nature of an organization influence the content, arrangement, and style of the writing. To write effectively you need to consider the organization, your audience, your role: in short, the writing context.

The Influence of the Organization

Whether they are large or small, private or public, profit-making or nonprofit, organizations have goals, hierarchy, politics, and an existence of their own.

Organizational Goals

All organizations have goals. These may be as diverse as making money or inspiring patriotic fervor, and they include developing markets, influencing legislation, setting policy, performing services, and proselytizing for a belief. Goals channel the activity of every organization and provide an identifiable and specific context for business and government writing. You don't write because you feel like it or because you want to; the goals of the organization require you to write.

As an organizational writer, you must differentiate between your own goals and those of your group. You may want higher wages, more power, or a different job. But writing on the job, you must reflect the organization's goals, not yours. In writing to a buyer, for instance, it is not in the interests of the organization to make yourself look good at the organization's expense: "Everything is falling apart here, but I'll make sure you get what you need on time." An organization won't (and can't) permit that attitude for long.

Organizational Hierarchy

All organizations, no matter how democratic, have organizational charts, decision-making flow sheets, and chains of command. What you write gets passed up, down, or across the organization with many different people reading it.

The hierarchy determines your audience. No matter what the destination of your writing is, your immediate supervisor will probably transmit it—and will most probably look it over before it leaves your office. Seldom will anything go directly from you up the chain of command, even if the subject of your writing is of no interest to your boss.

The structure of organizations leads to multiple audiences for at least two reasons. First, decision making is often multilevel. One group makes a decision which gets reviewed by that group's superiors—and on up the chain of command. This process allows shared responsibility for decisions.

Second, the entire organization needs to be kept informed. This leads to circulating writing FYI, For Your Information. Writing helps the hierarchy maintain itself through sharing responsibility and information.

Organizational Politics

A third influence on organizational writing is office politics. If you are a member of an organization where office politics doesn't exist, you are one of a lucky few (or you are naive), and you needn't be concerned about this aspect of organizations. If your organization is factional, you already know more about office politics than we want to discuss. Here are just a few reminders.

Politics may influence to whom, what, and how you write. For instance, office politics dictates that everything you produce be transmitted by superiors. They want to make sure you aren't undercutting their position. Office politics is partly to blame for multiple-level decision making because no one wants to bear complete responsibility for a mistake.

Organizations promote from within, making competition among employees keen. To protect yourself from misunderstandings, misinterpretations, or outright deceit, you may want to write memos and letters to clarify your position on important issues. Here is an example. As a state employee, you have been criticized by the governor's office for forcing a major political contributor to comply with employment security regulations. The director of your agency is in an uncomfortable position. A memo to your director pointing out the illegality of failing to enforce existing laws will clarify your position and bolster the position of the director with the governor's staff.

Finally, a considerable amount of organizational writing gets done to CYA: Cover Your Rear! The example above illustrates CYA as well as any. Before your director decides to make you the scapegoat for the governor's anger, put in writing the legal requirements for your actions. Both you and your director are aware of the importance of written records to a review panel or a court of law.

Organizational Life

Your organization probably existed before you joined it and will continue to exist long after you leave. While you may help to mold its growth, the organization is not you nor, for that matter, any one individual. IBM doesn't fold when the president or the messenger quits.

Organizations have lives of their own, and considerable energy goes into ensuring the health of that life. Your writing, every piece of it—including semiprivate correspondence on letterhead stationery—adds to or detracts from your organization's health or image. You are expected to foster goodwill for the organization and not indulge your own interests. For example, you might feel better if you wrote a rude letter to a client who has disregarded your previous four letters. Writing such a letter might be good for your mental health, but it wouldn't promote the interests of your organization in any way.

To sustain the health of an organization, group and individual achievements are shared. Newsletters, brochures, company papers, and corporate magazines increase internal communication and reduce in-house jealousies and squabbles.

The ongoing life of an organization emphasizes your job slot at the expense of your personal identity. When you write within the organization, people look to see what job slot the writing comes from—president of sales, business manager, administrative assistant to the chief clerk, or teller. The personal name on the writing becomes less important the further the writing travels in the organization and the older the writing becomes.

The continuation of organizations also encourages writing for the record, for the files, for an unknown historical audience. Because no one knows what information might be important in the future, many actions—important or not—are written up for the record. When employees are no longer around to answer questions, their files speak for them.

Audiences

In organizational writing, your task is to make things happen, to effect change, to influence thoughts and actions of others. Consequently, your audience helps to determine the content and arrangement of your writing. For instance, in writing a company memo to a friend, you could perhaps be flippant. But humor might be inappropriate to a supervisor, a wider audience, or in a letter to be filed for future reference.

The audience influences the structure of your writing. If a report is to go no further than your colleagues, you won't need a lengthy introduction, executive summary, glossary of terms, or technical appendices. Only include the information essential to your audience.

Audiences, Not Audience

The hierarchy, the chain of approval, and the need to keep everyone in the organization informed lead to multiple audiences for most business and government writing. If you remember that organizational writing usually has more than one audience, you may save yourself a lot of trouble.

Writers sometimes leave important facts out of their reports—the previous year's sales, the previous month's sales, and this month's projected sales figures—because they know the boss has that information. But they fail to think about where the report is headed. The company's owner doesn't have this detailed knowledge. And the owner must be fully informed to make correct decisions.

Analyzing your audiences is crucial. Before you begin to write, you should 1) identify your audiences and 2) define them.

Some of the analysis that follows may seem familiar to you, since every writer who thinks at all about a project considers the audience. But some of it may be new. The less you have written on the job or the less you have thought about audiences, the longer your audience analysis will take—at first. Remember, however, that analysis is not an end in itself although it is crucial to effective writing.

Audience Identification

There are several ways to determine all the people you may be writing for.

Traditional Identification. Traditional audience identification uses an organization's flow chart to discover who reads a piece of writing. The writer traces the writing up, down, or across the organization.

Using the flow chart to identify audiences has several defects:

1. *The flow-chart model assumes that all organizations have neat lines of authority.* They don't. The actual lines of authority may differ greatly from the theoretical flow chart, and the course a piece of writing follows may differ even more.

For example, a major law firm has over forty lawyers and a considerable staff. Four senior partners head the firm. Only one of those four is active in the firm, and he has retired from all decision making, leaving that responsibility to a younger associate. She, in turn, designates her office manager to review all office work before it comes to her desk. The office manager controls the movement of all in-house paper, yet he doesn't appear on any formal flow chart of the organization.

2. *Organizational charts make everyone on one level look equal.* The associate who has been designated to make all final decisions in the law firm has no more authority on paper than her twenty-four fellow associates. Even if all twenty-four were equal in decision-making matters, they still wouldn't have equal knowledge, training, or interest in every subject.

3. *Organizational charts are limited to the organization.* This model doesn't help identify audiences outside the organization. Yet much of your writing may be going beyond your own group.

Levels of Knowledge. Another key to help you identify your audiences is to think about how much knowledge people have about your project.

1. *People who are familiar with your project are easy to spot.* They probably include your supervisor, other members of your team or committee, people at work on a similar project, and people who know your project but are in a different department (for instance, someone in budgeting who doesn't know the intricacies of your work but has been kept up to date because of money considerations).

2. *A second group* doesn't know what you are writing about but wants to or has to know. These interested people will normally be decision-makers in your department or parallel ones: managers, administrators, executives, partners, owners. Writers who target their writing only to their supervisors frequently neglect this important group.

3. *The final audience knows nothing about your assignment.* This group consists of people inside and outside the organization who learn of the work through your writing. This group also includes the historical audience: people who in years to come may go to the records and read what you have written.

Egocentric Organization Chart. A more effective aid to identifying your audiences has been designed by Dwight Stevenson and J. C. Mathis (*Designing Technical Reports,* Bobbs-Merrill, 1976). Instead of locating the audiences on a flow chart or having the writer guess at some level of knowledge, Stevenson and Mathis recommend a model they call the "egocentric organization chart." This model positions you at the center of the writing act. From this position you identify where your writing actually goes and who really sees it. In doing this you will find several audiences that fan out from you. You may not write to each of these audiences every time, but they exist.

1. *Handlers.* We usually think of this group first when we write on the job. It consists of supervisors and other people of authority who pass our work along after first checking to make sure it is acceptable. (After all, your work reflects on them as well as on you.) This audience also includes people in the hierarchy who must sign off on a piece of writing for it to advance. Before the vice-president of sales gets to see your idea for a new promotional campaign, an assistant screens it to make sure it merits attention. Handlers may block something from going forward, but they seldom make positive decisions themselves.

2. *Decision-Makers.* These people have the power to act on the information you provide. They can put your recommendation into effect, okay your request, buy your idea or product, or promote you to vice-president. They may be inside or outside the organization. A sales promotion idea—to let customers vote on their favorite flavor of the month—gets the nod from the vice-president for sales. A proposal to supply the government with 250,000 highway signs gets approved by the undersecretary of transportation. Decision-makers need to be sold. They want clear and concise information—enough of it to make good decisions but not so much that you take up more of their time than necessary.

3. *Doers.* These people must carry out your proposal after it leaves the hands of the decision-makers. The vice-president decides your ice cream flavor promotion is good, but the ad department writes the copy, and the district managers supervise the contest. These people need specifics and details; they are less interested in the overall picture.

4. *Affected Parties.* These are the people affected by the project

that your writing initiates. This audience varies greatly depending on your subject. In the case of the flavor campaign, this audience could include several groups: another department in the home office (Budgeting must plan the cost of your promotion, Research must come up with a new flavor, and Public Relations must write press releases), other units in your organization (individual stores must find room for the displays and perhaps hire more cashiers, the manufacturing unit must produce the new flavor), or even suppliers and consumers.

5. *Historical Audience.* Almost all organizational writing ends up in someone's filing cabinet sooner or later. There it will probably remain undisturbed forever. But there is always the chance that years later, someone may remember your successful "Flavor of the Month" campaign and want information about it.

Audience Definition

Having identified your potential audiences, you'll want to define the basic characteristics of each so that you can understand their influence upon your writing and write more effectively. Try to figure out what each audience likes and dislikes, what prejudices they hold, how smart they are, how educated, how interested in the subject, how trusting of you. If you define your audiences carefully, you can determine what each needs to know, what style is appropriate, and how persuasive you must be.

For example, a disparaging remark about Social Security in a letter to retirees will probably defeat whatever purpose you have in mind. Or after you define the educational background of the decision-makers, you may discover that this group needs a style free of technical terms or in-house jargon. However, the handlers, concerned with the propriety of the writing, may be sensitive to grammatical correctness and punctuation.

Each audience you identified should next be defined according to their objective, personal, and situational characteristics.

Objective. Define each of your audiences as fully as you are able according to objective, demographic qualities. Is the audience predominantly male, female, old, young, black, white, Southern, Californian, Baptist, Moslem, Indian, German? Beware of stereotyping, but an allusion to a rock group is probably not appropriate for an older audience while an allusion to the Depression will probably mean little to young people. Objective qualities are those that your audience has little or no control over, but which may be very important to the reception of your writing.

Personal. Define each of your audiences by the personal choices it has made. Are members of your audiences educated? Do they have large families or small? enjoy sports or prefer fine arts? live luxuriously or simply? drink or abstain? Such matters of choice say much about a person's likes and dislikes. If you consider them, they will influence both what you write and how you say it. A good way to discover personal preferences is to find out what sorts of clubs or societies the members of an audience join—country clubs, church groups, social or community organizations.

Situational. Define the attitudes of your audiences toward your subject. Are your readers naturally interested in what you are writing about or must you spark their concern? Are they knowledgeable or must you define your terms and fully develop your thoughts? Are they predisposed to favor what you are writing about or do they tend to disapprove of your task? Are they enthusiastic? Can they help you? Your answers to these questions will help you determine how to organize your writing, what to include, and how to say it.

Individuals and Groups

When analyzing your audiences, you may want to identify individuals in each category and define them precisely by name, perhaps even making up a little chart. You know that your proposal will go from your supervisor to the vice-president of sales. If it is approved, you and the vice-president's assistant will work together with Mary Lee in budgeting, Bill in promotion, and Susan in personnel.

Sometimes, however, it may be convenient to think in terms of groups of people: the bookkeeping department or the sales team. The same sorts of questions pertain whether you are analyzing individuals or groups. With groups, you will be more general in your definitions.

You the Writer

Once you have identified and defined your audiences, you should try to understand how they see you—and how you see yourself. Before you begin to write, you must understand your position in the organization and your role in the project.

You and the Organization

When writing for an organization, what counts is the role you play in the organization. Since you as a person are less important than your organizational role—especially as your writing travels away from you in time and space—you should know the image your job title conveys.

The public expects the president of a large corporation to write more formally than a salesperson. We assume the vice-principal of a high school uses tough talk (sometimes the Vice-President of the United States does). The manager can be aggressive, but the floor-walker had better be temperate. In short, your job title carries with it expectations and responsibilities that you must consider.

How Others See You

Study the objective and personal qualities that other people see in you just as you studied those of your various audiences. Consider your sex, age, race, nationality, and religion compared to your audiences. Consider your education level, your personality type, your prejudices and likes. What sort of person do others see when they look at you?

In addition to how readers see you personally, ask yourself how they think about you in relation to your subject. Are you seen as an expert in the field? Or are you writing about something outside your area of competence? If you are an expert in the field, you will get by with less documentation.

How You See Yourself

How you see yourself is as important as how others see you. First, be honest with yourself and recognize why you are writing. If your writing is self-interested—to protect yourself, justify your actions, or even conduct reprisals—admit that to yourself. For example, if you want to make sure that a flawed design does not become your sole responsibility, your report should clearly indicate who else worked on the design. However, if you hide from yourself the real intent of your report, you may hide it from your readers too.

In addition to thinking about your own motivations, analyze your attitude toward your subject. If you lack confidence, stop writing; otherwise a diffident or qualified tone may creep in and undermine your presentation, no matter how strong your position. If you can't avoid writing even though you lack confidence, admit your doubts and try to create a confident attitude. Or are you overconfident and too aggressive? That attitude can make your writing sound overbearing and arrogant.

If you are not enthusiastic about your subject, don't pretend you are. Chances are you will sound insincere. If you are not an expert, don't pretend to be one. If you do and get caught, you will be embarrassed.

If you're not sure about your facts, check them out. When your name is on the writing, you are responsible for the content. If you include material whose accuracy you can't vouch for, say so. Similarly, if you present an interpretation, make clear the presence of opinion.

Be straightforward with yourself and as honest as possible with your reader. If you're sure of who you are, your tone will be relaxed and appropriate. If you're sure of your audience, you will be able to address them effectively. If you're sure of your material, the content will be easier to select and arrange.

You and Style

Although your personality may be irrelevant to your writing task, don't be bland. Create a pleasant voice in correspondence, an authoritative voice in proposals, a concerned voice in sales promotions, and a committed voice in position papers. Manipulate style for its effect without going beyond the boundaries of accepted business and government conventions. Be correct, but don't let correctness get in the way of effectiveness. (Unit VIII discusses such issues.)

Context

Before you begin to write, you should fully understand the context of your writing. Too often we assume we know why we are writing something, fail to think it through, and end up with the wrong content, arrangement, or style. Or we don't consider the context at all and end up with a hodgepodge of discussions and tones.

For example, a consumer advocacy group recently wrote to a state legislature asking for reform of certain laws. In the appeal the group got sidetracked, commenting at length about the existing laws and the fools who had made them. Those fools, of course, were some of the same legislators this group was lobbying. In their zeal, the consumer group forgot the context of their writing.

Causes

When trying to understand your writing context, consider what has goaded you to write. Ask yourself these questions:

1. *Am I responding to some other writing or verbal communication?* If so, be sure you know what that communication is and refer to it in your own writing. That communication will provide the

context for your writing. It might also help you to define your audience.

2. *Am I responding to a need of the organization?* If so, you should be able to identify the need clearly and precisely: the need for more customers, the need for clearer regulations, the need for a new waste disposal system.

3. *Am I responding to a personal need?* There is nothing wrong with wanting to be promoted, for instance, but don't confuse your personal goals with those of the organization.

Summary

Before you begin to write, consider:
1. the influence of the organization,
2. the identity and definition of your audiences,
3. how you see yourself and how others see you,
4. the context of your writing.

If you take the time to analyze your writing situation, you decrease the chances of a prejudicial statement, an inappropriate tone, or a superfluous discussion. Each part of the writing task—the content, the arrangement, and the style—is influenced by these circumstances.

2

Arranging Information

ONE IDEA INFLUENCES the arrangement of most organizational writing: Time is money. The less time a person must spend to get your message, the better your writing. The shape of business and government writing depends upon particulars of this idea:

1. *Different audiences need different amounts of information.* Some people won't need to read what you have written; the sooner they learn this, the happier they are. Others will need only enough information to know how to file your writing. Still others will need the general scope of your thought, and a few members of your audience will need all the details. Much of the effort that goes into organizational prose goes into addressing the different needs of these audiences.

2. *Readers are more likely to read the beginning than the middle of a piece of writing.* Titles, headings, captions—single words that stand alone on a page or underlined phrases—will get read first. The first sentence of a paragraph is more likely to be read than the following sentences. The concluding part of a piece of writing will get more attention than the middle.

3. *Readers do not resent judicious repetition.* Repetition reminds readers of important information and helps their understanding.

These observations lead to three important arranging devices: purpose statements, subject sentences, and formatting devices. Each summarizes and quickly communicates information, helping your audience spend as little time as necessary with your writing.

Purpose Statements

Most ineffective organizational writing can be helped immediately by the addition of a purpose statement to introduce what follows. There are times when you don't want to begin with a purpose statement: in form reports, in government proposals that must follow a specified structure, and in some persuasive writing, which is best begun more subtly than with a purpose statement. But these are the exceptions. The rule is to start all writing with a purpose statement unless there is a good reason not to.

Even if you don't include the purpose statement at the beginning of your writing, you should write one anyway.

Three Uses of a Purpose Statement

1. *A purpose statement immediately establishes your subject or problem, the purpose of the writing, and your conclusions.* It helps readers quickly determine if they must read further. Many times all a reader needs to know is your conclusion or recommendation; a purpose statement includes it at the very beginning.

2. *A purpose statement helps* you *to identify and define the subject, purpose, and scope of your writing task.* If you start to write before you know what you are writing about, you will not be able to put together a good purpose statement.

3. *A purpose statement helps you to decide what to include in your writing.* All of us find it easy to stray from our subject, to let one idea lead to another slightly off the subject, which leads to another that is totally off the mark. A good purpose statement keeps you from breaking the unity of your writing. All you have to do is refer back to it to judge what is or isn't appropriate.

The Four Parts of a Purpose Statement

A purpose statement introduces your subject and the writing that follows. For instance, a letter that notifies a supplier of several faulty components would begin with the four parts of a purpose statement:

1. *The subject or problem of the writing:* "On May 3, 1983, you shipped us fourteen component parts to convert our Model 3 viewer to a viewer and enlarger."

2. *The task that the writer had to perform:* "Francis Perkins, who ordered the components, asked me to supervise their unpacking and installation."

3. *The purpose (and scope) of the coming writing:* "The following report details those parts I found to be defective." (Note that this is the purpose of the report that follows, not the purpose of your task.)

4. *The conclusions (recommendations) that the writing reaches:* "We need these components immediately replaced."

Length

A purpose statement may be a sentence or two, or it may be three or four paragraphs. Keep in mind that a purpose statement is not a summary of the coming writing; it is a brief statement of subject, task, purpose, and conclusion.

Examples

Here is an ineffective purpose statement; it neither describes fully the purpose of the report nor offers any conclusion or recommendation:

> The General Accounting Office (GAO) recently initiated a significant program to identify cost overruns in the Department of Defense. Identifying cost overruns quickly and accurately will allow the GAO to take steps to ensure the legitimacy of such added expense. I was asked by the Director of GAO Budgeting to investigate the success of this new program. Following is my report.

A better purpose statement would include an overview of the report and mention the writer's conclusions.

The following purpose statement has a different problem: its author has not fully thought through the reason for the report; the purpose statement reflects this uncertainty.

> On March 3, I sent a memo to Mary Fredericks giving her the details about the promotional materials for the bicentennial celebration. I stressed that these materials were limited, poorly prepared, and purchased from an unreliable vendor. I suggested that unless we developed our own promo materials, we would not have the sort of bicentennial celebration the state expects.
>
> On March 25, I was given authority to prepare our own promotional materials.
>
> To this date, I have worked closely with David Barr of the State Planning Commission and Cindy Lee of PR to work out the snags in the promo package, its production, and its late distribution. The purpose of this report is to provide information about this project.

The report that follows continues this rambling self-justification. What exactly is the problem? What is the report supposed to present? This purpose statement doesn't say.

In fact, the problem was simple: to create a brochure and a video spot advertisement. The purpose of the report was to detail the progress and budget of these two projects. If the writer had written an effective purpose statement, the statement would have focused and narrowed the subsequent report.

Here is an effective purpose statement, succinct but complete:

> Thank you for submitting examples of your writing for my inspection. I have looked at these samples carefully and diagnosed several weaknesses. In the following report I call to your attention five major problems you have with organization and style. Finally, I suggest you contact Randall Cook for individual, in-depth help with your writing.

Subject Sentences

Subject sentences (or topic sentences) are great tools, clearly introducing the major divisions of your writing. A subject sentence allows readers to determine quickly if they want to (or have to) read further in a section or paragraph. If a section isn't important to them, they can skip it.

Subject sentences turn complex arguments into several single statements, one for each part of the argument. These single statements are more easily handled than the longer prose ideas. By looking at eight or ten subject sentences on a sheet, you can get a better idea of how to arrange them logically.

Subject sentences help you stick to the topic. If information doesn't relate to the subject sentence, don't include it in that section.

Subject sentences permit you to see parallel structures between sections. If one subject sentence says the section will present the need for and price of a brochure, it is easy to see that the next section might follow the same pattern—for example, discussing the need for and a price of a video spot advertisement.

Example

Subject or topic sentences act somewhat like minipurpose statements. Figures 2-1 and 2-2 illustrate the usefulness of subject

---

FIGURE 2-1. REPORT EXCERPT LACKING SUBJECT SENTENCES

FEE FOR MANAGEMENT COURSE

The current fee of $35 for our in-house remedial writing course pays for the equipment and materials we use. The course for management uses similar equipment and materials. Up to now, the Training Division has subsidized this cost. However, with the reduced financial support for Training from Headquarters, this is no longer possible. For example, currently we can't afford to repair fifteen readers and seven cassette recorders. The above proposed $35 fee for management courses would enable the Training Division to meet its equipment and materials cost.

FEE FOR SPECIAL SCHOOL

Reduced dollar support from Headquarters and the Training Division has coincided with increased demand for Special School because of salary incentives and more stringent certification guidelines. Together these two have led to an inability to pay for staffing the Special School. The Training Division in the past has funded several positions or parts of positions. They can now pay for only one. Headquarters has had to make up the difference. The proposed new fees for Special School will be used to cover these personnel costs. The fees will allow the Special School to continue service as before.

FIGURE 2-2. REPORT EXCERPT WITH SUBJECT SENTENCES INCLUDED

FEE FOR MANAGEMENT COURSE

A $35 fee for management courses is both justified and needed. Our in-house remedial writing course now charges $35 to pay for equipment and materials. The management courses use the same equipment and materials. The proposed $35 fee is an equitable solution to problems caused by the budget cuts from Headquarters. There is no doubt we need the money. Currently, we can't afford to repair fifteen readers and seven cassette recorders.

FEE FOR SPECIAL SCHOOL

A $35 fee for Special School can easily be justified and is badly needed. Most of the personnel attending Special School receive direct benefits from the service. They get salary increases or receive certification because of their successful completion of the courses. Since these employees personally benefit from the service, we think it reasonable to ask them to pay a small part of the cost. The need for fees is obvious. Training Unit hired four instructors before our budget cut. We will hire only one now. These new fees will allow the Special School to continue service at the level our employees expect and need.

---

sentences. The original report (figure 2-1) begins abruptly; it is disorganized and incomplete. The addition of subject sentences in the revision (figure 2-2) leads to a clearer presentation:

—The reader knows from the beginning what the paragraph is about.

—The division of content into "justify and need" provides an ordering device for the paragraphs.

—The mention of "justified" at the beginning of the second paragraph reveals a topic that will be developed.

—The subject sentences encourage parallelism between the two paragraphs and help simplify reading.

Using Subject Sentences

Before you arrange the body of your writing, turn each major section (or paragraph) into a subject sentence. Write all the subject sentences on a single sheet of paper. Look them over. Discover a logical arrangement. Order them, discarding any that are now unnecessary and creating any that are now needed to fill gaps.

As you write each section, let your subject sentence control the content. There are times when you'll discover you must add something that doesn't fit the subject sentence. Consider carefully if the addition belongs. If it does, rewrite and broaden your subject sentence.

Formatting

Formatting is one of the "secrets" of good organizational writing. The format outlines your writing, helping you see its overall shape and design—for better or worse. It also allows your reader to skim your work quickly and easily.

Types of Formatting

Three levels of formatting exist: overall, subhead, and series. All are available to the organizational writer.

Overall Formatting. Long reports and proposals may be formatted into chapters, units, or sections with a table of contents and appendices. This formatting occurs in many books. We are all familiar with this sort of formatting, rarely use it, and seldom give it a second thought. If you ever work on a long project, however, use it. Overall formatting breaks a complex project into manageable pieces for both you and your reader.

Subhead Formatting. Subhead formatting occurs within reports, proposals, letters, manuals, position papers, and minutes. Subheads break up a solid page of prose with a series of headings that offer single words or phrases summarizing what follows. Generally, you will need no more than three levels of subheads.

Subhead styles vary, but you must be consistent at each level within your work. For instance, if you choose to set one subhead in small caps with an empty line above and below, then all subheads of that level must follow the same pattern. The three most frequently used subhead styles are:

1. ALL LARGE CAPS SET OFF FROM TEXT
2. SMALL CAPS SET OFF FROM TEXT
3. *Italic type, followed by a period, and set at the beginning of a paragraph.*

Subheads should be short, succinct, and similar in tone. When possible, subheads should be meaningful words, not generic terms. Suppose, for instance, you are writing instructions for operating a duplicating machine. Rather than use the terms "Step 1," "Step 2," and "Step 3" as your headings, use meaningful heads: "Turn on Machine," "Test Paper Path," "Check Special Features."

In addition to offering a speedy outline of a piece of writing, subhead formatting has other benefits:

—It breaks up blocks of print and provides white space that is easy on the eye.

—It signals the equality of information. All topics that appear under the same subhead must somehow be equally related.

—It signals the superiority and subordination of material. The physical placement of information relates ideas without lots of explanation. The position of the following instructions clearly signals which idea is subordinate and which controlling:

TEST PAPER PATH
   CHECK PAPER STACK
   OPEN GATE #1
   REMOVE CYLINDER #1
     Lift Cap
     Unscrew Lever

One word about mechanics. Never end a page with a subhead. This destroys its usefulness. When the subhead falls alone at the close of the page, run a short page and begin the subhead on a new sheet.

Series Formatting. Within a section of a report, break a long prose statement into an indented series whenever possible. Our presentation of the three benefits of subhead formatting, above, illustrates this. We could have run those three points in a long prose paragraph, perhaps signaling each by "One," "Two," and "Three." Instead, we chose to break them out of narrative form and run them as a series. This form is easier to scan and, since it helps create white space on a page, is easier to read.

Examples

Figures 2-3 and 2-4 are abbreviated police reports, one fully formatted and one not. Readers of the second can easily find the information they need, the headings help to clarify the report, and the appearance is less foreboding.

FIGURE 2-3. UNFORMATTED POLICE REPORT

TO: Chief R. Goodman
FROM: Captain D. Riggins
RE: Complaint against Officer Smith
DATE: October 9, 198–

A complaint has been received against Officer Ronald Smith from Mr. Tom Hurley. Mr. Hurley is complaining of Officer Smith's actions last Friday night when Officer Smith stopped and forcibly held Mr. Hurley at the shopping mall, near Tony's Pizzeria. Officer Smith has been interviewed in reference to this incident. Mr. Hurley, the complainant, has also been interviewed. Mr. Calebra the owner of the pizzeria was interviewed as was the supervisor of Officer Smith. The tapes of the radio conversations that took place at the same time have also been reviewed. The following is my report.

Last Friday night Officer Smith received a call to a silent holdup alarm at Tony's Pizzeria. When he got there, he saw two male suspects running from the store. Simultaneously, he saw the store owner, Tony Calebra, shouting, waving, and pointing at the two men. . . .

Mr. Hurley contends in his sworn affidavit that he was roughly handled by Officer Smith for no reason and searched unlawfully. . . .

Officer Smith stated in the interview that he was responding to a silent alarm at the pizza parlor. . . .

After conducting the interviews with those involved in the incident at Tony's Pizzeria, listening to the tapes, and contacting the supervisor, I have reached a conclusion. It is first of all obvious that Officer Smith's version of the events surrounding the incident at Tony's Pizzeria is essentially correct. This is substantiated by the complainant, Mr. Hurley, both in his letter and during my interview with him. Secondly, although the events surrounding this incident and specifically the rough handling of Mr. Hurley were unfortunate, they could not have been helped. In fact, the final report could have been much worse had it not been for the level-headedness of Officer Smith in a stressful situation. Finally, Officer Smith not only acted within the guidelines for this department but responded as the state law dictates in performing his duty to attempt to apprehend what appeared to be fleeing felons. It is my recommendation, therefore, that a letter be placed in Officer Smith's file completely clearing him of any wrongdoing and that a copy also be sent to Mr. Hurley. I also recommend that copies be forwarded to the city manager, city attorney, and city council.

FIGURE 2-4. FORMATTED POLICE REPORT

TO: Chief R. Goodman
FROM: Captain D. Riggins
RE: Complaint against Officer Smith
DATE: October 9, 198–

INTRODUCTION

Problem: Mr. Tom Hurley filed a complaint against Officer Ronald Smith, charging him with undue force in Mr. Tom Hurley's arrest, October 2, 198–.

Task: On October 4, you instructed me to investigate this complaint, and I have interviewed all the people involved: Mr. Hurley, Officer Smith, Mr. Tony Calebra, and Officer Smith's supervisor. Attached to this report are transcriptions of those interviews and of the radio dispatches that night.

Purpose: The following report reviews the facts of the incident, summarizes the testimony, and arrives at recommendations.

Finding: After investigating this complaint, I have found Officer Smith innocent of the charges. I recommend no action be taken against him.

TESTIMONY OF EVENTS

The Incident: Last Friday night, Officer Smith received a silent holdup alarm from Tony's Pizzeria on the mall. Upon his arrival, Smith saw two men fleeing from the area, with Mr. Calebra pointing at them and yelling. Officer Smith took chase and caught Hurley. When Smith returned to the Pizzeria, Mr. Calebra informed him there had been no robbery. . . .

Hurley's Testimony: Mr. Hurley contends he was roughly treated by Smith, searched unlawfully, and falsely imprisoned in the squad car. Hurley admits that Smith apologized but says that isn't enough.

Calebra's Testimony: Mr. Calebra agreed with the report in all points. He admitted that he was unaware that the burglar alarm had gone off. . . .

Smith's Testimony: Smith stated that he was responding to a silent alarm at the pizza parlor and, when he arrived, thought he saw two men fleeing a crime. . . .

Captain's Testimony:	Smith's supervisor stated that Smith was level-headed and respected by his fellow officers. He also said that Smith was assigned to a utility car because of his maturity.
Smith's Previous File:	A search of Smith's file showed that he has been a reliable officer for fourteen years. He had one previous citizen complaint for undue force, but it was investigated and dismissed.

SMITH INNOCENT

Conclusion:

After conducting this investigation, I have reached the following conclusions:
1. Officer Smith's version of the incident is essentially correct and agreed to by Hurley, Calebra, and the tapes.
2. The rough handling of Hurley, while unfortunate, could not have been helped.
3. Officer Smith has acted within the guidelines of the department and state.

Recommendation:

It is my recommendation, therefore, that a letter be placed in Officer Smith's file completely clearing him of any wrongdoing in this matter, and that a copy be sent to Mr. Hurley with a letter of explanation. I also suggest copies be sent the city manager, city attorney, and city council.

PART TWO

The Handbook

UNIT II

Job Applications

3
Résumés

PREPARING A WINNING job application—a résumé and a covering letter of application—takes a good deal of time and effort. It doesn't require any secret tricks or knowledge, although professional résumé-writing services may want you to think you need their help. We aren't saying you can dash off an effective application with little thought or preparation. But you can do a good job without paying consultants—if you are willing to put in the necessary effort.

Research the Job

An effective résumé addresses the needs and concerns of a specific employer and job. To produce an effective résumé, consequently, you must fully research the employer and job. For instance, discover whether your employer has any specific likes or dislikes that you should know about before you produce your résumé. Find out what skills the company needs and emphasize those. You might even discover during this research that you wouldn't be happy with that company or in that job. A few hours of research can save you years of discontent.

To research a job, talk—in person if possible—to people who work for the firm. Drop in at the snack bar or a nearby lunch counter during coffee breaks and meet some employees. Most people are happy to talk about where they work, and you can quickly learn about working conditions, company morale, and the firm's needs.

Another way to investigate a job is to talk to the firm's personnel director. Question the director about the future needs and long-range plans of the organization. You will learn what to include and emphasize in your résumé and your letter of application. Talking to the director has another benefit. The more personal contact you have with representatives of the firm, the better your chances of getting an interview.

If you can't drop in and talk to employees or company officials, use the phone. While face-to-face contact is best, a call is better than no contact at all.

Letters of Reference

When you have finished researching the job you want—but before you construct your résumé—solicit letters of reference. While letters of reference are not formally a part of the résumé, they are mentioned in the résumé and must be ready when you submit it. Too often, job candidates put off asking people to write letters of recommendation. This delay inconveniences the people writing your recommendations and results in late or hurriedly written letters.

Good letters of reference can't get you a job if you don't have the right qualifications or if you fail to measure up in an interview. But good letters may help get you that interview.

Ask for letters from people who know you, your work, and your potential in the field. People who write letters for you but who have known you for only a few months or who don't understand your work are doubly harmful: their comments are practically useless and it may seem that no one knows you well enough to speak in your favor.

Give references as much information as possible about your goals, the particular job, and your qualifications. The more specific their letters, the more weight they will carry. If there is some special point you would like a writer to address, tell the person. For instance, if the job needs someone who can speak well and your reference knows that you are a persuasive public speaker, ask that the letter say so.

Assemble Your Materials

The final chore in preparing to write your résumé is to assemble all the materials pertinent to your job application. Gather refer-

ences, transcripts, copies of publications, examples of your work—
whatever you will need for a successful résumé.

In addition to gathering supporting evidence for your résumé,
collect any biographical information you need. Give yourself time
to locate this information; under no condition guess or make up
facts. If you can't remember a name or date, track it down. Incorrect information on a job application, no matter how trivial, may be
grounds for dismissal years later. Increasingly, firms research the
accuracy of your résumé.

The Résumé

The résumé is the most important document in your job application. It outlines your experience and abilities in detail but without
comment. It is factual, not interpretive.

Prospective employers look at your résumé before anything else.
They circulate it to other members of the firm. They stack it up
against others. They scan it, inspect it, then reinspect it, all the
while trying to read between its lines.

There is no *single* résumé of your past. You design a résumé to
fit the job for which you are applying. Suppose you decide to change
careers and leave your position as county clerk. Your résumé for
a position in hospital management will stress your management
experience, your understanding of budgeting, your integrity, responsibility, discipline, and industry. A résumé written for an administrative position at a convention center will emphasize your
public relations experience, your many contacts, your energy and
enthusiasm.

Purpose

The résumé by itself won't get you a job. Its purpose is to get you
an interview or an invitation to send more material. It makes sense,
then, that you don't have to—or want to—put everything about
yourself in a résumé. Leave some for later. Put in the résumé everything necessary to keep you in the race for the job.

Audiences

Usually, résumés are read by nonspecialists in your field—managers, administrators, and personnel directors. They decide whether to ask you for more information or to reject your application. These people are professional employers, experts at spotting strengths as well as weaknesses in résumés. For this audience write concisely and clearly; don't use specialized language or jargon.

Don't try anything too creative, cute, or novel, either. Résumés have a conventional form that professional employers expect you to follow. They want your résumé to provide information in the quickest way—not call attention to itself. Make your résumé stand out, not by gimmicks, but by the clarity of its organization, the cleanness of its layout and design, and the conciseness of its information.

For some jobs—professional firms and closely knit small businesses—applicants are hired not by professionals but by the members of the organization. For this audience you can be more daring in your design and more professional in your language. These people will care less that you are faithful to a standard résumé form. They do want evidence that you can speak their language.

Résumé Content

We can't tell you exactly what to put in your résumé—that will differ for each person and for each job—but we can make some general suggestions that may help you to decide what should be included. Generally, no matter what form your résumé takes, it will include these categories:

1. *Title*. Make the title informational. Not "Résumé," but "Résumé of John Smith, CPA" or "Nursing Credentials of John Smith."

2. *Job Line*. A job-description line identifies the type of job you want. Whether to include one is a disputed point these days. We think you should. Including this line forces you to consider your job objectives fully. Besides, you are designing individual résumés for

each different job; therefore, the job-objective line won't limit the use of the résumé. Place this information near the beginning.

3. *Personal Information.* Include your name, address, and telephone numbers (home and business). Any relevant physical or health information goes here. Keep personal information to a minimum and list only what is relevant to the job. We have seen résumés that include parents' names, monthly rent costs, and even clothing sizes! Keep to the point.

Because of federal regulations forbidding discrimination, you don't have to include your birthdate, sex, marital status, or race. If you decide to include such information, be honest. People sometimes want to hedge on their age—don't. If you decide to include your age, list your birthdate, not how old you are—you won't have to remember to update it every year.

4. *Work Experience.* List jobs, dates, skills, responsibilities, and other facts that will impress a future employer. Begin the list with your most recent job.

5. *Education.* Include the colleges you have gone to, the years you attended, your major field of study, the degrees earned, and your grade point average if superior. If you do not have a college degree, include your high school and any college work you have done. Begin your list with the last school you attended.

6. *Honors and Offices.* If you have received honors or if you hold offices of importance, list them under a separate category. These should be work-related or reflect significantly upon your character.

7. *Organizations.* If membership in professional societies or organizations attests to important skills or values, note such membership under a separate category.

8. *Hobbies or Interests.* List them if they are relevant to the job you seek. Don't be trivial.

9. *References.* Note that you have letters of reference available and the address where they can be sent for. You may want to give the names of your references, especially if they are well known in your field.

10. *Date.* For your convenience, date your résumé (month and year, probably at the end). During a career, people often produce many résumés. Having a date on your résumé may save you from an embarrassing error.

11. *Other.* Depending upon the particular job, you may want to

include special information on your résumé. Published scholarly articles, for instance, are important to teachers and are always recorded. If you hold a professional license that is necessary in your field, record that fact. If you're not sure about what may be conventional for résumés in your field, get someone's and look at it.

Using Your Judgment

If you are hunting for your first job, you may have trouble coming up with enough information for your resumé to demonstrate your aptitude and character. In this case, include hobbies and interests that give some sense of your skill, talent, intelligence, or personality.

For older résumé writers, the opposite is sometimes a problem: what to select from years of experience and many skills. Too much detail from too far back will obscure your recent, important pursuits.

How far back should you go? Use good judgment. For instance, an executive with a business degree and ten years of experience will not list odd jobs he held during high school or college. But if you are a recent college graduate, you may want to include those jobs. People with advanced degrees will not include their high-school transcripts because they have more recent educational documents.

Whatever you include, give details. In telling of your public relations skills, don't say you do press releases and special projects. List the sorts of releases you have produced: radio, television, newspaper; biographical, topical, human interest. Name the media you can work in: video, print, tape, billboard. Specify your skills in layout, design, paste-ups, jingles, slogans, logos. Give facts about the number of people you reached; prove that you are imaginative, inventive, aggressive, and energetic. Be precise and detailed; it sells.

Be certain you aren't trivial. We saw the résumé of a petroleum engineer that listed her Girl Scout troop and her Rainbow chapter. The business world does not care that you enjoy bridge or raising pigeons. What you include reflects your judgment, so choose carefully.

There are some things you should *not* include in your résumé:

1. *Your picture*. If you need to count on your appearance to sell, you don't have much that counts on the job—unless you are a model.

2. *Salary figures*. Former salaries are confidential and not a matter for your résumé.

3. *Reasons for leaving a job*. Even if your reasons reflect favorably upon your character, discussing them is straying into the field of interpretation and not sticking to facts. Save this for the interview.

Résumé Length

Your résumé should be no longer than one sheet, single-spaced. However, if a choice exists between creating a one-page résumé and leaving out essential information, use a second sheet. Personnel directors frown on anything longer. Needing more than two sheets is an excellent warning that you are not being selective enough in the materials you include.

If you do use two sheets, don't use the back side of the first sheet. Finally, don't staple the sheets together. Use a standard paper clip.

Résumé Style

Résumés are briefer and more direct than other organizational writing. Because a résumé is an outline, rely upon phrases and dependent clauses, not complete sentences.

The most frequent problem of style in writing résumés—a lack of parallelism—results from their outline form. If you begin a parallel series, continue it until you come to the end of that segment. In figure 3-1, for instance, John Carl's previous professional experience appears in parallel form: "Full-time Lecturer," "Part-time Instructor," "Lecturer," "Course Assistant," "Teaching Assistant." "Assistant for the Modern Novel Course" would have broken the parallel structure he created, as would having capitalized "Assistant" but not "instructor." If you set up parallel segments, maintain the parallelism throughout the résumé.

Don't avoid the pronoun *I*, but be sure not to overuse it. Keep your reader in mind. Relying on phrases and dependent clauses reduces the need for *I* in résumés.

The Truth

Always tell the truth in your résumé—but you don't have to tell the whole truth. If you left a job under less than ideal circumstances (and how many people who have had more than one job haven't quit or been fired?), you may want to ignore the job. However, you can be certain that most employers will ask you to account for any suspicious-looking gaps. Before you omit an item from your résumé, consider whether it will be more of a problem to have to account for the omission later.

Again, we emphasize, you may omit information but never lie, not if you want to keep the job. Pick and choose what you include on your résumé in your favor; your future employer expects you to do this. But be prepared for questions.

Throughout the construction of your résumé, ask friends and family to look over your work and make suggestions. Don't be shy. And don't try to explain away objections they raise. Listen and accept any criticism they give as the favor it is.

Formats

Figures 3-1, 3-2, and 3-3 illustrate the three basic résumé formats: the chronological, functional, and analytical. In addition, résumés in some artistic fields (arts, advertising, public relations) may be imaginative and unique to exhibit the creativity of the writer. Similar information (discussed above) appears on all résumés regardless of format.

Chronological. This form (figure 3-1) lists your previous activities from the most recent to the past, either in straight time sequence or in time sequence according to the different categories you use. The standard categories, in order of their appearance on the résumé, include 1) personal statistics, 2) previous employment, 3) education,

---

FIGURE 3-1. CHRONOLOGICAL RÉSUMÉ

Teaching Credentials of John Carl
7976 Schuylkill Ave.
Nashville, TN 37203

Birthdate:	June 30, 1945
Telephone:	University: (615) 555-1234 Home: (615) 555-9876
Present Employment:	Full-time Lecturer, Vanderbilt University, 1981– (Prose Fiction; British Authors I; British Authors II)
Previous Professional Experience:	Part-time Instructor, University of Tennessee at Nashville, 1979–1981 (Intro to Composition; Intro to Rhetoric; Intro to Literature)
	Lecturer, Turney Center of the Tennessee State Penal System, 1979–1981 (Intro to Composition; Intro to Rhetoric)
	Course Assistant, Vanderbilt University, 1971–1972 (The Modern American Novel)
	Teaching Assistant, Vanderbilt University, 1969–1971 (Freshman English; Poetry; Prose Fiction)
Education:	Ph.D. Vanderbilt University, May 1981 "Godwin and Shelley," W. P. Elledge, director
	M.A. Vanderbilt University, 1971
	B.A. Drew University, 1967
Specialization:	Major Field—British Romantic Literature Minor Field—Modern British and American Literature
Scholarships:	Vanderbilt University Scholarship 1968–1969 Rose Memorial Scholarship 1963–1964

FIGURE 3-1. CHRONOLOGICAL RÉSUMÉ (CONT.)

In Preparation
  Monograph: *The Evolution of a Concept: Decorum from Aristotle to
                 Johnson*

  Articles: "Shelley's Maddening Secret in *Julian and Maddalo*"
               "Unraveling Beatrice: Rhetorical Strategies in *The
               Cenci*"

Professional   Modern Language Association
Organizations: National Council Teachers of English
               Keats-Shelley Association

Credentials: A complete dossier from the Placement Service,
               Vanderbilt University, Nashville, TN 37203, includes
               these references:

               Professor W. P. Elledge
               Professor James Stathis
               Professor Vereen Bell
October 198–

---

4) honors and awards, 5) references. Though the most popular format, the chronological form is not always the most effective. It gives a good overview of where you spent your time in the past but not a good overview of what you can do.

Functional. Instead of telling when you did something, the functional résumé (figure 3-2) lists what you can do by job category. List each job title and follow it with a brief description of duties. Omit dates and start with the most significant duties and abilities. Education may be included after the list of "functions" that you have performed.

This type of résumé has become increasingly popular because it helps both you and the employer. It gives you a chance to think about what you learned from the jobs you have held. At the same time, an employer can read exactly what you are qualified to do.

We showed the functional résumé to a former personnel director

FIGURE 3-2. FUNCTIONAL RÉSUMÉ

Social Service Qualifications

C. P. Prink   Office: (901) 555-2345
92 Main Street   Home: (901) 555-8765
Alma, TN 38018

Job Objective   Social service staff position; working with people and
                      serving others; using administrative and program skills

Director of   —supervise and coordinate activities of 28 adult
Religious   volunteers serving over 350 program participants of all
Programming   ages in our church
                      —responsible for budget of $28,000 in 1981
                      —participate in the developing, planning, and
                      implementing of seven-level religious programming, 52
                      weeks a year, seven days a week, including such
                      various events as Teen Weekend, Senior Bible Study,
                      Married Club Baseball, and Toddler Camp
                      —Design and prepare all program publicity, including
                      newsletter, posters, and media press releases
                      —Supervise and direct yearly training courses for 85–90
                      religious programmers from around the state
                      —responsible for broad long-range plans and goal
                      setting for our religious program
                      —relate to people of all ages, races, and physical ability

Assistant   —directly responsible for special services for over 150
Director of   handicapped adults and children in pilot federal program
Special Services   that was city-wide
                      —created activities and projects for individual
                      handicaps
                      —sponsored social and cultural events for this audience
                      —counseled handicapped adults and children
                      —conducted sensitivity training workshops for staff and
                      volunteers of special services program

Insurance Clerk   —learned the importance of detail and discipline
and Agent   —responsible for ledgers and bookkeeping
                      —contact with the public took patience and goodwill

---

FIGURE 3-2. FUNCTIONAL RÉSUMÉ (CONT.)

Education	Perkins School of Theology, SMU, Dallas, Texas, Summers 1974–79 American Conservatory of Music, Chicago, 1968–70 Central High School, Little Rock, Arkansas, 1964–67
Hobbies	Choral singing, organ, folk music, camping
Letters	Letters of reference will be supplied on request

January 198–

---

who was reworking her own résumé and wanted some help. When we suggested this form, she immediately recognized its advantages even though she had never seen an example before: "I used to go through résumés with a yellow highlight pen and mark all the skills and talents applicants listed among the welter of unimportant details. Then I could go back and see exactly what they had done or knew how to do. That is exactly what this form of résumé does."

Analytical. Figure 3-3 illustrates an analytical résumé, really a variation of a functional résumé. Instead of reviewing previous jobs and experience, however, this type of résumé lists skills, beginning with the most important. Sometimes education is omitted from the analytical résumé, though we think it should be included.

The analytical résumé is useful if you want to change careers. It shows what you can do, not where you have been.

Creative. If you are sure that your audience is not opposed to creativity and experimentation, you might design your own résumé form. You should do this only in extraordinary cases, for instance, if the job you are applying for is in advertising or design, where initiative and creativity are essential. In some organizations such individualism will threaten your chances for a job. If there is any doubt in your mind about using a creative résumé, use a standard format.

FIGURE 3-3. ANALYTICAL RÉSUMÉ

PUBLIC RELATIONS
CREDENTIALS OF:

Catherine Reimer
47 Pennsylvania Avenue
Wyomissing, PA 19601
(215) 555-3456

PROFESSIONAL OBJECTIVE
Public Relations Administrator for municipal or state government

SUMMARY OF EXPERIENCE

Public Relations:
Created, directed, and administered special "awareness" projects for five public-service agencies in the Philadelphia area. One of these was a year-long campaign to improve the image of the Philadelphia Airport. Polls proved a 15% improvement in local image. Two of the agencies became full-time clients as a result of the special projects. Put together successful presentation for the LPR Fund before the Philadelphia Bank Group, which subsequently accepted the LPR account. Named Public Relations Person of Pennsylvania for 1981.

Press Relations:
My undergraduate degree in Journalism prepared me for many writing situations. Placed news releases in all the major media in Philadelphia Metropolitan Area. Have written for in-house journals, newsletters, and brochures. Designed brochures and ad copy. Supervised an in-house newsletter for Philadelphia Airport for two years.

Client Relations:
Work has made me aware of persuasive aspects of business and government work. Can strongly identify with client needs and problems. Convinced that the client knows more about situation and knows better how to proceed than even the client realizes.

Single Project:
Proposed, designed, administered the winning "Hopewell Is a Natural" project for the Hopewell

---

FIGURE 3-3. ANALYTICAL RÉSUMÉ (CONT.)

State Park. The theme, logo, slogans, and special projects were chosen in a national competition. The campaign included TV spots, T-shirts, brochures, and on-site programs.

EDUCATION

1965   Penn State University
        M.B.A. in Management
1961   Kutztown State College
        B.S. in Journalism, *summa cum laude*

PROFESSIONAL ORGANIZATIONS

Vice-President, Pennsylvania Society for Public Relations
Member, American Association for Public Relations

References and Portfolio upon request   6/8–

Layout and Design

After a few reminders about layout and design, you're on your own.

1. *Be consistent in your formatting throughout.* For instance, if a major category first appears in capital letters, all parallel categories should appear in capital letters.

2. *Be consistent in your indentation.* If under one category, a sentence that continues onto the next line is indented three more spaces, indent three spaces every line in a similar position.

3. *Use white space carefully and often.* The eye doesn't feel comfortable with too much type too close on the page. Use margins and spacing to help the reader follow the organization of your résumé as well as to relieve the heaviness of the page.

Mechanical Details

It is still best to have a printed résumé, preferably on twenty-four pound paper. You may choose a conservative, inoffensive shade that makes your résumé slightly distinctive: a light gray, for instance, or an off-white. Don't use a primary color; someone may view it as in bad taste.

If you type your own résumé, be sure to use a carbon ribbon, not a cloth one. Also use an elite typeface (that is, a small type face, 12 characters per inch).

Photocopied résumés are becoming more common because of the improved quality of photocopying and the increased expense of printing. The copy must be clean and sharp and on good paper.

Finally, remember that your résumé must be error-free. There are no exceptions and no excuses. Proofread and proofread and proofread.

4

Letters of Application

THE JOB APPLICATION letter is a persuasive cover letter that interprets the facts of your résumé and fills in the gaps. The letter of application will not have the permanence of your résumé. But this letter—your introduction to a prospective employer—helps to influence the way people respond to your application. It does in writing what you want to do in an interview: convince the recruiter that you are the person for the job.

Purpose

The purpose of the letter of application—like the purpose of the résumé—is to help you get an interview. First, the letter fleshes out the bare bones of your résumé and explains things that need explaining. For instance, in the résumé of John Carl (figure 3-1) there is a gap between 1972 and 1979 in his work experience. A close look at C. P. Prink's résumé (figure 3-2) discloses that her education and vocation are not in the same area. Both applicants use their letters to address these issues (figures 4-1 and 4-2).

A letter of application is also the place to create a sense of your personality. Résumés are outlines; as such they are flat and lifeless. Use your letter to communicate aspects of your character that you think will help you get the job. Carl's letter, for instance, creates a tone of whimsy and self-effacement, including such expressions as "older and wiser (in that order)," "its largess is only seemingly endless," "a semblance of modesty." These stylistic additions try to give a sense of the writer and to separate his application from the hundreds of others.

FIGURE 4-1. LETTER OF APPLICATION (JOHN CARL)

John Carl
7976 Schuylkill Ave.
Nashville, TN 37203

October 22, 198–

Professor Matilda Wynne, Chairperson
Department of English
Barton School
Warren, AR 71671

Dear Professor Wynne:

Please consider my application for the junior position in nineteenth-century literature that you advertised in the October MLA Job Information list. Enclosed is my résumé.

My graduate studies began in 1968, when Vanderbilt University granted me a University Scholarship. After passing my Ph.D. qualifying exams in 1972, I left the university for the alluring world of private business, running and owning several restaurants. Older and wiser (in that order), I returned to Vanderbilt in the fall of 1979 to complete my dissertation.

Last year I accepted a part-time position as instructor of composition and rhetoric at the University of Tennessee at Nashville, which included an unexpected bonus, the opportunity to teach at a nearby prison. One opportunity followed another. This year Vanderbilt University has again employed me—its largess is only seemingly endless—and I presently hold a one-year appointment that finds me honing my teaching skills.

In the interests of brevity and a semblance of modesty, I offer my résumé and credentials as sources of additional information. I welcome any inquiries and am, of course, available for an interview at your convenience.

Thank you for this consideration.

Sincerely,

John Carl

FIGURE 4-2. LETTER OF APPLICATION (C. P. PRINK)

C. P. Prink
92 Main Street
Alma, TN 38018

February 3, 198–

Mr. George Jones, Chairman
Board of Directors
Christian Life Summer Camp
4848 Broadway
Knoxville, TN 37912

Dear Mr. Jones:

Handicapped children often have two burdens to bear: their physical
handicap and our neglect. A six-year-old paraplegic doesn't gladden our
hearts the way a happy child running and playing does. We shunt the
handicapped child off: out of sight, out of mind.

I have seen the boredom and tedium that is the lot of many handicapped
children. For this reason, I would like to establish a handicapped
children's unit at the Christian Life Summer Camp. The healthy as well as
the handicapped would benefit. Healthy children would be able to learn
from the handicapped; the disadvantaged would have the pleasure of
activities and the challenge of competition all summer.

My credentials indicate that I have the administrative skills and the
commitment to establish such a camp. As a bonus, I will bring to Christian
Life Summer Camp my musical talents, talents I had planned to make a
career until my young brother was crippled in a car accident.

I will be happy to discuss the many positive aspects of this suggestion and
my employment on the staff of the Christian Life Summer Camp. I spend
most of my time at the First Church of Alma and can be reached there,
(615) 555-1234.

Thank you,

C. P. Prink

Finally, the letter is an example of the quality of your work. A personnel director who has five equally trained and experienced applicants to choose from might well use your letter to judge your ability. If the letter is carelessly written, poorly structured, sloppily prepared, or just too short to be of any use, the employer may pass up an interview with you in favor of someone else. For this reason a letter should be a full page long. Your prospective employer expects a substantial writing sample.

Some letters of application do little more than highlight information that appears on the résumé. For instance, you received a special honor or have an unusual skill, and you don't want a prospective employer to miss it on your résumé, so you repeat the information in your letter. Judicious highlighting is all right, but highlighting alone fails to exploit the full potential of the cover letter.

Highlight information only when such highlighting is important or when your letter needs greater length to be useful as a writing sample. A letter should be more than repeated information. Unless you add something that isn't in your résumé, you are wasting the time of your reader and losing an opportunity to sell yourself.

Content

The content of your letter will vary with the résumé it accompanies. You should design each letter to fit the résumé as well as the job and audience.

When applying for an advertised position, open your letter by clearly stating the job you are applying for (the business might be filling several positions) and where you learned about it (they may have placed ads in different media). Carl's letter does just this: "Please consider my application for the junior position in nineteenth-century literature that you advertised in the October MLA Job Information list."

If you are sending out an unsolicited job inquiry, you might try to make your letter more persuasive and begin with a "hook" or "grabber" rather than information. The Prink letter (figure 4-2) tries to get the attention of the reader while it begins to build a case for employment.

Be careful, however. The "grabber" is one place where you

might become cute or trite, calling your judgment into question. Don't begin with a rhetorical question such as "Are you looking for a skilled employee who is industrious and will work for low wages?" Such a cliché will only elicit a groan of disbelief and a polite rejection.

The body of your letter gives you a chance to answer questions that someone reading your résumé might have. Look at your own résumé as objectively as possible (or even better, get a friend to look it over). Try to see if there is anything in it that creates a negative impression or that leads to questions. Pretend you are a cynical and distrustful employment agency director; look for trouble, assume the worst. Does being single make you less reliable than a married person, or maybe even antisocial? Those two jobs you held in the same year, do they indicate a tendency to quit a project instead of sticking with it when it gets tough? That career switch, does it suggest that you still might not know what you want to do?

After a close inspection of your letter, try to turn any potential liability into an asset. For instance, as a single employee you will be able to put more time into your job—maybe even make the job your life. From the two jobs you had in one year you learned the importance of getting along with people. Your career change gives you a second field of knowledge and an unusual combination of skills.

If there is nothing in your résumé that needs to be addressed in your letter (and this is uncommon), then use your letter to sell yourself. Persuade the reader that you are uncommonly suited for the job and that no one else can do for the organization what you can do. A letter of application is not the place to practice modesty, though be careful not to sound arrogant or pushy.

One word of warning if you are trying to relocate. You may feel like giving some reason for your job change, but don't insult your present employer. The person hiring you is aware that an employee who is disloyal once may be disloyal again. Instead, present a positive reason for wanting to leave the firm, one that will reflect well on you. Say, for instance, that you have accomplished all you can at the present job and you want a new challenge or that your present employer has a young and intelligent staff and your room for promotion is limited.

Don't complain about your present situation. The fact that you are looking for a job indicates your unhappiness; don't let it sound as if you are an employee who can't be satisfied.

End your letter with a close that requests (not demands) an interview at the convenience of the employer. Don't put conditions on the interview. When you are offered the interview, you can make suitable arrangements.

Close by thanking the personnel director for taking the time to read your letter.

Style

In a letter of application, tone is important. Decide what sort of personality you want to reflect, what will make you stand out in the crowd, then choose your words and your sentence structures to create that character. Be correct. But don't be so formal that the letter loses a personal tone.

When you think your letter is ready, show it to several friends for comment. Listen carefully to what they say, to what they don't say, and to what they almost say. They won't want to hurt your feelings and so will try to be nice. But you want to know how your letter works, so listen to their ideas and read between the lines. You may disagree with them or ignore their advice, but you do want to listen.

Mechanics

Each letter of application should be separately typed. It is not yet accepted practice to photocopy letters and type in the inside addresses and greetings. And no matter how good your photocopy is, someone examining your letter can tell that it is a copy.

Type your letter on good bond paper using a carbon ribbon. Don't use erasable bond (it smears), onion-skin paper (it wrinkles), or a cloth ribbon (it blurs). Sign your letter in black ink.

Be sure there are no typos. Proofread the letter an extra time.

UNIT III

Correspondence

5

Letter Style and Format

LETTERS are more personal than other writing you do on the job. You write them to individuals rather than to a general audience, to people you know or have talked with on the telephone. Still, letters are businesslike. They often have several audiences, and they often wind up in permanent files.

A letter may be as simple as "Here's the report on furnace filters that you asked for." It may be as delicate as a response to a customer who is threatening a lawsuit. It may contain a questionnaire, a report, or instructions.

Understand Your Purpose

Letters deal with issues. They request information, make demands, clarify positions, express thanks, and ask for action, money, or votes. Your purpose in writing usually determines your tone as well as your attitude toward the reader.

You must clearly understand why you are writing. While recommending that a proposal be adopted, you may, for instance, find yourself complaining about the funding agency's priorities or reviewing an argument you lost about the proposal. But your purpose is to recommend the grant, not to chastise the agency or to replay a lost battle.

If your real motivation for writing is to let someone have it, to blow off steam, or to indulge self-righteous indignation, *don't* write, not even for the files. Don't create more hostility. Let off steam, then *consider* writing if you find real issues that should be addressed.

Most effective business and government correspondence has a single purpose. If you are an employer, you may need to stipulate conditions of the job you are offering. If you are on a grants committee, you may want to encourage a rejected applicant to resubmit a grant. But you are primarily offering a job or declining the application. That purpose must be clear in your mind so that it can be clear in your writing. (Purpose statements are discussed on pages 19–21.)

If the purpose is not clear to you, your writing will be garbled. This happened recently when a nursing home sent out a letter to the families of its patients. The bulk of the letter requested that relatives keep prescription drugs and aerosol cans from the patients. The letter explained that this was a state code and that the staff would remove any drugs or cans within the week. If the letter had stopped there, all would have been well, but the letter also announced the hiring of a new administrator and that the home was immediately switching from whole milk to 2 percent milk.

What should have been an effective persuasive letter—do this now for the sake of the patients and to comply with the law—turned into a newsletter. All the persuasion was lost. The state-code problem, the one item needing action, was forgotten.

Purposes

Writing a letter that offers a job is very different from writing a letter that turns down an applicant. Both are very different from writing to someone asking for an adjustment on an incorrect order or asking someone to send a donation to support your cause.

As you begin writing, recognize whether you are presenting good news (you won the contract), bad news (your proposal was turned down), or trying to persuade the reader to do something (send a contribution).

Good-News and Courtesy Letters. The news is good—we want to hire you; here is your back-ordered merchandise; your grant has won;

you won the contract—even though the news may contain conditions or qualifications. And letters written as business or social courtesies—thank-you letters, obviously, but also letters acknowledging orders, requests, or agreements, and notes written for someone's files (*see* Chapter 6).

Bad-News Letters. These letters are dominated by bad news—we hired someone else; your merchandise is back-ordered; your grant has been turned down; you did not get the contract. In bad-news letters, you need to work to keep the goodwill of the person you are writing to (*see* Chapter 7).

Persuasive Letters. These letters ask for action—send money to our cause, pay your bills, vote differently at the upcoming session, adopt this proposal, implement that procedure, give me a job interview. Many letters, not obviously persuasive, nevertheless require you to be persuasive (*see* Chapter 8).

Create Goodwill

Every letter you write adds to or detracts from your organization's image. An underlying purpose in all your correspondence is to maintain and enhance the goodwill of your organization.

Your letter may be the first contact someone has with your organization, but whether or not it is, the image you project, the tone you adopt, and the concern you have for your reader should create and maintain goodwill. Project a positive image even if you are turning down an application or registering a complaint.

This point is briefly stated, but it is crucial. The sarcastic jab you want to take at a late supplier, that irritated tone you are tempted to use on the confused policyholder—these let you have a laugh, but they do not add to your organization's image; they do not promote goodwill.

Letters are very often between you, your reader, and the files. Assuming that issues of fact and policy are correct, the potential audiences within your organization, who may spot-check your letters, will be primarily concerned with the image that you project.

Consider Your Audience

Creating goodwill depends greatly on how you treat your reader. Letters are very forceful; they are directed at individuals, to *you*s. Even if you are trying to persuade someone to send you money, keep the reader's needs in mind. Treat the reader as you want to be treated—the Golden Rule of letter writing.

This is not simply a platitude; it is an effective way to develop your writing strategy. If you were writing to yourself, what would make the presentation effective? a rational or an emotional approach or both? what tone? which facts would be crucial? What would make you send money? give yourself an interview? respond favorably to your complaint? What would make you feel thanked for the job you did?

When writers give way to their irritations, their letters can be counterproductive. We think this happened with a letter the Defense Department sent out during the neutron-bomb debate.

In response to the letters, telegrams, and phone calls protesting further development and planned deployment, the Pentagon sent out a letter and information package. We expected the letter to defend and explain the official position, as it did. But we did not expect it to insult its readers, as it did by implying that people opposed to the plan, which included the people getting the letter, were either fools or knaves, who had been taken in by "a well-orchestrated propaganda campaign based in Moscow."

Even if the writer believed that people had been duped into being part of such a campaign, the writer should have addressed readers as individuals making individual political decisions. Individuals wrote, telegraphed, and phoned; individuals will change their minds. The writer should have acknowledged doubts, and then directly dealt with differences in understanding, addressing the reader as one would address a friend. As it was, this expensive mailing was wasted; the letter and "information" increased anger and concern rather than decreased them.

Treating the reader as you would want to be treated is simply practicing the traditional American Indian advice to spend some time in the other's moccasins. If you will do that, you should avoid most of the mistakes in tone that letter writers make.

Style

Letters are generally short, sometimes one page, seldom over two pages unless they are actually reports or proposals in a letter format.

Because they are concise, because they are read in the midst of office routines and office distractions, and because they should focus on a single purpose, letters usually take more time and effort per page than other kinds of business and government writing.

Even a routine letter demands that over half of your writing effort be spent on phrasing, tone, and style—getting the words right.

Let's consider the unique style problems and possibilities of letters and memos.

Tone

The tone of letters ranges from informal to the most formal. Informal does not necessarily mean colloquial and formal does not necessarily mean stuffy. There is no single right tone for a business letter.

Informality is seldom the danger. For most of us the danger is that we will make letters that should be friendly and informal sound cold and distant, businesslike in the worst sense of the word—stuffy, pompous, full of clichés and "traditional phrasing."

Use your knowledge of your reader and of your task to help you develop the most effective tone for your letter.

If you are speaking for a corporation that chooses not to be bothered with a "trivial" complaint, you will select a distant and formal tone. But if that same corporation wants to project itself into the affairs of the people around it, then you must take off your coat, roll up your sleeves, and be one of the folk. In asking for money, for instance, whether donations or new orders, you will speak directly to your reader with personal pronouns and involve your reader through illustrations.

Paragraphs

Because letters are short and concise, you sometimes have one-sentence paragraphs. The first paragraph is often a single-sentence reference to a past letter and the last paragraph a good-luck-with-your-current-project, goodwill closing. Trying to stretch these paragraphs by adding a filler sentence or two usually seems clumsy.

Letterese

Letters seem to invite clichés and formula phrases probably because they are concise and often deal with routine matters. These phrases make your letters stale. The list in figure 5-1 contains a sampling of stock phrases and some useful substitutes. If you are willing to eliminate such words and phrases from your letters, your writing will be fresher and more readable. These stock phrases seem to cluster at the beginning or the end of the letter. Most are easily deleted.

FIGURE 5-1. STOCK WORDS AND PHRASES

Stock Word or Phrase	Substitute
aforementioned	this, that, previously mentioned
as per our conversation	as we discussed (agreed, informed you, etc.)
at hand	*omit*
attached hereto	attached
at your earliest convenience	soon, *or specify: e.g.,* next week
be advised that	*omit*
check in the amount of	check for
deem it advisable	believe

enclosed herewith	enclosed
enclosed please find	we have enclosed, *or* a *(blank)* is enclosed
find enclosed	find
hereto	*omit*
herewith	*omit*
in due course	soon, *or state specific time*
kindly advise	advise *or* tell
permit me to say	*omit*
purpose of this letter is to (invite, acknowledge, etc.)	*omit; simply* we invite, we acknowledge, etc.
pursuant to this matter	in response to this matter, *or be specific:* following up on this, because of this
pursuant to your request	as you requested
re *or* in re	regarding *or* in regard *(save* Re *for memo headings)*
receipt is acknowledged	we have received
said matter, said letter	this matter, this letter
thanking you in advance for	thank you for
under separate cover	separately

Remember that only words and phrases found almost exclusively in letters and memos are included in this list. (Particular "problem" words for reports are discussed on pages 201–202; many general style problems are considered in Unit VIII.)

Loaded Language

Since letters address a specific person about a specific situation, it is often tempting to use strong language. Sometimes you need strong language. If you mean "You are responsible and you will be hearing from our lawyer," you should usually say that directly and forthrightly, without calling names or being sarcastic. Most of us recognize sarcasm easily, but we don't always recognize the words that seem to indirectly call someone's behavior or judgment into question. The words and phrases in figure 5-2 are warning flags. The presence of these words warns you that you *may* be drifting toward insinuation and name-calling. But the individual words can only be judged in context.

FIGURE 5-2. LOADED WORDS

---

apparently, *as in* apparently you haven't noticed
assume, *as in* perhaps you assumed
claim, *as in* it has been claimed; you claim; the company wants to claim
contend, *as in* you contend
feel, *as in* you feel
perhaps, *as in* perhaps the problem is not apparent to you
you, *as in* you failed to notice; you do not realize; you told us; you
    contend; you apparently believe

The word *you* runs through the list. When you are talking about a problem, be very careful about pointing, about how you assign blame. Names—individual, group, and organization—need to be used carefully also.

The tone is the issue more than the words themselves, and controlling your tone is the basic issue. You may need to say to someone challenging you, "Our records show . . ." but you need to say it without anger, indignation, or sarcasm, and you need to invite the reader to respond with what the reader's records show.

Standard Letter Formats

Readers expect letters to follow standard formats. These formats encourage readers to focus on the contents of your letter quickly and accurately.

We present only the basic letter formats here. (Memo formats are in Chapter 9.) For information beyond these basic formats or for more detailed information, consult a good secretarial manual, such as *Webster's Secretarial Handbook* (Springfield, Mass.: Merriam-Webster, 1976).

The Parts of the Letter

Without covering every possibility, this brief guide to the basic parts of the letter should serve for most situations.

Inside Heading

The inside heading consists of the date, file numbers, the inside address, and any attention lines and subject lines that you need.

Abbreviations. Use only the very common abbreviations. You may use abbreviations in courtesy titles *(Mr., Dr., Esq.)*, in degrees *(Ph.D., M.S.W., M.D.)*, in street designations *(Ave., Blvd., St.)*, (although these are often spelled out) and in post office box addresses *(P.O. Box)*.

Street directions *(North, South)* are usually spelled in full as are the names of numbered streets *(First, Fifty-second)*.

Names. Use the full name, including the given name. Generally, use the name the person goes by. Nicknames seldom belong in the heading; you may use them in the salutation.

Job Titles. Put one-word job titles on the same line as the name: name, comma, title. Put titles of two or more words on the line following the name.

File Numbers

Place file numbers, yours and theirs, one or two spaces below the dateline and above the address.

Attention Lines

Use attention lines to address letters to individuals without limiting the letter to that individual. An attention line helps ensure that the letter does not sit in someone's in-basket through several weeks of vacation.

Place an attention line between the inside address and the salutation. When you use an attention line, you may omit the salutation.

Salutations

Coming up with the "right" salutation troubles many people. You can find detailed lists of salutations for individuals of rank or title in desk dictionaries, yearly almanacs, and secretarial guides (look in the Table of Contents or Index for a listing like "Salutations" or "Forms of Address"). Guidelines for more ordinary situations are straightforward.

Dear Title Name is always correct. Use *Mr., Miss, Mrs.,* or *Ms.* as appropriate. (Be careful using *Ms.* While some women prefer it, it offends others. If you know a woman's preference, follow it, even if you prefer a different title. If you do not know her preference, you must guess or resort to a different salutation.)

In a formal salutation, you will usually omit the first name, *Dear Senator Wimsey, Dear Mrs. Marple.* A nickname is appropriate only if the person uses it regularly. In a slightly less formal situation you might use a nickname in the salutation even though you have used the full name in the address. You might have *Robert H. Cleveland, Editor,* in the address, for instance, but *Dear Bob,* in the salutation.

Courtesy titles, job titles, and titles of rank or honor are often used in the salutation: *Dear President Ellison, Dear Editor Esposito, Dear Doctor Chisenbaum,* and *Dear Foreman Wright.* Using these titles avoids the *Ms.* problem.

When you do not know the name of a specific person to write to, use an impersonal salutation. The traditional ones still work well,

Dear Sir or Madam or *Dear Ladies and Gentlemen*. The objection to using only *Sir* or *Gentlemen* seems valid. You can circumvent most problems by addressing the group by name: *Dear Complaint Department* or *Dear Executive Committee Members*.

You may omit the salutation entirely, particularly in routine correspondence to unknown people. Simply begin with a statement of the problem or request. Some writers begin with *Greetings* or *Hi*. This borders on being cute.

Closings

Complimentary closings haven't changed much in recent years, but some writers now omit them. The last line of the letter becomes in effect a closing line. If you do omit the complimentary close, be certain that your letter closes pleasantly, perhaps with a thank-you line.

Build traditional closings around the words *sincerely* or *truly*. Use *cordially* only with acquaintances. Closings built around *respectfully* show deference; use them only when deference is appropriate.

Signature Block

The signature block consists of the signature, the typed name, and title if appropriate, and sometimes a typed company name.

If you are acting as the agent of a company in making a proposal, for instance, or denying a claim, you should type the company name (customarily, entirely in caps) below the complimentary close and above your signature. This legally interposes the company between you and any liability. You are then acting, without question, on behalf of the company.

Have the signature line (the typed line below the signature) typed as you want to be known.

Indicate degrees either by the appropriate courtesy title preceding the name (seldom anything other than *Doctor* is used) or by the usual degree abbreviations following the name (*Ph.D., M.S.W.,* or *J.D.,* for example), but not by both.

One-word titles of positions held in the organization *(President* or *Treasurer)* appear immediately after the name. Titles of two or more words *(President and Chairman of the Board)* appear on the line below the typed name.

Always sign letters in ink, of course. Letters signed by proxy, by a secretary or co-worker, should be initialed by the person who signed.

Your signature may be less formal than the signature line; sometimes you may sign only a first name or a nickname. Be certain that the signature is in keeping with the tone and occasion of the letter, however.

The conventions about how a woman signs her name are no longer strictly followed. Women as well as men may call themselves what they choose. If a woman has a preferred courtesy title *(Miss, Ms.,* or *Mrs.),* she should place the title in parentheses in front of the typed signature. Courtesy titles may be omitted entirely.

Signing either a degree designation or the courtesy title indicating a degree seems pretentious. Never sign both the courtesy title and the degree abbreviation.

Postscripts

Don't use postscripts in business letters to add a thought. Use them only to reinforce a point already made.

Letterhead

All letters relating to your job, including semiofficial letters such as job recommendations, should be written on letterhead. Of course, you will not abuse the use of letterhead; it is not for personal correspondence.

When letters run longer than one page, use blank stock of the same sort as the letterhead for the following pages. In a heading in the upper-left corner on the second page, include the name of the addressee, the date of the letter, and the page number.

Spacing

The body of a letter is normally typed single-spaced with a blank line inserted between paragraphs. Very short letters—one paragraph, fewer than ten lines—may be typed double-spaced.

Typing Formats

Many organizations and agencies use detailed typing manuals (often called "style guides") to standardize correspondence. If your office has such a guide, follow it. If there is none, choose between the block and modified-block formats in figures 5-3 and 5-4. Almost all letters in business and government follow one of these.

Punctuation patterns used in letters are illustrated and discussed in the same figures.

Block Format

In the block format (figure 5-3), place all elements of the letter against the left-hand margin: dateline, inside address including any attention line, salutation, body, complimentary close, and the signature line.

Figure 5-3 also illustrates open punctuation. This style omits many traditional marks.

Block format and open punctuation are both quick to type, but they are not particularly pleasing in appearance.

Modified Block Format

The modified block (figure 5-4) presents a more balanced appearance. It is the most common typing format, although it is not so quick to position on the page as the full block. In using the modified block, place the inside address, the attention line, the salutation,

---

FIGURE 5-3. BLOCK FORMAT SHOWING OPEN PUNCTUATION

[Organization Letterhead]

[Month, day, year]

[Name of Addressee
Title, if not on line above
Organization Name
Specific Department or Suite Number
Street Number or P.O. Box Number
City, State   Zip]

[Salutation]

This is an example of block format with open punctuation. Block format
has been touted at various times as the way of the future because it
requires less typing time. Although widely adopted, it has not displaced
the modified block format. This is probably because of the more pleasing
appearance that the modified block presents on the page.

Open punctuation, as seen here, omits punctuation after the salutation and
complimentary close.

[Complimentary close]

[Typed signature line
Title as appropriate]

---

and the body of the letter at the left-hand margin, but begin the
dateline, the complimentary close, and the signature line slightly
over halfway toward the right-hand margin.

   Figure 5-4 also illustrates mixed punctuation. This is the punctuation most widely used today.

FIGURE 5-4. MODIFIED BLOCK FORMAT SHOWING MIXED PUNCTUATION

[Organization Letterhead]

[Month, day, year]

[Name of Addressee
Title, if not on line above
Organization Name
Specific Department or Suite Number
Street Number or P.O. Box Number
City, State   Zip]

[Salutation,]

This is an example of modified block typing format. It is the most widely used typing format in business and government. It presents a pleasing appearance. Because it is traditional, it draws no attention to itself. The reader's attention will be on your message, not on the pyrotechnics of your format.

Mixed punctuation, the most generally used punctuation style, is also used in this example. Commas appear in the dateline, following the salutation, and following the complimentary closing. Commas are sometimes necessary within an address—between name and title, for instance—but they do not follow each line of the address. In formal letters, a colon follows the salutation.

Closed punctuation, a more formal style of punctuation, places commas after each line of the address and a period at the end of the address. Commas follow the salutation and the complimentary close. A colon is more likely to follow the salutation in closed style than in open style.

[Complimentary close,]

[Typed signature line
Title as appropriate]

6

Good-News and Courtesy Letters

GOOD-NEWS AND COURTESY letters (which include letters of acknowledgment and letters for someone's files) should be easy to write. But sometimes we get stuck trying to attach conditions to the good news or trying not to sound like just another thank-you letter.

Good-News Letters

Writing a good-news letter is usually a pleasant task. We all enjoy offering someone a job, accepting a manuscript, or awarding a grant or contract. We enjoy congratulating the winner, especially when the competition has been rugged.

But a good-news letter often has conditions attached: Here's the offer " . . . but demonstrate that you are an affirmative-action employer"; ". . . but the computer must be delivered by October 1"; ". . . but we expect you to provide ten hours of training for our staff"; . . . and on and on. You must qualify the good news without putting off your reader. After all, you want the reader to accept the job or follow through on the proposal.

Even if you are not attaching qualifications, you must sometimes sell yourself and your organization. If the applicant has had another job offer, you must make the applicant want to accept your offer.

Outline

A good-news letter usually conforms to the following outline:

Congratulations. The good news—loud and clear—begins the letter. Any reluctance you may have about the applicant or the proposal must not show. If you have decided to make the offer, make it gladly.

Even if serious qualifications come later, open with the good news. Presenting the good news positively helps convince the reader to accept the qualifications or to make the changes you present later.

Share the Excitement. Explain the reasons for the good news. For instance, "Your proposal represented a unique combination of experience, technical knowledge, and innovative design." Make all compliments specific; make them refer to this offer, not offers in general. These specific comments will help convince your reader that you and your organization have taken a personal interest in the good news.

The Qualifications, the Problems, the Ifs. These need to be spelled out clearly, whether you are asking for revisions (what kind, to what extent, by what date) or you are offering a smaller salary or later starting date than expected. If the conditions or changes are significant, you will need to quietly sell yourself and your organization here.

Acceptance. Clearly spell out anything that your reader must do to accept the good news ("sign and return this letter" or "phone us by the first of the month"). This is especially important when conditions accompany the good news. For your sake and for your reader's sake, be clear about the reader's obligations and your deadlines.

Good News Again. Restate the good news and close by looking to the future—to the prospective employee's contribution to the company, to the significance of the article in the field, to the impact of the completed project. Sell your reader again, especially if there have been conditions attached to the good news. Close with an active welcome to your dynamic organization or program.

This outline generally works well. Of course you won't always have five paragraphs. Some of the "points" may become two or more paragraphs in your letter; others may be combined or deleted.

Tone Problems

Any trouble you have in writing a good-news letter will usually be with tone. The writer of the following good-news letter let the problems bury the good news. The applicant will think twice about taking this job:

Dear Carla Sims:

We are pleased to be able to offer you a job as Programmer with Central Farm Management.

In all candor, you were not our first choice. We had hoped to find a programmer with an accounting or actuarial background. But we hope that your willingness to learn and your fine background will make up for your lack of experience.

However, since you will be learning on the job for some months, and because of these very difficult economic times, we are not able to offer you the full salary we discussed. Rather we are offering you a beginning salary of $— a month. We hope that you will agree with us that that is a reasonable salary, all things considered.

After you have been with us for a few months, we can renegotiate the salary, if that seems proper. After one year, as you know, you will be eligible to join our profit-sharing plan.

I hope you find this offer attractive, even though I realize it is probably not all you had hoped it would be.

Please call me at your earliest convenience so we can arrange your starting date.

Sincerely yours,

You may have altered the job offer, the candidate may be your second choice, but put the best face on things. If this candidate is your choice now, offer the job happily and without regret. Let the applicant have the best chance possible coming into your organization. Figure 6-1 shows a letter that welcomes the applicant.

FIGURE 6-1. EFFECTIVE GOOD-NEWS LETTER WITH QUALIFICATIONS

CENTRAL FARM MANAGEMENT
Managing Farms Throughout the Midwest Since 1952

July 16, 198–

Ms. Carla Sims
Apartment G-3
1433 Decatur Way
West Urbana, IL 60185

Dear Carla Sims:

Congratulations. On behalf of Central Farm Management I am pleased to offer you the position of Programmer that we discussed two weeks ago.

Your wide-ranging background and your fine academic record were decisive. Although you lack accounting experience, you impressed us with your proven ability to handle new and challenging situations.

Unfortunately, the continuing recession means that we must offer you less than we discussed. Your starting salary will be $— a month. I apologize for any disappointment this causes.

We do expect the economy to improve soon, so we will shorten your probation period to four months. If, at the end of that time, you have progressed, as we expect you will, we will be able to make up the salary deficiency.

Please call me soon so we can arrange your company physical and your starting date. If I have not heard from you within ten days, I will call you in case this letter has gone astray.

FIGURE 6-I. EFFECTIVE GOOD-NEWS LETTER WITH QUALIFICATIONS (CONT.)

I look forward to hearing from you. You are the kind of bright, energetic person that has made Central Farm a leader in its field. I think you will find the Programmer position both exciting and challenging, with possibilities for developing software that suits the needs of our company and our customers.

> Sincerely yours,
> CENTRAL FARM MANAGEMENT
>
> W. Ralph Anderson
> Personnel Director

The proposal you are accepting may not be everything you had hoped for or the price may be higher than you expected. Negotiate changes, but when you accept, accept wholeheartedly.

The writer of the following letter, for instance, seems as interested in being annoyed as in telling the good news.

Dear Iris Blassingame,

Your computer printer has finally arrived, and we are shipping it to you tomorrow. I know you thought it would never get here. It has been a long time coming, but as I explained to you several times, it is a very popular printer and is back-ordered all over the country. I think you found that out when you couldn't get it from anyone else.

At any rate, it will be arriving shortly. I hope you won't have trouble getting it running. Some of our customers have. But if you pay attention to the manual this time, you should be able to get it running. Please, read the manual before you call me.

I know three months is a long time, but you better believe I did everything I could to get the printer to you as fast as possible. At any rate, good luck.

> Sincerely yours,

The letter may be full of good news, but the tone is tired and sour. The customer has been an irritation and the writer lets her know it. Having let off this steam, the writer may feel better, but he has lost a customer. Even if this customer has finished making major computer purchases for a while, she may have friends who are thinking about buying computers. Don't begrudge the good news.

The letter should be honestly friendly. If it can't be friendly, it should be brief instead of dwelling, as this one does, on the problems the writer has had. By shifting the attitude slightly, the writer can make this the good-news letter that it should be (*see* figure 6-2).

FIGURE 6-2. EFFECTIVE GOOD-NEWS LETTER

COMPUTER ACRES
For All Your Computer Needs

April 18, 198–

Iris Blassingame,
1452 South Vermont Avenue
West Vicksburg, LA 71285

Dear Iris Blassingame,

Your Brite-Print 255 Printer has arrived! We will be shipping it tomorrow morning, and you should have it within two days, as we are shipping it express (at our expense).

I know you will enjoy the printer, especially its high speed and graphics capability. I think you will also be delighted by many small features that make it an excellent machine.

Some of our customers have had a few problems getting their 255 printers running. Pay close attention to the manual, and you should be all right. Incorrectly positioned "dip" switches have usually caused the problems. Page 14 of the manual describes these switches and lists the settings. Generally, setting a baud rate of 1200 seems to work best.

If you do have a problem, please call me. You may also want to use the toll-free number for the distributor. They have an excellent

---

FIGURE 6-2. EFFECTIVE GOOD-NEWS LETTER (CONT.)

---

technical support department to answer user questions. That number is
800-555-1234. Technical assistance is available from 9 a.m. until 7 p.m.,
Monday through Friday.

I am glad that I was able to give you such a good deal on this very popular
printer, and I am sorry for the delay. If the distributor had accurately
warned me of the length of the back-order, we might have done something
else.

Let me know how you like the printer. The more I know about how
products work for customers, the more helpful I can be. Let me hear from
you again.

Sincerely yours,

Joe Blankenship

Courtesy Letters

Business courtesies include acknowledgments, thank-yous of all
sorts, and file letters, whether written for your files or for someone
else's. These letters are seldom written to convey information; their
primary purpose is creating goodwill. You create goodwill by thanking someone for a good job or a courtesy, by acknowledging a
customer's order, by keeping the customer informed of any problems or delays. Finally, you create goodwill and prevent misunderstandings by putting into writing the results of telephone
conversations and informal meetings, then sending on copies for
people's files.

Letters of Acknowledgment

Acknowledging an order from a customer or a phone call from a
client is much like a file letter, written for the customer's files. The

major difference is that in acknowledging an order or a request, you are often also actively working to maintain or create goodwill for your organization.

The basic outline for an acknowledgment is simple:

The Background. Thank you for the order, we have your inquiry, we talked about this problem yesterday—followed by the acknowledgment, the details of the order, the inquiry, or the conversation, and the action being taken.

Follow-Up. Perhaps with more details of the action being taken or with discussion about the situation.

Closing. Thank you for your order, good luck, or whatever else is appropriate.

The acknowledgment letter is straightforward. It seldom has news for the reader. It recounts what has already been agreed to. Because of this, it begins with the issue under discussion, then adds whatever else seems appropriate. Still, it must be concerned with maintaining the reader's goodwill. When dealing with customers who seem unable to keep their checkbooks balanced, you may be tempted to add a sarcastic barb. The writer of the following letter forgot to actively work at keeping the reader's goodwill.

Dear Mr. Samuelson:

I have reinstated your policy, as we discussed this morning on the phone. We will bill your checking account each month in the future. I trust that we can count on you to have the money available so that these mix-ups will not occur again. After all, this is the second time this year that I have had to reinstate this policy.

I hope that you can be prompt in the future and that we won't have to discuss this matter again.

Sincerely yours,

The facts are fine, but the tone is abrupt and almost bitter. The writer sounds like a third-grade teacher shaking a finger at a naughty child. The letter in figure 6-3 acknowledges the telephone call and discusses the problem without berating the reader.

FIGURE 6-3. EFFECTIVE LETTER OF ACKNOWLEDGMENT

WORLD LIFE AND CASUALTY

February 15, 198–

Quentin R. Samuelson
1577 Marvel Lane
Northgate, MA 01536

Policy No: 42-A-5986-55

Dear Mr. Samuelson:

Thank you for the telephone call this morning. As we agreed, I have reinstated your life-insurance policy and the automatic premium payment provision through your First National account #78-945-432-35.

Beginning with the current premiums, your checking account will again be billed directly each month. If you will be sure that there are sufficient funds to cover these billings, the procedure will run as smoothly for you as it has for many others.

We understand that a person will occasionally have a mix-up in financial matters. We are sorry that our letter about the returned checks alarmed you, but you can understand our need to find out about these payments.

If you discover a problem in the future, a call to a policy correspondent here at the home office will help us deal with the problem so that we can help you keep your insurance in force.

Please call or write to us again if we can serve you in any way.

Sincerely,

Sandra Holloway
Policy Correspondent

Thank-You Letters

We often think that writing a thank-you letter is a chore, even when we sincerely appreciate what has been done. But an effective thank-you letter is an excellent way of bringing you and your organization to someone's mind in a positive and personal way. Such a letter is a strong image-building tool.

A thank-you letter has one obvious purpose—to make someone feel good for doing something for you or your organization: giving a speech, writing a letter of recommendation, reviewing a proposal, providing services, or giving money.

Thank-you letters fit less traditional occasions also. You may even use a thank-you letter as a follow-up letter, thanking a potential customer for visiting your showroom or for the telephone inquiry, or thanking a new customer for an order, telling when the merchandise can be expected—and of course reminding the reader of your presence.

A thank-you letter is brief. It thanks a specific person for a specific task. Making the thanks and praise specific will keep you from falling into the gushy, boring thank-you-letter style. Make your praise genuine; make your reader feel good (after all, that's why you are writing).

The outline for a thank-you letter is often this:

General Thank You. Identify the specific task and occasion, whether a gift to an endowment fund or an inquiry about a new checking/ savings account.

Specific Follow-Up. Mention something that was particularly enjoyed or particularly successful, something that the gift will be used for, perhaps sending some requested information.

Close Out Any Left-Over "Business." Briefly explain how the remainder of the reader's pledge may be donated or when your reader can expect the honorarium check or the ordered merchandise.

A Final Thank You. This may be coupled with a hope that you can use the service again, that you can assist the reader or customer again, or some other appropriate and specific offer or wish.

You will modify this outline to suit your needs, often combining the third and fourth points.

Tone

Most thank-you letters are not specific enough to create the kind of goodwill they intend. As you write, ask yourself, How can I make this person feel good about what has been done? Even the most traditional of thank yous—for the after-dinner speech—should be specific.

> Dear Sylvia Washington,
>
> On behalf of the people attending the awards banquet the other evening, I want to thank you for your speech about Yosemite.
>
> I know that the people at the awards banquet enjoyed the evening much more because of you.
>
> Your honorarium has been processed and you should receive your check shortly. Again, thank you for the fine talk.
>
> Sincerely yours,

This writer must think that the check is a sufficient thank you because there is no other personal touch here. A good thank-you letter should be personal above all else (*see* figure 6-4).

FIGURE 6-4. EFFECTIVE THANK-YOU LETTER

Western Distributors
Door-to-Door and Person-to-Person Sales

June 18, 198–

Dr. Sylvia Washington
Chief Botanist
California Wilderness Preservation Society
2651 West Dandelion Road
South Sonora, CA 95373

Dear Doctor Washington:

On behalf of the people attending the awards banquet, I want to thank you for your presentation, ''Along John Muir's Trail.''

Several people have remarked how much they enjoyed your stories of the old days in Yosemite, especially the anecdotes about John Muir. Your excellent photographs of the region and your storytelling ability made the banquet a treat for us all.

Again, thank you. Your honorarium has been processed; you should receive your check shortly. Best wishes on the book you are currently writing on John Muir; I look forward to reading it.

Sincerely yours,

Bernard G. Moore
Awards Committee

Here is a second thank-you letter. It is passable but not as good as it should have been. Perhaps the writer got bogged down because she was writing a form letter.

Dear Contributor:

Thank you for your donation to the Friends of the Museum annual fundraising auction.

You contributors have provided a wonderful catalog of items for auction this year, from original paintings to evenings at local restaurants. The money we raise will be spent on numerous worthwhile projects to enhance the museum.

Enclosed are two complimentary tickets for you. We hope that you can attend the auction. Unfortunately, we can provide only two tickets to a donor.

Again, thank you for your donation.

Sincerely yours,

To be an effective thank you, the letter should be much stronger. This letter seems to emphasize that it is a form letter almost every chance it gets, from the salutation to the vague way it tries to be specific about donations and projects. The letter in figure 6-5 is a positive thank you throughout, even though it is a form letter.

FIGURE 6-5. EFFECTIVE FORM THANK-YOU LETTER

CITY MUSEUM OF SCIENCE AND HISTORY

June 18, 198–

Tom Murphy
Suite 612
4516 College Way
Sunset City, MD 21430

Dear Tom Murphy,

Thank you for your donation to the Friends of the Museum annual auction.

Because of you and many others like you, we have a wonderful catalog of items for auction. We have exciting plans for the money this year, including restoring the prehistoric exhibits and developing hands-on and walk-through exhibits depicting many different cultures and civilizations.

We are enclosing two complimentary tickets for you. We hope that you will attend and enjoy the evening along with the Museum members and supporters from throughout the area. Tickets will be available at the door if your party includes more than two.

Again, thank you for your generosity.

Very sincerely yours,

Cornelia Jones, Director

File Letters

A file letter puts into writing the results of a meeting or telephone conversation. Although writing such a letter is a "courtesy," it is often important.

The file letter turns into paper those conversations and understandings that may evaporate. The file letter allows understandings to be verified, then filed where they can later explain why something was done a particular way.

There is no particular outline for a file letter. Generally it begins by setting the stage: "In our meeting yesterday, we agreed that . . ." The agreements might be outlined chronologically or grouped by topic.

Because this letter reports completed agreements, you are seldom concerned with the reader's response to the agreements themselves. The meeting was the place for the discussion and negotiation. If more negotiations are needed, another meeting will be needed. Do not alter agreements as you write a file letter.

You will want to be certain that you have been complete and that you have reported each item fairly. You may want to downplay some particularly sensitive issue, but if it has been agreed to, it must be a part of the letter.

Although you are writing for the files and your letter will probably only be seen by the person you are writing to, be certain not to let snide remarks or inside jokes slip into the letter. You and your reader may have an understanding about these things, but others may not. These relatively private letters have a way of unexpectedly being seen by others.

7

Bad-News Letters

You write bad-news letters for many reasons: to turn down job applicants and promotions, to reject manuscripts and proposals, and to disclaim liability. In writing any bad-news letter, your challenge is to tell someone No while maintaining that person's goodwill toward you and your organization.

Your No must be clear. No matter how much you want to ask a person to try again, no matter how close the person was in the competition, you must not waffle or hedge. To hold out false hopes simply because you are afraid to say No is cruel.

Your No must be pleasant, never snide or sarcastic. You may be turning down what seems to be a poorly conceived and hastily written proposal, but five years from now the person who submitted it may have an idea that will make your company rich. You want that person to think well of you and your organization even though you turned down the proposal.

Outline

The following outline will generally work for a bad-news letter, but you must be exceedingly careful about the tone.

Buffer or Introduction. Set the background for the bad news—the thousands of proposals, the hundreds of applicants, the rules of the company, the current economy. This is the backdrop for the bad news, but it is not the bad news itself. Sophisticated readers will know that bad news is coming, but still they will be better prepared for it by the buffer.

The Bad News. The No must be clear; it must be unequivocable. Read your letter as if you were the recipient. The No should be clear, firm, and polite.

Follow-Up, Further Explanation. Present the reasons for your decision. Let applicants know where they stood, let job candidates know what factors were decisive. If you can provide a useful pointer or offer positive encouragement, do so. If you can be helpful, you will be well remembered.

Close. Do not repeat the bad news; don't rub it in. The bad news should be clear in the second paragraph. If it is not, or if you have undercut it too much, go back and correct that. The close may be a simple "best wishes" or a hope that things will work out differently another time.

Tone

The tone in a bad-news letter is critical. Too blunt a tone invites ill will and may create hostility in a customer you are trying to mollify. But being too gentle is equally bad, whether you hide the bad news in a welter of detail or so praise the applicant or proposal that the reader does not understand why you are saying No.

Overly Blunt Tone

An overly blunt letter, such as this one an insurance company sent, invites a hostile reaction.

Dear Mr. Thomas L. Brown:

Our investigation reveals that the Eat-A-Burger restaurant has no liability for the damage to your bus or for the wrecker company charges. We therefore deny any claim you may have against Eat-A-Burger.

Very truly yours,

The No is certainly clear, and so is the writer's lack of concern for the reader. The claimant, Mr. Brown, will respond to this with irritation and possibly court action.

The writer may have intended to be brusque in hopes of stopping further discussion—the big insurance company telling the small claimant not to waste its time. This tactic may work, but it will create resentment and hostility even if it "resolves" this particular claim. With a little thought, it is possible to write an effective letter (*see* figure 7-1).

FIGURE 7-I. EFFECTIVE BAD-NEWS LETTER: DENYING A CLAIM

Worldly Insurance Co.

November 3, 198–

Claim No: ABC-83-456
Insured: Eat-A-Burger
D/Loss: 9-18-8–

Mr. Thomas L. Brown
Charter Bus Lines
125 North White Oak Avenue
South Des Moines, IA 50261

Dear Mr. Thomas L. Brown:

We have received your letter about your driver's accident at Eat-A-Burger. I apologize for the delay in answering, but as I am certain you can understand, we needed to investigate thoroughly before writing.

In our investigation we found no liability on the part of Eat-A-Burger for the damage to your bus, the loss of its use, the wrecker charges, or any other damages either actual or compensatory.

We do agree that the driveway your bus was attempting to negotiate is inadequate for your bus. However, common sense should have prevented your driver from attempting to use the driveway and the drive-through window. While the beginning of the driveway does not have a width warning, as you pointed out, it does have a height warning, which your bus exceeds by eighteen inches, and which your driver failed to heed. Had your driver been able to proceed around the corner, the bus would have run into the canopy over the drive-through window, doing extensive damage to the canopy and further damage to your bus.

Fortunately no one was hurt in the accident and neither the bus nor the building was seriously damaged. Still, even these minor accidents are inconvenient and surprisingly expensive. The towing charge that you reported, for instance, seems excessive; however, that is a matter for you to take up with your insurance carrier and with the wrecking company.

> Sincerely yours,
> WORLDLY INSURANCE
>
> John R. G. Ross
> Claims Investigator

Burying the Bad News

Writers sometimes bury the bad news so well that the reader must guess what is happening. Only the apologies and sympathies indicate that the letter contains bad news. The reader must sift through the letter several times to find the specifics. Here is a letter sent out by a major company to its employees. They had to guess at the point of the letter.

Dear Cynthia Mackey:

The economic conditions of our country over this last year are far from encouraging. Until recently, business shutdowns and curtailed activities were not affecting areas in which we operate.

During the first part of the year, it appeared that our total business for 198– would reflect another growth year; however, with industry closing and cutbacks in our operating areas, we have had to revise our projections to reflect current market conditions. We must take action to maintain and improve our position so that when the economic turnaround occurs, we can continue our growth. If this is done, our employees, customers, and stockholders will continue to remain secure.

I am pleased that not one of our employees has been laid off or received a reduction in wages due to the economic conditions. We have chosen to avoid such drastic measures. Instead, we believe a more prudent step is to postpone our September 1 scheduled salary review for all employees. This action, along with others, such as increasing our sales efforts to large industries and our cost-improvement efforts, will improve our financial stability during these difficult times.

Our intent remains to continue our steadfast course of improving benefits and providing equitable and competitive salaries for all employees.

Thank you for your understanding and support of this difficult decision.

                                        Sincerely yours,

After reading the letter, many employees were unsure what "difficult decision" had been made. But it's there, buried in one sentence in the middle of the third paragraph: routine raises were postponed three months. Most people would agree that postponing raises is better than laying off workers, shutting down the plant, or reducing wages, but the bad news is still bad news.

Admittedly, such a letter is difficult to write. No one wants to tell employees that they are not getting something they have been promised. When writing becomes difficult, it is natural to hide behind generalizations and side-issues, as this writer did. It is easier and more pleasant to talk about the economy in general than to talk about someone's raise in particular. If you were speaking this news, you would mumble. This letter is the written equivalent of a mumble.

By following the outline for a bad-news letter and doing some straightforward editing (eliminating some of the vague hopes for the future and replacing them with some specific plans and goals), this letter can be made effective (*see* figure 7-2).

FIGURE 7-2. EFFECTIVE BAD-NEWS LETTER: DELAYING EXPECTED ACTION

OKLAHOMA TOOL & DIE

August 1, 198–

Ms. Cynthia Mackey
879 North Oak Drive
Ravine, OK 74603

Dear Cynthia Mackey:

Through most of the current economic hard times, Oklahoma Tool and Die has been relatively prosperous. Large back-orders and our several unique tools have kept us from having some of the difficulties of our competitors. Unfortunately, the back-orders have been filled, and new orders are slow coming in.

To avoid taking the drastic measures that many companies in our field have taken, we are postponing for three months the employee review and merit raises scheduled for September 1. This decision applies to all employees.

This was a difficult decision to make and we realize that it will work a hardship on many. Our company remains "a small company" in many fine ways; we feel the hurt of our friends. We have shared good times through profit-sharing and production bonuses. Now that times are bad, it seems best to share the necessary sacrifice rather than having it fall on a few.

Economists expect the recovery to begin soon. We know that because of our quality products, we will be one of the first companies to feel the

---

FIGURE 7-2. EFFECTIVE BAD-NEWS LETTER: DELAYING EXPECTED ACTION
(CONT.)

---

renewed vigor of the economy. When we do, we will continue with our past policies of maintaining competitive salaries for all positions.

Thank you for your understanding and support in these hard times.

Sincerely yours,

Marjorie Kineavy, President

Being Overly Solicitous

Sometimes writers are overly solicitous. The No is clear, firm, and prominent, but there is so much concern for the reader, so much praise for the turned-down applicant or proposal, that the reader screams, "If I'm so good, why didn't you hire me!" or "Why didn't you accept my proposal!"

If the writer begins to praise the reader before saying No, the reader gets a nasty shock in addition to the bad news.

Dear Mr. Garth:

Thank you for applying to Natural Gas and Pipeline as a technical writer. Your academic record—both the courses and the quality of your work—is outstanding. Your references are stunning, and your writing samples show a wide range of skill and experience, especially considering that your work experience has been very limited.

Unfortunately, you do not appear to have all the background that you need to meet our requirements. Consequently, we have hired someone else.

We wish that we could have hired you, and we wish you the best of luck at finding a job that will match your talents and potential.

Sincerely yours,

The applicant must wonder why he wasn't hired. The writer has been overly solicitous. To rewrite, we will follow the outline and put the news into an honest perspective (figure 7-3).

FIGURE 7-3. EFFECTIVE BAD-NEWS LETTER: TURNING DOWN
AN APPLICANT

NATURAL GAS AND PIPELINE

October 28, 198–

Mr. C. David Garth
709 Ohio Road
Indiano, IN 47378

Dear Mr. Garth:

Thank you for applying to Natural Gas and Pipeline as a technical writer. Of the more than forty applications we received, yours was one of the half-dozen given very serious consideration.

Unfortunately, as you know from the ad and from our interview, we need a writer with an extensive background in the pipeline industry. Because of your lack of experience with pipelines, we are unable to offer you the position.

Your educational background, your outstanding references, and the materials that you presented—both your application and your samples—suggest that you will be an excellent technical writer.

I enjoyed interviewing you, and I am sure that you will find a job that will suit your needs and let you get that often elusive first actual experience.

Sincerely yours,

Joanna R. Bixby
Personnel Director

Tragic News

We have been discussing the kind of news that makes people unhappy, but not tragic news, not life-and-death news. If you must write such news to someone, ignore most of what we have said. Present tragic news directly. Attempts to buffer it are unintentionally cruel. Follow this outline:

The Tragic News Itself, without Adornment. "We regret to inform you that your daughter is missing and presumed drowned. . . ." Give the details and the facts. It is a horrible shock, but it is better than accidentally misleading a reader by buffering the news.

Amelioration or Commendation, If Possible. Here belong the details about what happened and the nobility or heroism of the people involved, as appropriate.

Help Available. Include one or two people or telephone numbers to contact for help—counseling, insurance, funeral arrangements, and whatever else is available. *Briefly* outline the services and help that the reader can easily get. Giving too much information is as bad as giving too little; too much information may confuse the distraught reader.

Regrets and Close. Your task is finished. Nudge the reader to get help or take advantage of services; say that someone from the chaplain's office or from the airline will be contacting the reader next week; say whatever else is appropriate and end.

That's all you can do.

8

Persuasive Letters

PERSUASIVE LETTERS ask someone to do something: complete a form, give money, buy something, correct a problem, pay a bill, adopt a procedure, or hire an applicant. Even cover letters may be persuasive, if they argue that recommendations in a report be adopted or procedures be changed.

This chapter discusses persuasion in letters—getting the reader's attention, keeping that attention, getting the reader to adopt the action you want. Most of what we say here has its roots in classical rhetoric, but we do not want to review classical rhetoric; we want to help you write effective persuasive letters.

Before you begin writing, estimate your chances for success. Writing a good persuasive letter is work. If you know your cause is hopeless and you still want to put your views on record, consider writing a position paper (*see* Chapter 18). You will need much less time and effort to write a clear, informal position paper than to write something to sway a long-fixed mind.

Understand Your Purpose

As you begin, spell out for yourself your *specific purpose* for writing. Spell it out even more exactly than when you write a purpose statement (*see* pages 19–21). What *exactly* do you want your reader to do after reading your letter? Send a check for $45.10 to bring an account up to date, change a vote on this issue, call this phone number for more information about these services, or award this company this contract?

Your purpose is not to berate your client about the overdue account, but to collect the money. Focus on your specific purpose as you write; everything you include should support that purpose in some way.

If you are to persuade your audience, you must find a point of agreement, a point where you can sense them nodding their heads and saying, "Yes, that's right."

The point may be a truism ("We all have a stake in protecting freedom") or it may be very specific ("We must defeat the Lobster party in the election"). It may be better profits, decreased turnover and increased morale, or more effective and efficient service. You must analyze your audience to determine what the point of agreement will be.

Types of Audiences

You must carefully identify and define your audience (*see* pages 8–14) when writing a persuasive letter. For this discussion, we will look briefly at three possible sets of audiences, focusing on how much you know about them rather than on their positions on your issue.

Friends

Knowing people well does not necessarily improve your chances of persuading them. When trying to persuade friends, writers often lose sight of their purpose. First, they may become overly concerned with what friends will think of them or of their performance. Second, they sometimes try to anticipate all the likely reactions and objections. They lose themselves in a jungle of guesses, suppositions, and second-guesses.

But you should be able to focus on some useful facts. You should know the *kinds* of arguments friends respond to—emotional or logical?—and the *kinds* of issues that sway them—profits or reputation? principles or utility? Knowing how they are usually swayed, you should be able to write an effective letter.

Identified Groups

Often you will be writing to a group that you know in general—people belonging to a specific organization, who have a specific job, who have responded to a plea or questionnaire.

Even though you do not know individuals, you do know why their names are on your list. Use that information and make some broad assumptions about your audience as you write.

Suppose you are marketing a new line of cosmetics. Your approach will depend on whether you are writing to consumers or to retailers. Consumers care about featured colors, skin care, and creating a new image for themselves. But retailers care about profit margins, advertising campaigns, and point-of-purchase displays. Retailers want a good product, of course, but they will choose the one that will help the balance sheet.

Do not make overly specific assumptions. A person whose name shows up on the save-the-whales mailing list still must be persuaded to send you money to help save the Kodiak bear. Showing retailers a hefty profit margin and a terrific advertising campaign does not mean they will be willing to stock something that might hurt their reputations.

Strangers

Canvassing letters are often sent to large groups of people about whom you know nothing: strangers. You may be asked to write a letter to people on many mailing lists and in many parts of the country, so you will not even have demographic data.

When you know nothing about the people getting the letter, let the issue select your readers. Many of your letters will be thrown away unread; you can't prevent that. But if your letter is effective, interested people will read it. Find those readers by beginning your letter directly; ignore those readers who won't agree.

If you are selling children's books, for instance, assume that people who will buy them are already interested in children and education. Making a plea for books in the home—in an effort to convert the heathen (that is, to sell books to the bookless)—may insult your most receptive readers. You want to convince people to buy your books, and your audience already believes in the value of education.

But don't narrow your audience unnecessarily. It includes many people without children currently in the home—grandparents, aunts, uncles, friends, and teachers—and perhaps people who have never had children but who might give such books to a children's hospital.

Define your issue in broad, relevant terms: education—not schools public or private, not busing, not anything except giving a child the best opportunities. In your terms, that means books. Show how your books enhance opportunities; then develop secondary issues such as value, binding, and the classical tradition.

Tone

There is no single tone for all persuasive letters. A series of collection letters might begin with a very friendly letter and progress toward a firm, perhaps even a curt letter. The right tone is crucial for an effective letter.

Your tone reveals and reinforces your attitude toward your subject, your audience, and yourself. Occasionally you may, as you write, fall into the best tone for your letter. More often you must choose from a variety of tones that seem to be emerging as you write. Analyze your tone and take conscious control of it.

A Confident Tone

Use a confident, positive tone. Things may be bad, they may get worse, but something can be done, if your reader is willing to help.

Recently a political group sent out a plea letter full of gloom and doom. Indeed it was so full of gloom and doom—the end of everything true, good, and beautiful was so near—that we wondered why anyone would send money to their cause. If the letter was accurate, the only thing left to do was to turn everything into freeze-dried food and head for the hills.

Your reader must feel your confidence and determination. You may have been trying to collect an account for ninety days, but if you write with a whine, expecting not to get paid, your expectations will be fulfilled. To sound uncertain is to invite failure.

Avoid a threatening tone, however. If you are ready to turn an account over to a collection agency, say so, and then help the reader avoid having that happen. Here is an effective closing from a firm but polite collection letter:

> . . . We would like to work with you on this bill and arrange a payment schedule we both can live with. We are prepared, however, to submit your account to a collection agency.
>
> As soon as you receive this letter, give our bookkeeper, Phil Gordon, a call at 555-1234. Let him help you arrange a payment schedule. We want to work with you to maintain your credit rating.

Keep the tone positive and confident.

Maintaining Goodwill

The tone you choose can do much to help you maintain the reader's goodwill or to help you lose it.

A home heating company sent out its annual get-your-pre-season-heating-checkup promotional letter. The letter included this paragraph:

> We are currently finding a serious problem in old heating systems: cracked heat exchangers. This can cause a dangerous situation because it allows the fan to blow air into the combustion chamber, either blowing the pilot out or "rolling" the flame out the front of the furnace. The only real solution for the cracked heat exchanger is to replace the furnace.

The writer seems to know the business, but the reader with a ten-year-old furnace may feel that the low-cost pre-season checkup is a setup for the sale of a new furnace.

You want your readers to trust you. It is not enough to have your reader's best interests at heart. You must *seem* a reasonable person interested in your reader's welfare.

Be careful with negative language of all sorts. Appeal to the hopes of your audience. The more negative your language, the more strident your tone, the more likely you are to lose readers who may have agreed with you. You may feel good about telling them "the hard facts," but your goal is to persuade your audience to do something particular, not to make yourself feel good for "sockin' it to 'em."

And, surprisingly, avoid most humor. Humor is very tricky. When writing within your organization, you may find yourself effectively using a self-deprecating tone. Otherwise, humor is almost always at someone's expense. Readers often resent it. Concluding your argument for day-care centers with a barb directed at probable opponents will cost you points, no matter how worthy your position. Take on the opposition directly. If the opposition to day-care centers focuses on cost, then argue costs. Show how the centers can pay for themselves with nominal fees, increased productivity, and less sick-time.

You may not win, but if you resort to sarcasm, you will lose.

Your Credibility

To be persuasive you must be believed. If you are not believed, nothing else matters, including the quality of your thought and your evidence. This is not simply a matter of having your facts right, although you must do that too.

You create credibility with your expertise, your background, and with the tone and evidence you bring to the letter. You maintain it by demonstrating (not parading) your knowledge of the subject, both factual and emotional, by sticking to germane points and treating your evidence honestly.

Your organization's image may advance your cause or handicap you. The most compelling evidence becomes suspect if your organization is suspect.

When research sponsored by a tobacco company institute fails to show a link between smoking and lung cancer, for instance, most of us are skeptical. We are suspicious of the baby-food company, its sales declining, sponsoring research that "shows" homemade baby food creates a greater desire for salt. Indeed, each company may be right and its research beyond reproach, but most readers are suspicious.

Sometimes you may want to rely on your own expertise. You understand how personnel procedures should be written and here are your suggestions. You have been a teacher for many years and understand how administrators should be evaluated. You have been a volunteer in a hospital as well as an accountant and have seen several kinds of waste.

Such expertise may include your experiences and your understandings as an outside observer or as a participant. If your audience does not know you well by name or job title, you need to make clear the basis of your expertise. Don't be bashful, but don't be overbearing.

Be very careful of the you-have-no-right-to-question-me tone. This is usually an attempt to hide fear and insecurity, to avoid questions and discussion. In a crisis, agencies and bureaucracies often adopt this stance, sometimes deliberately. If you find this tone creeping into your writing, examine your attitude very carefully. The mere presence of this tone will create suspicion and hostility with some readers.

Unless your audience has negative associations with your name or your organization, they will generally pick up your letter in a neutral frame of mind. Then you can establish both your goodwill and your credibility. To do this, use your evidence and the tone of the letter. Both goodwill and credibility are much easier to maintain than to establish. If you have them, be careful not to lose them.

Your Evidence

Your evidence may consist of statistics, trends, profit-and-loss statements, and the results of surveys and questionnaires, as well as the logic of the situation. Your evidence may also consist of anecdotes, personal observations, and these, too, constitute facts and a kind of logic. Examine the presentations that sway you. Assume that your audience can be swayed in similar ways. Generally you will use both rational and emotional arguments in every persuasive situation.

Rational Arguments

Our society prides itself on being rational and logical. We argue that one procedure or one product is more cost-efficient than another; we argue that one product is of better quality and should be bought even though it costs slightly more. "This person will do the job well because of experience and educational background." "Please pay this bill so that I can pay my bills and so we can continue to do business." "Please reconsider my claim for these reasons."

There are several major kinds of rational evidence, including data, authority, and logic.

Data. Look at the facts, the numbers, the statistics. Take surveys and tally the results; then try to interpret them. In using data, you are dispassionate and objective. The facts may scream for action, but the writer does not. Let the facts "speak for themselves."

Authority. Look at experts in the field. On the basis of their expertise, what do they say, what do they believe? An expert in one field is not an expert in all fields, of course; football players are not necessarily experts on panty hose, for instance.

Logic. Look at the logic of situations and possible alternatives. Also look at the logic of arguments. Do these facts actually relate to one another as you say? Do the arguments fit together?

Emotional Arguments

Emotional speakers and writers are often distrusted. Yet an appeal to emotions—to hopes and fears—can persuade people. Emotional arguments are seldom appropriate *within* government and business organizations, but they can be used in making public appeals—whether for money, votes, or support. Just be careful that an emotional approach does not lead to ranting and raving.

Combining Arguments

In writing a persuasive letter, you must combine rational and emotional arguments. The current debate on nuclear arms, for instance, deals in both kinds of arguments. Stories of the burned and dying in Hiroshima or hypothetical stories of the impact of a nuclear blast on Detroit appeal to our emotions, as do stories of enemy invasions and calls for a strong deterrence, and a renewed spirit of patriotic duty and sacrifice. But these concerns may involve rational arguments also.

An opening emotional argument often effectively gets the reader's attention, allowing you to persuade with the logic of your position and your factual information. After a logical presentation of the argument, urge the reader to action with a final emotional argument —another starving child or another glimpse of the future as it can be.

Writing the Letter

Keeping your reader in mind throughout the writing and editing process may help you reconcile the sometimes troublesome conflict between your desires and the reader's interests. While persuasive letters vary widely, we can present a useful way to organize one: reader—writer—reader.

Open and close with the reader's interests. Develop your interests in the middle. If you open with a point of agreement, it should be easy to develop the reader's interests.

To keep the most readers, open not with the world going to the dogs but with a concern for saving the world from the course it is on. Establish contact with the reader: "I am answering your ad," "This is our country," or "We all believe in people getting what they pay for."

Then develop your interest, your point. "Here is how I fit your ad," "Here's what we can do for our country," or "I too think I should get what I pay for."

Then your interest and the reader's interest should merge at the end to focus on your specific purpose: "I am available for an interview," "Join us in fighting this swelling tide by sending money," or "Correct the order so we can continue to do business."

Balancing your interests and the reader's interests can be challenging. If you are collecting an overdue bill, you may discuss the problems of cash flow, sympathizing with the person trying to do business in uncertain economic times. But don't invent excuses for the client; you want the bill paid.

The Hook or Grabber

In letters to people you know or do business with, let your reader quickly know why you are writing and get to your point.

But in letters you are sending to strangers, you must get your reader's attention. You do this with a hook or grabber, a direct attempt to capture the reader's attention. Sometimes you do it visually, with a picture, the letterhead, or overall appearance. Usually you do it in the first sentence.

While the hook or grabber is the first thing the reader reads or sees, it is usually the last thing you write. Look at your letter and ask how you can hook the reader. Often the hook can be lifted from a thought or image in your letter; sometimes you will need to create a new one.

Recently an investment firm sent out letters inviting people to a financial planning seminar. It had no hook.

Dear Investor:

A few days ago we sent you an invitation to our newest Financial Planning Seminar at the Monterey Hotel, 238 Airport Road, Boulder, New Mexico, on Tuesdays April 5 and 12, 198– at 7:30 P.M. Not having heard from you, we felt this invitation may have gone astray.

There is nothing here to grab attention. The possibility that a letter might have gone astray was not enough to intrigue us. Neither the paper (cheap) nor the letterhead (drab) conveyed any feeling of wealth or power—the things that people expect investment services to understand.

In addition to investing another penny in a better sheet of paper (which would have also made the letterhead look better), the writer needed a grabber. Many are possible:

> You no longer have to be rich to get rich.

or

> Now you can invest with the wealthy. You can shelter income and earn the same tax breaks they do.

or

> Now you may be able to turn your middle-class wage into upper-class retirement.

Get the reader's attention; then make your pitch.

The Close

In saleswork, people speak of "the close," the tricks used to get the interested customer to stop being interested and to buy. Your letter too will have a close, where you will try to motivate the reader to act. You want your reader to buy the product, send the check, interview the applicant, or vote for the candidate.

Move things along, if that's appropriate. Remove obstacles. Tell the reader what to do and how to do it. Provide an envelope. Push a little bit. "I will be in Detroit next week and can arrange to see you then." "Write out a check now so that we can close our books on this matter." "So let me hear from you today. Just indicate—on the enclosed card—the number of fun and fact-filled issues of *'TEEN* you want to receive, and return it along with a check or money order."

Gimmicks

Persuasive letters, especially plea letters, use many gimmicks to get the reader's attention and to get action.

Most of the attention-getting gimmicks are obvious: colored envelopes, overprinted envelopes saying "dated material" or "urgent action required," even beginning the letter on the outside of the envelope so that the reader will begin reading instead of routinely throwing away this piece of "junk mail."

Other gimmicks push the reader to act as you want. Ask the reader to fill out a survey or questionnaire, position a token, lick a sticker, or mail in a sweepstakes chance. These gimmicks all start the reader doing something positive about your letter.

We cannot tell you what gimmicks will work on your readers, but we can give you two cautions. First, be sure that you are attracting a kind of attention in keeping with your cause and your audience. Second, beware of overused gimmicks. Your own taste should be an appropriate guide if you once again see yourself as the reader.

Enclosures

Especially in plea letters, writers often enclose brochures, flyers, or other materials. Sometimes these are gimmicks to get attention; sometimes they help set up the close; sometimes they provide more information. These materials are extra. They should reinforce your point, but they will not substitute for the persuasion of your letter.

Generally, do not refer to enclosures until late in the letter; you may omit mention of some enclosures altogether. Keep the reader's attention on your words. Once your readers get onto the other materials, you may have trouble getting them back to your point.

Writing Technique

Writing a persuasive letter is a ruthlessly rational process. What is your specific purpose? what issue will relate to the audience?

what has been done to focus on the reader's needs?—all these questions must be answered, and the material that detracts from the purpose must be excised.

Two examples illustrate the variety of persuasive letters. An architectural firm wrote the letter in figure 8-1 while awaiting a contract decision. Since the letter followed the proposal and bid interview, a grabber would have seemed out of order. Still the letter begins with the reader's interests—thank you for the interview—and closes with them—do you want more information? I hope we can help you.

FIGURE 8-1. PERSUASIVE LETTER FOLLOWING INTERVIEW

WILLIS, READ, & MAY, INC.
Architect and Designers

Joseph S. Collins, Administrator
Brookside Medical Center
2614 East Donaghey Avenue
Brookside, KY 42711

Dear Mr. Collins:

On behalf of Willis, Read, & May, I want to thank you for considering our presentation on the proposed Brookside Medical Center Psychiatric Facility. We enjoyed the interview, and we want to reaffirm our interest in working with you on the project.

The following is a very brief summary of major points made in our presentation:

—Willis, Read, & May is firmly committed to achieving excellence. We are particularly interested in projects where architecture contributes to the health of the individual.

—Our hospital experience is enhanced by extensive design experience in the highly specialized area of mental-health-care facilities. Much of our success has resulted from close communication with our clients.

FIGURE 8-1. PERSUASIVE LETTER FOLLOWING INTERVIEW (CONT.)

This is achieved through our "on site" design sessions at which the client participates in the actual details of the design process.

—Careful scheduling of projects has resulted in savings of time and money on major medical projects. Our proposed schedule for the Brookside Psychiatric Facility is just ten months from design start-up to construction.

—Willis, Read, & May has demonstrated repeatedly its ability to meet and control budgets, particularly in types of projects that often go over budget.

We believe that a private psychiatric-care facility such as that proposed by Brookside Medical Center will be a major asset to mental health care in your region. We want to reiterate our interest in the project, our qualifications, and our desire to be of professional service.

Please contact me at any time if we may provide you with additional information. Again, thank you for your attention and consideration.

Sincerely,
WILLIS, READ, & MAY, INC.

Judith C. May, AIA

Asking a teen-ager to renew a magazine subscription is very different. Here (figure 8-2) the letterhead, complete with picture, hooks the reader, as does the promotional layout. The tone of this letter fits the letterhead—bright and breezy. Again, the outline of the letter moves from the reader—hi—to the writer—look at our magazine—and back to the reader—send in your renewal.

Throughout both of these letters, the writers focus on what they can do for the reader. The writer's self-interest is presented as uniquely filling the reader's need. The two letters differ greatly in tone and content, but each is effective in its own way.

FIGURE 8-2. PERSUASIVE LETTER: SUBSCRIPTION RENEWAL

ROXIE CAMRON
6725 SUNSET BLVD.
LOS ANGELES, CA 90028

Hi!

I'm Roxie, 'TEEN's Editor

The guys in the subscription department tell me <u>your 'TEEN subscription is about to expire—only two more issues to go!</u>

I hope you won't let that happen 'cause we've got so many exciting things planned for you in the months ahead, and you won't want to miss <u>ANY</u> of them!

That's why I'm writing—to give you a personal preview of what's coming up and up-'n-coming in future 'TEEN issues. Of course, there'll be <u>Dear Jack</u>, <u>Dear Jill</u>, <u>Reader Write-On</u>, <u>Dear Doctor</u>, <u>Dear Beauty Editor</u>, and all your other favorite columns. But there's a lot more in the works, too!

   *** In-depth features on SEX AND DATING PROBLEMS
   *** CAREER GUIDES to help you plan a beautiful future
   *** MONEY-MAKING IDEAS to finance your boundless energy and enthusiasm
   *** Exciting PEN-PAL EXCHANGES that help you share and compare your world with others
   *** In-the-know and behind-the-scenes features on your FAVORITE ENTERTAINERS
   *** HOME SEWING AND CRAFTS to brighten your denims and decor
   *** Answers to your biggest BEAUTY PROBLEMS
   *** RECIPES AND COOKING HINTS to tantalize a party of 2 or 20
   *** FABULOUS FICTION that's fun, fancy and fitting

You name it! Every issue of 'TEEN will be full and fuller of everything you want to know about. (We get over 25,000 letters a month from teens that tell us what's on your mind! And what's on your mind is on our pages.)

FIGURE 8-2. PERSUASIVE LETTER: SUBSCRIPTION RENEWAL (CONT.)

So let me hear from you today. Just indicate—on the enclosed card—the number of fun and fact-filled issues of 'TEEN you want to receive, and return it along with a check or money order. Do it today! Keep us coming your way and we'll keep coming up with more, more, and MORE that you won't want to miss out on!

Sincerely,

9
Memos

MANY PEOPLE THINK of memos as short, informal letters that stay within a department or organization and are written on memo paper instead of letterhead.

Most memos are shorter and less formal than letters; most are written on memo paper and stay within your organization. But memos are not simply second-rate letters.

Memos do most of the things that letters do, of course. They convey messages of all sorts including good and bad news, thank yous, and file summaries. Lengthy memos may actually be reports or manuals.

Most often memos remind or announce. They seldom persuade. You may write to alert readers to problems, to suggest solutions, or to set out the merits of competing positions, but seldom to change someone's mind. Within organizations, people usually settle issues in person—at conferences, on the telephone, and in meetings. Then they report the outcomes through memos announcing new policies, changed procedures, transfers, and retirement parties.

Memo or Letter?

Sometimes you need to choose between sending a memo and a letter. In practice the choice is seldom based only on how far the correspondence is traveling. It is based on the tone and the appearance you seek. Letters are structured and personalized, addressed to individuals (even if the individual is only Dear Customer), and written to individuals, not a group.

Choose a letter when
—you want a more formal tone, including a formal salutation, closing, and signature, as you usually want when writing to specific people outside your organization (but *see* Informal Memos, below).
—you want to structure your correspondence as a letter is structured, with opening, body, and closing—when you are being persuasive, for instance.

Choose a memo when
—the letter format seems stuffy, as when writing to a group in your organization or an immediate superior.
—the information is the primary concern rather than the tone with which it is delivered (even if the information is going outside of your organization).

Informal Memos

For greater efficiency, many companies now use memo forms to respond to customers. These commercially available forms contain space for two or three messages. The forms have several sheets of paper and carbons so that messages can be written back and forth, with each sender keeping a copy of each message. Because the original question or problem stays with the reply, information passes back and forth as efficiently as notes being passed around a schoolroom.

These memo forms look very informal but they allow an organization to handle routine matters, including customer inquiries or requests, quickly and inexpensively.

Some organizations reply to routine inquiries and requests with notes written on the bottom of a letter. Again, this is quick and lets the reader know exactly what the writer is responding to. Such informal memos are sometimes sent between organizations even at the executive level.

You must, of course, follow your own organization's policy in using informal memos of any sort.

You need to keep copies of informal memos just as you do regular memos and letters.

Purpose

Memos are information documents (the deadline has been changed; we need a meeting; your report was deficient in these ways; here are our options). Memos should yield their information —good, bad, or indifferent—quickly and easily.

Memos are office writing—brief and direct, even terse—to be read, understood, and acted on in the midst of the noise and the sometimes mind-deadening routines of the office. The memo itself should be written for the convenience of the reader—message first, background later.

Audiences

Your audiences for a memo are almost always inside the organization and usually close to you—your supervisor or someone in the next office. Often you write to groups of people: the receiving clerks, the sales staff, or the research clerks. Often you write about situations that you have already discussed with your readers. However, even when you are dealing with a touchy subject, you should be direct about it. Indirectness in a memo always stands out.

Tone

Memos—memorandums, notes—are usually less formal in tone than letters. You naturally use fewer job titles, more abbreviations,

and more in-house jargon than you would in letters on similar subjects.

The memo format itself—without salutation and closing, with a
subject line—encourages both directness and familiarity.

Typing

Normally, type memos single-spaced on memo paper, with a double space between paragraphs. Short memos—one paragraph—are
sometimes double-spaced.

Typing a memo on letterhead makes it seem much more formal.

Some large bureaucracies, both private and governmental, have
style manuals—sometimes called correspondence guides or manuals—that prescribe the format for all but the most informal memos.
If your organization has such a manual, you should follow it.

Format

Memo paper generally has To, From, Re, and Date lines printed
on it. These are usually aligned under each other at the left margin.

Traditional form calls for aligning the names, the subject, and the
date under each other, usually like this:

    To: All Sales Agents
    From: Sarah Jossings, Sales Manager
    Re: New Memo Formats
    Date: April 30, 198–

To and From Lines

To and From lines take the place of salutations and closings. They
may refer to individuals by title or by name, or they may refer to
groups by rank, job title, or classification.

Job titles are usually used with names in the To and From lines except in very informal memos.

Memos rarely use salutations or complimentary closings.

Initials and Signatures

Initial or sign only those memos out of the routine or those which may raise legal or organizational issues. By doing so you accept responsibility for the content. Initial or sign a memo near your typed name on the From line.

Initialing or signing routine memos, especially to colleagues, seems overbearing.

Re or Subject Line

The Re line (from the Latin *res,* meaning "thing" or "matter") should reflect the point of the memo, not the general topic—"Saturday Parking" or "Change in Sick Leave Policy" rather than "Weekend Use of Facilities" or "Employee Benefits."

Sometimes the line is labeled Subject instead of Re.

Date Line

The date line is usually the last line of the heading. The date is written in the style used in the organization: *January 12, 198–* or *12 January 198–.*

Writing the Memo

Because you can assume that the audience knows of the situation, because your memo is often a follow-up to a conversation or meeting, your information is the most important item.

Begin the memo with the new information. Then explain the information, add details as needed, and finally fill in the background for people or the files.

This allows your reader to decide how far into the memo to read. After reading the first line, at most the first paragraph, your reader should know whether to toss your memo out, to act on it, to file it for reference, or to read on. Readers expect memos to be to the point.

Occasionally you may feel compelled to structure a memo in some other way. However you structure it, think about the person who must read it.

First Line

Announce the specific purpose of the memo in the first line. Don't refer to the Re line or use it as an antecedent.

Avoid opening with a general point: "The purpose of this memo is to announce new shipping procedures"; instead begin with the specific point, "We are initiating new shipping procedures immediately. These procedures will increase office efficiency and speed customer deliveries."

Thank-You Line

Memos that contain inquiries or request favors often close with a thank-you line even though there is no complimentary close or signature.

Style Problems

Memos that focus on the writer and background instead of the needed information are ineffective. Memos should be direct. Anything else is annoying, as the following example proves:

This year Personnel sponsored a very successful lunchtime speakers series on many topics, including recreational and motivational topics. The topics ranged from repairing and reupholstering a sofa to sailboating.

Next year the Office of the President will join Personnel to co-sponsor an expanded lunchtime series. The range of topics can be even larger and the speakers may include some local celebrities as well as professionais to discuss stress management, family growth, and self-help and life-management topics of all sorts in addition to the hobby and leisure-time programs.

It is possible for the series to include some entertainment—local bands or choirs, for instance. Ms. Dodger in Personnel and I expect to take turns introducing the programs.

I am asking you for suggestions about specific programs and speakers. If you have a topic in mind but don't know of someone to present it, please suggest the program anyway. We will try to find a speaker. Please send your suggestions to Ms. Dodger in Personnel.

This is an inefficient memo. The memo buries the request for suggestions, the crux of the memo. The other information is background. Some of it, such as who is going to introduce the programs, is completely irrelevant.

Information about expanding the program is necessary, of course, if people are to make useful suggestions. But the memo contains little detail. Figure 9-1 shows a concise and direct version of the memo.

The rewritten memo includes all the pertinent facts and still creates an inviting tone. Even in this memo, paragraphs three and four could be omitted. Thanking Ms. Dodger is not required but does add to the pleasant tone.

FIGURE 9-1. EFFECTIVE MEMO

MEMO

TO: All Unit Heads
FROM: The Office of the President
RE: Suggestion for Lunchtime Programs
DATE: October 28, 198–

We are asking employees to suggest programs for an expanded lunchtime series. Programs will be presented weekly instead of twice a month and will include a great variety of topics. Suggestions for program topics or specific speakers should be sent to Ms. Elaine Dodger in Personnel.

In addition to the self-help and leisure-time programs of the past few months, we anticipate adding programs in life-management, such as budgeting time and dealing with family changes and stresses, and perhaps some entertainment programs, including talks by local celebrities and performances by local bands and choirs.

This lunchtime series has been extremely popular. We owe a large Thank You to Ms. Dodger and the others in Personnel who organized it. I think the expanded program will be even more enjoyable.

Thank you for your suggestions.

UNIT IV

Proposals

10
Proposal Writing

So YOU WANT to (or maybe you have to) write a proposal. Congratulations! Proposals win contracts and jobs; contracts and jobs make money. Proposal writing is an important assignment, and you should welcome it as an opportunity.

Good proposal writing is not the jealously guarded secret of some elite profession. It doesn't take years of training or a Ph.D. in technical composition. True, some pitfalls exist, but some timely advice may help you avoid mistakes before you make them. This chapter presents concerns common to all proposals. The following chapters discuss three frequently written kinds of proposals: procurement, grant, and sales.

Classifying Proposals

Proposals offer services or products in a specified time, usually for a set fee. The different classifications of proposals help define their nature.

Solicited and Unsolicited

Proposals originate in different ways. If someone comes to your organization and requests a proposal, that proposal is said to be solicited. For example, if your local fire department is unhappy with the increasing costs and decreasing coverage of its insurance package, it might look into changing insurance companies. The chief comes to your insurance agency with a list of requirements and asks you to propose new coverage. If you are working on this solicited proposal, you must be certain your solution meets all the requirements listed by the chief.

Unsolicited proposals—ones that have not been invited—are harder to write. True, you aren't obligated to meet the desires or demands of an outside source. But neither have you been asked for a solution. An unsolicited proposal offers a workable solution to a problem, but it must first convince someone that a problem exists. Unsolicited proposals, because they have no audience waiting for them, are less common than solicited proposals and must be twice as persuasive.

Internal and External

Proposals, like memos or correspondence, are said to be internal or external; that is, they either remain within an organization or travel outside it. Internal proposals may be relatively minor, dealing, for example, with purchasing procedures or streamlining an operation—"Suggestion Box" ideas. Others may be the result of years of study and lead to radical changes within a corporation. Right now a multivolume proposal is circulating in one of the major automobile companies. If implemented, it will drastically change the relationship between labor and management. At another corporation—one of the country's largest cosmetics manufacturers—an internal proposal led to relocating the research and development department to a different state.

When we talk about proposals, however, we usually are referring to external proposals, proposals written by one organization or individual for another organization. (Our discussion focuses on such proposals.) One group has a need or a problem that another can fill or solve. This need might be quite specific: feeding two hundred employees three times a day. Or it might be a problem that the funder can only describe and hope some other expert can solve: to produce a strong yet flexible material that will last a hundred years and be resistant to salt water, drying, barnacles, and powerful tides. In this case, the funder advertises and the proposer responds.

Different Forms

Proposals come in several shapes. The simplest proposal is one yelled across the room: "Hey, why don't you try plugging it in!" The most complex might propose the design and construction of a space station to circle the earth. The first takes no writing skill; the second would fill volumes.

A proposal can appear in a memo, a letter, a report, or on a standard form. Memos and letters propose relatively simple projects. More complex projects require more complex proposals and have a title page, table of contents, introduction, discussion, conclusion, and appendices. Such proposals follow usual report procedures modified by the unique features of a proposal.

Standard-form proposals—in which the buyer dictates to the proposer the form that the proposal must follow—often appear in government, which seeks uniformity for the sake of standard evaluation.

Purpose of Proposals

Proposals have two ends: to sell a solution and to sell the ability of your organization to produce the solution.

Sell Your Solution

Proposals may propose anything, though they usually offer a specific solution to a specific problem, to be provided within a specific time at a specific price. Selling your solution to a problem requires two different skills:

1. finding a feasible, economically viable solution;
2. communicating that solution in clear, concise, and convincing language.

If either is missing, you have trouble.

We repeated "specific" deliberately. Almost all proposals are detailed, concrete, and precise—not philosophical abstractions or general statements of intent. They lead to legally binding contracts. They contain details, facts, dates, and budgets. So always include the details: the more precise a proposal, the better.

Sell Yourself

A proposal also sells the proposer as the one to implement the solution. Your organization doesn't make any money if someone else wins the contract. Selling yourself is a two-step job:

1. Document that your firm has performed well in the past, can do so now, and is likely to do so in the future.

2. Show by the professionalism of your proposal that the work of your firm is expert.

Proposals and Persuasion

Your proposal must compete with other proposals, convincing the requester that your solution and your firm are best. If a proposal is dull, you probably won't get the contract, no matter how effective the solution. Proposal writers must do a lot more than just supply information.

1. *Begin your proposal with an attention-getting device.* Sometimes you have to hit the mule on the head with a two-by-four to get its attention. But choose your two-by-four carefully. Don't be cute; don't be trite. Maintain a businesslike tone. The most successful attention-getting devices for business center on profits; for government, on competence and reliability.

2. *When appropriate, find a theme for your proposal and weave it throughout.* Your theme might be the high quality of your firm's work or the uniqueness, efficiency, or economy of your solution. Use a key word in the title, in the introduction, and throughout the proposal to communicate your theme.

3. *As often as possible, document what you say with statistics, facts, and testimony from well-known experts.* The appearance of authority is persuasive.

4. *Put yourself in the place of the people who will evaluate your*

proposal and try to write positively. An example of this is replacing the No Smoking in the Theater sign with Smoking Permitted in the Lobby. Both messages convey the same idea, but the second is written positively and more persuasively.

5. *Remember your reader when you write the proposal*. Repeat key words and ideas. Signal all transitions. Structure your work and reveal the structural logic to your readers.

Proposal Stages

In casual conversation we often talk about "writing a proposal." In fact, writing is only one part of the process—and often *not* the most difficult or the most time-consuming part. At least four stages occur in the proposal process. Two deal with solving the problem: the analysis and design stages; two more with creating your proposal: the strategy and writing stages.

Solving the Problem: Analysis

Carefully study the proposal package (also known as the "bid-set" or the "solicitation" package). Are you and your organization qualified to submit a proposal? Are you able and willing to perform the work requested? Can you respond to everything in the proposal package? Can you meet the deadlines?

At this stage you should get in touch with the contracting agency. Be sure nothing has been added or changed since the publication of the proposal package. Ask for any necessary clarifications. Even if you don't have any questions, call and discuss the proposal. Let the contracting agent learn of your interest and intent.

Solving the Problem: Design

Organize a team of interested and qualified employees to work on a solution. Even if the solution is relatively simple, it is best to assemble a team. Unless the proposal is strictly personal (a research fellowship or training stipend, for example) mentioning a team adds credibility to the final document. Also, someone on the team may have an idea or discover a problem that you missed.

In designing your solution, go back to the proposal package. Study all the instructions. Look closely at the evaluation procedures; find out what the requester is emphasizing. Then go back and study all the instructions once more.

Creating the Proposal: Strategy

Once you have a workable solution, choose a persuasive strategy that sells. If you infer that the contracting agency is primarily interested in an economical solution, stress economy. If the contracting agency seems most interested in the longevity of the solution, stress that. Find a winning, persuasive strategy around which to organize your workable solution.

Creating the Proposal: Writing

The final stage is the actual writing. Once you understand the demands of the request, have found a feasible solution to the problem, and have devised a strategy to sell your solution, writing the proposal is almost a mechanical operation—but one that includes all the skills every writing task demands! Just follow the "simple" rules of clarity, conciseness, and coherence (*see* Unit VIII). While easy to say, this is, unfortunately, like telling someone to do good and reject evil—a lot of decisions and judgments must be made along the way.

Proposal Length

This question often comes up: "How long should a proposal be?" If the funder limits the length, the answer is easy. You must not exceed the stated page limit. More often, however, an easy answer is impossible. One thing is certain, don't pad. Time is too valuable to be wasted on unnecessary length. We can only agree with Abe Lincoln when he was asked how long a person's legs should be. He answered, "Long enough to touch the ground." In proposal writing: long enough to get the job done.

Nonresponsiveness

The most frequent reason for the rejection of proposals is nonresponsiveness. This is government talk for "failure to follow directions." If the directions for a proposal call for twenty pages and yours is twenty-one pages, you are "nonresponsive." Your proposal will be disqualified no matter how good everything else is.

Similarly, if the directions say that you must have a licensed electrical engineer on your payroll, and you do not prove that an electrical engineer works for you, you are nonresponsive. Your proposal will be disqualified.

Government agencies are usually required by regulation to disqualify nonresponsive proposals regardless of their quality. Therefore, follow all directions and answer all questions. If you can't meet all the requirements, you are probably wasting your time submitting the proposal.

Other Sources of Help

Other proposals—winning and losing ones—are often your most valuable source of help. If you can, get several proposals similar to the one you must write. Study them. Compare the winners and losers. Look at any comments made by the evaluators. What led to one's success and the other's failure? Spending an hour examining other proposals can often be more useful than anything else.

Other proposal writers are also excellent sources of help. Find someone who has a good track record in putting proposals together and get the value of first-hand experience. But be careful. There are self-styled experts, who give advice freely, but have never written a successful proposal. The advice they give is worth exactly what they charge for it. Talk to someone who has written winning proposals.

11

Procurement Proposals

THE LARGEST CUSTOMER in the world for goods and services is the United States government. Each year, thousands of government offices and agencies solicit an astounding array of products and services—from anvils to psychic predictions, stuffed animals to salmon inseminators, spy satellites to financial analyses.

No one knows the amount spent each year on federal procurements. Estimates in 1980 placed it at well over $100 billion a year. Another statistic illustrates the importance of this economy. The United States employs more than 128,000 people whose sole job is managing the government's buying!

How does this huge buying operation work? Experts think that only 15 percent of the buying is done by competitive bid. That leaves about $85 billion a year to be allocated by proposals. The government announces it needs a product or a service, invites proposals, evaluates them, then negotiates the work, time, and cost with the finalists.

Such procurement practices are not limited to the federal government; the standards and methods of federal proposals are models for many state and large local governments. We will use federal procurement practices for our discussion.

Bids *versus* Proposals

A bid occurs when there is no doubt about the product or service to be purchased, when no elaborate or special conditions have to be met by the bidder, and when price is the only variable factor in determining who will win the contract. For instance, the government wants to buy ten thousand No. 10 cans of Grade-A Tom Terrific Tomatoes. The only variable is price. The agent for the purchase publishes the specifications, announces the due date, looks at the bids, and awards the contract to the lowest bidder.

But more and more often federal agencies judge the awarding of a contract upon criteria other than price. For example, a proposal is called for when it is impossible to estimate a cost. The price of a new jet bomber, for instance, can't be determined until it has been designed and developed. So the government initiates the project by inviting a proposal.

The contractor offers a technical response to the Defense Department request. The contractor promises to research and develop a plane that can do what it must do, and deliver that plane within a specified period. The Defense Department agrees to pay for the cost and design of the plane plus a predetermined fee. A proposal has been submitted and accepted.

Other situations also encourage proposals rather than bids. For instance, a problem exists but the government doesn't know what solution to request; it's not sure of the service or product to purchase. The agency which has the problem asks experts outside of government to analyze the situation and submit a proposal.

Congress and regulatory bodies frequently forbid a federal agency from awarding contracts on the basis of low price alone. Congress restricts most agencies by a host of regulations that establish standards which must be met before a company can do work for the government.

Here is an example of how federal regulations encourage proposals. The Small Business Act of 1958 says, "It is a declared policy of Congress that . . . a fair proportion of the total purchases and services for the government . . . be placed with small business enterprises." To meet this goal, some work can be given only to companies with limited capitalization; this requirement leads to proposals rather than bids.

Request for Proposal

Whenever the purchase of a product or service is more complicated than just finding the lowest price in the marketplace, the government publishes an RFP, Request for Proposal. For a large and complicated contract, the government may give advance notice of an RFP. Otherwise, it publishes the RFP in the *Commerce Business Daily*. The government may also publish the RFP where it hopes qualified responders will see it: in trade journals, professional publications, industry newsletters. Figure 11-1 shows a recent RFP from a newspaper.

FIGURE II-I. SAMPLE REQUEST FOR PROPOSALS

Request for Proposals

Notice is hereby given that in accordance with EPA Grant Regulations 40 CFR 35.936-7 and 40 CFR Part 33 (42 FR 8090 February 8, 1977) proposals are hereby requested from qualified approved Minority Business Enterprise engineering consultant firms to perform the following services:

Performance of all necessary services for the sampling and Laboratory Analyses of Wastewater for the City of Lincoln Wastewater Treatment Facilities, EPA Project No. C-050600-01. The Laboratory Analyses shall be completed in accordance with EPA guidelines and be subject to review and approval by the EPA, Arkansas Department of Pollution Control and Ecology, and Furgusson and Stapleton, Inc., prior to completion of the engineering services requested herein.

Interested qualified MBE consultant firms are invited to submit proposals to be received not later than 5:00 p.m. local time, Friday, October 15, 198–, at the office of Furgusson and Stapleton, Inc., 1402 Marked Tree Road, Syracuse, Arkansas, 72701.

Specific information pertaining to the form of the proposal, including required data to be submitted, will be provided upon written request.

Two features of this advertisement are noteworthy. First, the job is apparently small, appropriate for local concerns. Second, the advertisement gives enough information to limit the number of inquiries to qualified proposers, in this case Minority Business Enterprise consultant firms. If you had responded to this RFP, you would have received a letter, shown in figure 11-2, revealing the concerns of the contracting agency.

FIGURE 11-2. SHORT RFP RESPONSE

Fergusson and Stapleton, Inc.
1402 Marked Tree Road
Syracuse, Arkansas 72701

October 4, 198–

Mr. John Sandalman
Sandalman Engineers, Inc.
2727 "P" Street
Little Rock, Arkansas 72204

Re: Request for Proposals—MBE Consulting Firms
     Wastewater Treatment Facility Plan
     Lincoln, Arkansas
     EPA Project No. C-050600-01

Dear Mr. Sandalman:

We appreciate your interest and response to our request for proposals from qualified MBE consultant firms to provide engineering services relative to the sampling and laboratory analysis of wastewater.

During the wastewater sampling and analysis phase of the facilities planning process, the consultant, as a minimum, must be capable and qualified to perform the following appropriate sampling methods and laboratory analyses for the following wastewater parameters:

   BOD_5 (must dechlorinate effluent sample)
   Total Suspended Solids
   Total Settleable Solids...

We request the following information to be included in your proposal . . .

a) <u>MBE Qualifications.</u> Submit a statement certifying MBE status and basis for recognition as MBE. The MBE firm is required to submit a self-certification statement that they are qualified in conformance with the Region 6 MBE Policy of the EPA National Policy as set out in 40 CFR 35.936-7 and 40 CFR Part 33 (42 FR 8090 February 8, 1977).

b) <u>Contract Type.</u> The contract type will be a unit cost per each sample and per each type of laboratory analysis . . . The MBE firm will be required to complete and furnish to our office EPA Form 5700-41. However, if a firm figure cannot be provided, a cost plus fixed fee might be considered.

c) <u>Proposal Contents.</u> The proposal should include the following information:

 1) <u>Qualifications.</u> Information reflecting qualifications of the person or persons assigned to provide services.

 2) <u>Experience and Competence.</u> Information indicating specialized experience and technical competence . . .

 3) <u>Capacity for Performance.</u> Identify a number and title of staff available and specific time frame for completion of the work.

We trust the information provided will be adequate for the submission of your proposal. Please contact me if additional information is required. We appreciate your interest and look forward to reviewing your proposal.

Cordially yours,

James C. Jones, P.E.
Project Manager

Clearly, neither the cost nor the technological solution is of great concern to the contracting agent. In fact, the government agency doesn't specify how the service is to be performed and sets few standards. That's up to the contractor. Of greatest concern in this reply is the identity of the bidder; that gets attention in the letter.

Technical, Management, and Cost Proposals

The project described in figures 11-1 and 11-2 is a small one, but most government contracts are not so small. Because proposals in response to RFPs include—by definition—more than just the cost of a product or service, they are often long and complicated. In fact, it is common (though not mandatory) for the federal government to ask for three proposals: a technical, a management, and a cost proposal. Sometimes the technical and management proposals appear together and the cost proposal is separate. On small jobs, the three are submitted as one.

The Technical Proposal

The technical proposal tells how the job will be done. It details the solution, lists the facts and figures, and proves that the solution will work. The government evaluates the technical proposal first, rejecting all proposals that are unworkable or nonresponsive. Next, the government examines the management proposals of those remaining.

The Management Proposal

The management proposal establishes the contractor's willingness and ability to meet the regulations set forth in the solicitation package and to complete the proposed project. A variety of management issues may influence the successful completion of a project, including a firm's organizational structure, finances, present work load, trade union relations, and record-keeping systems. After all, an ingenious solution to a difficult problem is worthless if the organization is unable to carry it out. Information about your company's policies, personnel, finances, past performance, and overall stability is vital to the procurement officer.

The Cost Proposal

If several proposals remain in the running, the cost proposals come into play. But the least expensive proposal is not the automatic winner. The cost and the solution are examined together, and the organization that makes the best total presentation will be invited by the agent to attend a "best and final" session.

The best and final session allows government representatives to ask questions, verify prices, and sometimes ask the contractor to reconsider prices. Sometimes, all the bidders who make the final short list are invited to the best and final, and they all have a chance to argue their case and change their price. The best and final session is the final opportunity for the government to question the effectiveness of your proposed solution, to determine the viability of your organization, and to whittle away at your charges. Following the best and final, the government awards a contract or cancels the RFP.

The Time Element

One of the most annoying features of working on proposals—and one of the most critical—is the brief time you have to produce the final document. All too often the RFP gets published only weeks— or even days—before the due date.

Short deadlines reward companies poised to act upon an RFP. Rumors abound that the limited lead time is an intentional move to limit the number of bidders and to aid favored companies, which get early notice. Whatever the reason for short due dates, be prepared to meet deadlines that are too close.

Don't get frustrated; parcel out as much work as possible; be prepared to work weekends.

Your First Procurement Proposal

The easiest and most effective way to discuss producing a procurement proposal is to walk through the various stages, noting what goes on and pointing out hidden traps.

Solicitation Package

In response to the government's RFP, you will receive a solicitation package (also known as the "bid-set" or the "proposal" package). For a small proposal, a brief letter may set out the requirements, as in figure 11-2. If a major proposal is being solicited, the package may be the length of a book.

For instance, a solicitation package from the Department of Health and Human Services advertises for "an Employee Counseling Service to be made available to federal employees at two Queens, New York, locations." The project is to run for ninety days with an option for an additional twelve months. The solicitation package is fifty-seven pages long.

The following outline of the package from the Department of Health and Human Services illustrates the kinds of information a bid-set package may offer.

1. *Federal "Regs."* Copies of all regulations affecting the proposal, or a general statement about the regulations in effect, the "regs by reference." Here is one example of the regs you might find: "The applicant hereby assures and certifies that it will comply with the flood insurance purchase requirements of Section 102(a) of the Federal Disaster Protection Act of 1973, P.L. 93:234, 87 Stat. 975, approved December 31, 1976."

You as contractor should read all the regs to guarantee compliance. Most are perfunctory.

2. *Checkoff Forms.* Forms that need only a check in the requisite boxes and a signature. The check signifies that you meet the criteria

of the regulations in question: small business status, minority own-ership, geographical location, equal employment opportunity, or environmental impact studies are a few possibilities.

3. *Contract Form*. Your organization must sign this form and submit it with the proposal. If the government agency accepts the proposal, it will countersign the contract, making it legally binding.

4. *A Cover Letter*. The letter introduces the solicitation package; it also gives the due dates, the names and phone numbers of the people to call for questions, and the place to send the proposal.

The letter sometimes contains other significant information. The cover letter of the package for the counseling service in Queens, for example, adds information important to the technical solution. And while it contains a disclaimer that the content is "for the offerer's information only and not considered restrictive for the proposal purposes," the letter says the government thinks the work can be done in "approximately sixty-five professional workdays." You had better thoroughly justify a budget based on seventy days.

The importance of cover letters can't be overemphasized. The cover letter to one project, for example, announces, "This package represents a competition of a contract currently being performed satisfactorily and the incumbent is expected to respond." Don't put much time into this proposal.

5. *Instructions to Contractors*. These tell you what sort of con-tract will be accepted (fixed-price or cost-plus-profit), how to format the proposal, and what to include.

6. *Background to the Statement of Work*. This section defines terminology in the statement of work (*see* below), details the prob-lem that exists, and states the objective of the solution and the policy concepts that apply.

7. *Evaluation Standards*. This document lists the standards by which the "source evaluation board" will judge the proposal. The criteria are individually weighted. The source evaluation board uses these criteria to score the proposal. You should pay attention to the relative value of each category. We discuss the importance of the evaluation criteria below.

8. *The Statement of Work (SOW)*. The SOW is the most impor-tant document in the solicitation package. It describes the product or service the government wants to buy or the problem the govern-ment wants solved. The SOW may be general, even vague, or it

may be concrete and specific. In either case, pay careful attention to it.

The statement of work for the counseling center in Queens runs twenty pages and covers many issues, each of which must be responded to. Here are the headings from that SOW: 1) Objective, 2) Tasks to be Performed, 3) ECS Training for Key Personnel, 4) Diagnostic Counseling, 5) Referral Counseling, 6) Follow-Up Responsibility, 7) Case Report Keeping, 8) Project Progress Reports, 9) Due Dates, 10) Staff Qualifications, 11) Office Space and Facilities, 11) Payment Provisions, 12) Excusable Delays, 12) Privacy Act.

Analysis Stage

Prepare yourself for your writing task by carefully studying the SOW and the evaluation criteria.

Statement of Work

The SOW is the key to any successful proposal. Before doing any work, study the SOW to be sure that you and your firm are able to meet the requirements as well as to perform the task which the government requests. Don't put in hundreds of hours of work on a proposal that will be immediately dismissed for being "nonresponsive."

Should you have any doubts about your ability to meet the requirements set forth in the statement of work, *stop!* Call the federal agent and talk over your questions.

Ideally, the SOW tells you what product or service the government wants. But the world of government procurement is seldom ideal. Sometimes, for instance, the contracting agency may not be sure what it wants, knowing only that a problem exists that needs solving. Perhaps too many injuries are occurring in a steel-fabrication mill. What can be done to remedy the situation? The SOW may be vague.

Other times, the contracting agency may think it knows what it wants when it doesn't. One example of such a mistake occurred a few years back. A consulting firm in Tennessee recommended—and a federal agency agreed—to replace a turbine on an electrical generator at considerable expense and downtime. The agency wrote an elaborate SOW. When the contractors surveyed the job, however, they found only some clogged intake valves that needed cleaning. So much for the SOW.

Remember that you are the expert in the field; that's why the government is asking for your services. If you find errors, flaws, or holes in the SOW, it is up to you to make the necessary modifications so you can produce a workable solution.

The Evaluation Criteria

The evelution criteria define the categories by which your proposal will be judged. Figure 11-3 shows some of the criteria for the counseling project in Queens. Each category to be evaluated has a numerical value; the categories together total 100 points. Seldom will a proposal receive 100 points, but the ones that come closest are those invited to the final and best session. It is more important, consequently, to do well in all the categories than to excel in one at the cost of several others.

FIGURE 11-3. PROCUREMENT EVALUATION CRITERIA

Representations and Certifications

One copy of the attached Representations and Certifications must be completed and be signed by an official authorized to bind your organization. This shall be made a part of the original business proposal.

Section VI

A. Technical Proposal Evaluation Criteria

The following criteria will be used in the proposal evaluation, with each criterion weighted as indicated. Within each grouping the items are listed in descending order of importance.

FIGURE II-3. PROCUREMENT EVALUATION CRITERIA (CONT.)

	Weight

1. Technical Approach: Understanding the Problem   30 points
    a. Knowledge of and/or experience in ECS concepts, policy and operations.
    b. Knowledge of and/or experience in the principles of counseling in employee-labor-management situations.
    c. Knowledge and use of existing area community treatment/rehabilitation resources.
    d. Methods of maintaining required confidentiality of client information and problems . . .
2. Proposed Methodology of Presenting Required   10 Points
   Training Courses
    a. Prior relevant training experience.
    b. Means for reinforcing initial training message.
3. Qualifications of Personnel Performing Training,   30 Points
   Problem Evaluation, and Casework Management
   (Personnel includes proposed subcontractors or
   consultants, if any).

   Specifically:
    a. Counseling experience with alcohol- and drug-dependent persons and their families . . .
    b. General counseling experience
    c. Training experience

B. Award Basis

Concerning the basis for contract award, technical quality shall account for 70% of the basis and price for 30%. "Price" shall be evaluated by adding the option price . . .

Any bid or proposal which is materially unbalanced as to prices for basic and option quantities will be rejected as nonresponsive. An unbalanced bid or proposal is one . . .

The evaluation page alerts you to the relative importance the contracting agency gives different criteria. In the counseling-center example, the price is less than half as important (30 points) as the project design (70 points). In another project the design component of a proposal is worth 30 points, minority participation 25, and standard purchasing procedures only 5. It stands to reason that your Affirmative Action plans will need to be as detailed as the proposal design itself.

The value of a category helps determine the amount of discussion that category gets. Usually, a category that is worth 30 points will be three times longer than one worth 10 points.

The evaluation standards also influence how you word your proposal. Repeat key words, phrases, even sentences from the evaluation portion of the guidelines. Members of the source evaluation board may not be reading as closely as they should. By using the words from the evaluation criteria in your writing, you help them realize which criteria you are responding to.

Only the SOW is more important than the evaluation standards. If it is not clear who will be doing the evaluation, call the agent in charge of the project and ask. Government lawyers and accountants evaluate proposals differently than do experts in the field.

Meet the Agent in Charge

You probably will have questions—perhaps lots of questions—about what to include in your proposal, questions whose answers will influence what you write and how you write it. Meet or at least call the agent in charge.

You may have some questions that cannot—or should not—be directly answered by the procurement agent. But that shouldn't stop you from trying to get a sense of what you want to know. For instance, how stiff is the competition for the job? How many inquiries has the agent had and from whom? (One way to find out this information is to lead the agent a bit: "Well, I guess L&M Aluminum will try to use their new process for this project." If L&M has been talking to the agent, you might inadvertently get some valuable information.)

Another unanswerable question you should try to get a feel for is the amount of money the government is willing to spend for this project. If you know how much the government expects to pay, you may be able to increase your profit margin and still win the project.

A surprising amount of useful information can be obtained by finding a chatty agent.

In talking to the agent in charge, try to discover if there are any "hidden agendas" involved in the RFP. Is everything as it seems, or is there something else lurking behind the apparent? Has the RFP been designed with a specific customer in mind? Does the contracting agency know exactly what is wanted? Is the money authorized for the project? Sometimes a tone, an attitude, or a revealing word will give some insight into what is really behind the RFP and help you design your proposal. Don't be naive. As Alice learned in Wonderland, everything is not always as it seems.

Design Stage

After analyzing the entire solicitation package, you have decided that your firm might be able to get the job. The next step is to try to arrive at a feasible, practical, cost-effective solution to the problem in the RFP.

The Proposal Committee

To help design a solution to the problem announced in the RFP, form a committee. Before you reject our suggestion—"No committee has ever come up with a good idea, and besides a committee means long meetings and wasted time"—hear us out.

If the proposal you write will be only two or three pages long, then forget the committee. Obviously the problem is an easy one and the extenuating circumstances few. After you finish your proposal, simply pass it around to four or five colleagues to get their suggestions and for their information.

But if your proposal will be substantial, set up a committee to:

—generate a range of ideas for solving the problem,

—increase the chance of finding any problems in the SOW,

—help spot holes or errors in your solution,
—spread the workload when time is at a premium,
—help you draft and write the final proposal,
—protect you from sole responsibility for the proposal.

Probably most of us have had bad experiences with committees and committee work. Too often, however, we forget the times when a committee was essential to solving a problem.

One problem with committees is their tendency to dilute responsibility, leading to late completion of assignments. To forestall this, first agree to some realistic deadlines for work on the proposal. Then stick to them.

For large proposals, the design and writing work is parceled out according to the major parts of the final proposal. A director oversees the whole project and is responsible for coordinating all phases of the proposal. Each part of the proposal—the technical, management, and cost components—is the responsibility, respectively, of the engineers, managers, and accountants. The director, however, must pull all the parts together, make sure they cohere, and complete the final work.

Your Solution

Keep the SOW and the evaluation criteria directly in front of you. You may arrive at an ingenious solution, but it will be tossed out if it ignores the SOW and the evaluation criteria.

To make sure you fully understand the problem posed in the package, write out the problem in your own words. The writing act itself encourages you to define the problem. And if you have the problem fully defined, you increase your chances of finding a comprehensive solution.

A cautionary note. Common wisdom has it that any solution to an RFP should not be too unconventional or radical. You should survey your area and discover what seems to be selling—what is "in" or "hot." For instance, in the 1960s a proposal for synthetic fuel made from corn would have been absurd, but by 1980, with huge farm surpluses, it was feasible. On the other hand, if you play too safe you may lose to a better, trend-setting idea.

Strategy Stage

After you and your committee have reached a solution that meets the demands of the SOW and considers the evaluation criteria, you must decide how to sell the solution. Before you begin to write the proposal, decide upon a proposal strategy.

Know Your Agency

Review the technical vocabulary and style of the agency you are writing for. If you are responding to a request from an agency in the Department of Interior, you had better know the jargon of that department. If you are writing a proposal for the military, your language and style should reflect military practice.

Think Ahead

Begin now to assemble the supporting evidence you need to bolster your proposal. Contact other departments in your organization for management procedures, standard purchasing practices, Affirmative Action plans, cost and quality-control guidelines, proof of safety and health-regulation compliance, environmental-impact statements, labor-union agreements.

Begin to document previous projects—preferably other federal contracts—that demonstrate your organization's successful track record. If no such projects exist, use work in the private sector to prove your organization's skill and dependability. Also, assemble résumés of key project personnel.

Persuasive Tactics

Plan your persuasive strategy. Persuasion is subjective and variable; no rules exist to ensure success. Instead, you must analyze each situation for the best persuasive tactics. There are four different concerns of any written work: what you say, how you structure or arrange your content, the style you use, and the physical presentation of the final writing. Each of these may reflect the three ways to persuade: by logic, by emotion, and by the image or reputation of your organization. (Persuasive tactics in letters are discussed in Chapter 8.)

Persuade by Logic. Procurement agents (and evaluation boards) think of themselves as reasonable people, so create and maintain a rational tone.

Try to determine the most important factor in the project. Read between the lines of the SOW as well as between the lines of your conversations with the contracting agent. Make the primary concern of the agency the controlling theme of the proposal and let it unify the proposal. For example, if the contracting agency is more concerned with your firm's experience than with its solution, build the proposal around experience and how it guarantees a workable solution. A proposal unified around a single idea is easy to grasp; it sounds logical.

Another way to appear logical is to include facts, figures, and authority. The more concrete the proposal, the more rational it seems. Take every opportunity to include specific and detailed data.

Finally, consciously assume a disinterested and businesslike attitude. Think logically; be uninvolved and objective. The tone of your writing will reflect your attitude.

Persuade by Emotion. One usual place to include an emotional appeal is at the start of the proposal. Beginning with a ''grabber''—an attention-getting device—is so standard that it's often difficult not to be trite. The old rhetorical-question grabber—''How would you like to have the whole Washington, D.C., Post Office renovated at almost no cost to the taxpayer?''—is as novel and effective as ads showing a ''typical housewife'' from a hidden camera.

Be more subtle. When you present your solution, work out a strategy that makes the contracting agent desire your project. Create the perception that your product or service will satisfy a need of the reader. Appeal to the civic pride of Washington residents or show how they will benefit from the new post office. Don't present your proposal as just a solution; present it as a solution whose primary end is the reader's well-being. Appealing to the self-interest of the audience is potent.

People prefer to think they are persuaded by logic, but they are more easily convinced by emotion. Include emotional ploys, but disguise them carefully. Word choices that are obviously biased will boomerang, but words that have subtle positive or negative connotations will work to your advantage.

Persuade by Image. Another way to convince your audience is through the image of your organization. An advertiser who hires a baseball player to sell razor blades or a movie star to hawk automobiles relies upon image. In each instance, the advertiser hopes that you will be persuaded by the public image of the person selling the product.

Similarly, persuade the procurement agent by your organizational image. The agent is often as concerned with the reliability of the contractor—the character of the bidder—as with the soundness of the solution or even the cost of the job. Do everything you can to create and communicate a good organizational image. Include your firm's successful past record; parade the credentials and honors of key personnel; attach a financial statement that proves your firm's solvency; append important managerial documentation that illustrates sound business practices. Do whatever you must to prove your company's strength, resolve, skill, and reliability.

A sound image includes the image that the written proposal projects. The final proposal must be error-free, and it should be professionally reproduced. The proposal becomes part of the successful, proficient image you wish to project.

Writing the Proposal

The design of the final proposal depends upon many factors, including the complexity of the project, the requirements of the proposal package, and the instructions for writing the proposal. For example, if the solicitation package recommends that the technical, management, and cost proposals be submitted separately, then you must have separate cover letters, tables of contents, and purpose statements for each.

Standard Forms

A major influence on the design of the final proposal may be the guidelines themselves; many will contain "Technical Proposal Instructions," "Business Proposal Instructions," and a "Budget Form."

While you must follow any suggested form, don't let it trap you. Creativity and persuasiveness become more difficult, but turn that difficulty to your benefit. Other proposal writers will despair of writing anything better than clear prose. Consequently, if you write persuasively within the limitations presented by the guidelines, you gain the advantage.

If your solicitation package recommends a standardized proposal format (like the one in figure 11-4), you must follow it. In this example you will see that five categories are to be included in the "Scope" section of the technical proposal. Make each a separate heading in the final proposal. In the five discussions, include specific phrases from the guidelines to clearly signal your reader what you are responding to.

FIGURE 11-4. PROPOSAL FORMAT

PART III—Instructions to Offerors ..... Technical Proposal Instructions

1. *Recommended Technical Proposal Format.* The following format is recommended for submission of technical proposals.

    I. <u>TABLE OF CONTENTS</u>

    II. <u>INTRODUCTION.</u> Summarize the importance that this project and your proposed approaches will have . . .

    III. <u>TECHNICAL.</u> Prepare technical proposal in response to the Technical Evaluation Criteria and to instructions below . . .

FIGURE 11-4. PROPOSAL FORMAT (CONT.)

A. Scope of Subpart
1. Objectives. State the overall objectives and the specific accomplishments you hope to achieve. Indicate the rationale for your plan, and relation to comparable work in progress elsewhere. Review pertinent work already published . . .
2. Approach. Use as many subparagraphs, appropriately titled, as needed to clearly outline the general plan of work, discuss phasing of research . . .
3. Materials and Methods. Describe in detail the methodologies you will use for the project, indicating your level of experience with each, areas of anticipated difficulties . . .
4. Accomplishments in the First Year. Explain the accomplishments you propose to achieve in the first year.
5. Schedule. Provide a schedule for completion of the work and delivery of items specified in the technical scope . . .
B. Qualifications
1. Experience. General background, experience, and qualifications of the offeror. Special notation should be made of similar or related programs performed . . .
a. Other Support. Describe other support being received . . .
2. Personnel. Describe the experience and qualifications of personnel who are available for work . . .
a. Principal Investigator. List name of Principal Investigator/Project Director responsible for overall implementation of the contract, and key contact for technical aspects . . .

Some of the "Instructions to Offerors" in our example are precise while others ask you to respond to more general ideas. For instance, "Approach" urges you to "use as many subparagraphs, appropriately titled, as needed to clearly outline the general plan of work." "Accomplishments," however, is less open-ended: "Explain the accomplishments you propose to achieve in the first year." Whether the guidelines are specific or general, keep in mind that you are selling your solution and your company. Write persuasively; keep your audiences in mind; present things from their perspective.

If your solicitation package does not include a proposal form to follow, design your own. Make it persuasive, but include the conventional proposal elements in the conventional order.

1. Cover materials: the cover itself, a letter of transmittal, and a table of contents.

2. Begin your narrative with an effective "hook" or "grabber," one that establishes your overall theme and strategy.

3. Define the problem, give your technical solution, review your organization's management systems, and detail the budget.

4. Close with a strong and convincing statement proving that your solution and your organization are preferable to all others.

5. In appendices attach testimony and evidence to support your proposal.

The conventional form contains many potential headings and features. Figure 11-5 lists some likely ones.

FIGURE 11-5. POSSIBLE PROPOSAL FEATURES

Cover Materials
    Letter of Transmittal
    Title Page
    Table of Contents
    Table of Illustrations
    Abstract or Summary

Introductory Materials
    Grabber
    Purpose Statement
    Reference to Earlier Association with Agency
    Reference to Earlier Association with Problem
    Definition and Restatement of the Problem
    Background to the Problem
    Subject and Purpose
    Needs Analysis
    Benefits to be Gained from Solution

Technical Response
    Scope of Solution
    Technical Solution

FIGURE 11-5. POSSIBLE PROPOSAL FEATURES (CONT.)

Methods to be Used
Feasibility of Solution
Staffing Plan
Organization of Design and Development Team
Technical Personnel Qualifications
Testing
Task Breakdown
Time and Work Schedule
Evaluation Procedures
Progress Reports

Management System
    Project Organization and Management
    Organizational and Administrative Structure
    Pertinent Management Policies
    Cost-Accounting Methods
    Payroll and Timekeeping Methods
    Dun and Bradstreet Rating
    Facilities Available
    Quality-Assurance Guidelines
    Personnel Qualifications
    Previous Experience
    Financial Viability
    Organizational Support

Budget
    Direct Costs
    Indirect Costs
    Subcontracts
    Type of Contract
    Method of Payment
    Late Penalties

Close
    Summary
    Conclusion
    Urge to Action

Appendices
    Letters of Reference
    Letters of Support
    Résumés of Key Personnel
    Applicable Management Policies

The Seven Parts of a Proposal

Whether you must follow a prescribed form or have the liberty to create your own, your proposal will usually include seven elements. These will not always be separated into the same divisions or appear in any predetermined order. We will discuss each of these seven in general terms, however, because each will almost always appear in a proposal.

Frontal Material

A letter of transmittal accompanies every proposal. Although this letter is not part of the proposal, custom requires that a copy of the letter appear in the proposal before the title page.

This letter is addressed to the contracting agent, and it may be the only part of the proposal the agent looks at. Therefore, you may want to include in the letter the essential features of the proposal, briefly stressing what is unique about your proposal.

The letter should contain at least three important pieces of information:

1. The last date the proposal can be considered. No proposal is offered indefinitely.

2. The name and address of your company's representative who is able to answer any questions that might come up.

3. An assurance that your company is willing and able to meet the conditions of the proposal.

In addition to the letter of transmittal, every proposal will have a cover, a title page, a table of contents, and a table of figures if necessary. Include a summary or abstract if your proposal is long.

Introduction

The introduction is one of the most important parts of the proposal. Write it last, after you are certain of your proposal. Use the introduction to anticipate your technical solution and your management proposal—and sell them. In marketing terms, here is where you create interest for the solution that is going to appear and where you begin to persuade the contracting agency that your solution is best.

The introduction might begin with an attention-getting device that begins to build the case for your solution. For instance, if your solution uses a new approach, you might use the introduction to point out the shortcomings of the usual techniques (the ones probably being proposed by your competition). The introduction also contains a complete purpose statement (*see* pages 19–21). The purpose statement (probably three to six paragraphs) discusses what the proposal responds to, what special tasks if any went into the proposal, and the scope and organization of the proposal.

This section also includes a clear and detailed definition of the problem, a definition carefully written to reflect the SOW and to anticipate your solution. This precise statement of the problem convinces your audience that you understand the issue while it makes sure that you have, indeed, thoroughly studied the SOW. But most important, the introduction sets up your audience for what comes later in the proposal.

Technical Solution

The technical solution is the heart of any procurement proposal. It varies greatly, according to the project's size, complexity, and scope.

Begin your technical proposal with a restatement of the problem and a concise discussion of your objectives. If you can define the work to be done in such a way that only your solution is suitable, you have won the contract. If the agency accepts your objectives—

and you have designed them to complement your solution—no other proposer can fully achieve those objectives.

Next, review the theoretical premise of your solution. Here you try to convince your audience that your solution is firmly anchored in the latest findings of the field. Review research; show how your solution is better than alternatives; prove yours is a winning idea.

If the proposal is not scientifically oriented and a review of research is inappropriate, discuss the strengths of your solution, whatever they might be.

Having established the viability of your solution, fully describe how you will perform the job. This section of the proposal is likely to contain graphs, time lines, charts, and illustrations. Describe the methods and materials you will use, the main tasks and minor tasks, the expected result of each stage, a schedule for the completion of each step, specifications for any product produced, the qualifications of all key personnel, and the legitimacy of your organization. This section will probably appear under a series of subheadings.

The technical solution section also includes résumés of the personnel most important to the project. Keep away from "boilerplate" résumés; that is, file only those résumés designed for your specific proposal. Also, be wary of "paper-hanging"—the practice of including in a proposal the impressive résumé of a highly qualified employee who will not, in fact, be involved in the project. You may get caught.

Management Profile

The management profile you include depends upon your organization and the job. We offer only a few general observations.

Include in almost any proposal a flow chart depicting the relationships among key personnel. For any project to be successful, clear lines of authority must exist. Evaluators believe that flow charts (organizational charts) clearly reveal any weaknesses in the chain of authority. We once worked on a project whose chain of command was not fully thought through. When we started to produce the flow chart for the project, we realized there were at least three possible supervisors. We went back and redesigned the workload structure.

Include an organizational chart that shows the relationship between the personnel in this project and the overall organization. An evaluator wants assurance that the people involved in the project are ranking members of the organization, or at least close to the people who make decisions.

In addition to human resources, this section should specify any pertinent facilities or natural resources. According to the solution you present, any number of documents might be appropriate. For instance, if the contract calls for the production of a commodity, include a summary of your firm's manufacturing facilities and quality-control methods.

The management profile includes a review of the record-keeping methods of your firm. Every government contract produces paperwork, for the product and for the proposal itself. The government expects records and progress reports to be accurate and complete. Discuss this phase of the work.

Finally, prove your firm's viability. Discuss financial stability, labor relations, past experience, present expertise, and organizational support.

Budget

The budget items usually appear on a form provided by the contracting agent. Fill out the budget form carefully and completely. The government is not as intransigent as private industry if a mistake is made, but an error may affect your profit margin.

Proposal Conclusion

The reader who likes to skim a document will expect a conclusion. Make it persuasive. Take one last opportunity to convince your reader that this solution and your organization are the only logical choices for the contract.

Appendix

The Appendix contains important information too bulky or too specific for the body of the proposal. For example, you mention your impressive and effective Affirmative Action plan in the body of the proposal. The Affirmative Action guidelines and a report of its effectiveness are appropriate for the Appendix.

The Appendix traditionally holds the glossary of important terms, if you need one.

When the guidelines limit the number of pages in a proposal, they exclude the appendices from that count.

Style

In addition to the traits of government and business style discussed in Unit VIII of this book, procurement proposals are persuasive (discussed above) and use visuals—illustrations, figures, graphs, charts, time lines. Contracting agents seem to love charts. Turning everything into some sort of chart or figure, however, is not the answer. Turning simple concepts into charts or figures can obscure their simplicity.

But we don't evaluate government procurement proposals, and it seems clear that people who do evaluate them think that charts and graphs are better than prose. Don't fight city hall. Give 'em what they want.

12

Grants

BUSINESS AND INDUSTRY exist to make a profit for their stockholders, not to invest in scholarly activities, artistic endeavors, social experiments, or humane causes—no matter how worthy or needy. Scholarly, artistic, social, and humane projects will in the long run, however, benefit business as they enrich the quality of our life. Aware of the gains to be had, the federal government encourages such funding by giving tax relief to private and corporate foundations engaged in grant-in-aid programs (commonly shortened to "grants"). At the same time, the federal government sponsors many grant programs.

Since World War II, the grant economy has become a major factor in correcting some dislocations inherent in our capitalistic system. Few people will deny the worth of cancer research, but few profit-making organizations can defend to their stockholders the funding of such long-term, pure research. But tax codes encourage corporations and individuals to support such public service projects; everyone benefits.

Grantsmanship and Grant Writing

Writing a letter, report, or position paper is relatively straightforward. You select, organize, and style your information. In applying for a grant, however, factors seemingly unrelated to the actual writing of the grant become important. In fact, writing the grant is only one part (and not even a crucial part, according to some) of the larger art of grantsmanship—obtaining a grant-in-aid.

Grantsmanship includes understanding various issues: funding sources, the evaluation methods, project designs, and your organization's plans. For instance, discovering the preferences of your funding source will help determine what you stress or de-emphasize in your grant application. Whether your funding source is public or private will influence your proposal design. Establishing an advisory board for your project will strengthen both the project and the final proposal. In short, mastering the art of grantsmanship is essential for writing successful grant applications.

Essential Criteria for Obtaining a Grant

If you or your organization want to submit a grant application, first consider three things:

1. whether you and your organization qualify for a grant;
2. whether your project is eligible for a grant;
3. whether your organization can execute the grant.

Do You Qualify? Grants-in-aid usually go to public or private non-profit groups or to individuals associated with such organizations. To apply for a grant, you must prove your nonprofit status. Usually your state's attorney general, the franchise tax board, or the Internal Revenue Service can provide such documentation.

In addition to proving nonprofit status, you or your organization may have to meet special eligibility requirements set by the granting body. For instance, the Levi Strauss Foundation limits its awards "to organizations which provide direct services in communities where Levi Strauss & Co. has production and distribution facilities."

Is Your Project Eligible? Foundations, corporations, and government agencies fund ideas and projects that are worthwhile but not necessarily profitable, projects that have social relevance but cannot be justified on the profit-and-loss statements of business or industry. A project designed for personal financial gain has little chance of being funded. While project eligibility differs among funding sources, the 1980 Kellogg Foundation statement of aims indicates the kinds of projects popular with many private granting organizations: "The Foundation is committed to improving educational opportunities that prepare individuals for work and citizenship and to improve services which benefit people. In some instances the approaches must also include defining public policy where it is inadequately stated or ineffectual in meeting its responsibility for the public's well being."

Can Your Organization Carry Out the Grant? Having an idea that can be funded does not require you to seek a grant. Consider the time, expense, and energy you and your organization will have to invest in the grant process and the project itself. Too often the allure of funds tempts an organization into commitments that are not in its best interests. Be sure the project complements the goals of your group before you seek the grant.

Competition and Time

To write a public or private grant is to enter a contest. In 1978, the federal government estimated that only five out of one hundred grant requests were funded. Today, more people are writing grants. At every stage of the grant-writing process, you must get the edge on your competition.

To compete successfully, you need time. A good grant proposal cannot be assembled in a few days or even a week. In addition to the time it takes to write and produce the proposal itself, it takes weeks to make the necessary contacts with the granting agency, to study all the pertinent documents, to document need and ability, and to organize the project and its personnel. Because many people are involved, managing and coordinating their contributions may take longer than you estimate. Give yourself plenty of time; then set deadlines—realistic ones—and stick to them.

Projects That Get Funded

The thousands of private and public foundations that award grants would seem to ensure a source of funding for any project. And foundations do support some strange ones. One private foundation limits itself to financing better breeds of animal stock; another funds only projects that lead to the creation of new musical instruments.

But it only *seems* as if any idea can find a sponsor. In truth, certain qualities increase the chances of winning a grant. Consider the following criteria as you design and write your grant proposal:

1. *Your idea is needed, and you can prove that need.* Money is scarce; no one will pay to reinvent the wheel. Moreover, you must be able to document need. A college education for convicted felons would seem to decrease the chances of their returning to jail. But a granting agency would want proof that this assumption is accurate.

2. *Your idea is timely.* Like it or not, ideas and concepts go in and out of fashion: some get "hot" while others—equally deserving —are ignored. Back in the 1960s, for instance, heroin maintenance programs were popular. Methadone and other experimental treatments found ready funds from public and private sources. Today, such programs are in disfavor; other causes have captured the public's fancy. Your project should not be too out of step with current trends.

3. *Your idea is innovative but not radical.* Funding sources gain prestige through the projects they sponsor. Little prestige accrues to a funder for giving money to an old idea, no matter how successful the idea may have been. The demand for innovation—for new approaches—is one shortcoming of the grant economy. Innovative: yes. Radical: no. Few funding sources want to gain notoriety for supporting radical or controversial solutions.

4. *Your idea leads to a finished project.* For the same reason that a funding agency avoids controversy, it prefers projects that lead to finished products. The funding agency itself is an organization with instincts for self-preservation, and a finished project enhances its reputation. One federal agency that supports scholarly research, for

instance, is reputed to refuse all grant requests for projects just getting off the ground (though this appears nowhere in its guidelines). A research project near completion, however, gets favorable attention. At the end of each year, this agency prints a list of its sponsored projects that have found a publisher.

5. *Your idea will find continued support after the grant expires.* Funding organizations prefer projects that continue after the grant runs out. Too, funding organizations like to get credit for beginning a successful, ongoing project. The Carnegie Foundation reminds everyone that they were the first to fund *Sesame Street*.

Funding Sources

Assuming that your project warrants funding, you must locate an appropriate funding source. There are three primary funding sources: the federal government, private foundations, and corporations.

The Federal Government

Washington is the biggest source of grants in the world, allocating as much as $40 billion annually. The federal government directs many of its grants to public bodies: municipalities, school districts, courts, and county agricultural agents, to name a few.

In addition, the federal government distributes billions of dollars to nonprofit groups outside of government. About twelve-hundred federal agencies have elaborate grant programs available to semi-private and private nonprofit groups, including schools and universities, orphanages, hospitals and hospices, and health and welfare groups of all types (from the Heart Foundation to the Salvation Army).

The government provides research tools to help you find a likely source of funding. Even if you know your funding source, researching that source will help you design your grant application. The annual *Catalogue of Federal Domestic Assistance (CFDA)* lists and discusses over one thousand grant-making programs. Figure 12-1 (a page from the *CFDA*) illustrates the information about one agency listed there.

FIGURE 12-1. PAGE FROM *CATALOGUE OF FEDERAL DOMESTIC ASSISTANCE*

OFFICE OF WATER RESEARCH AND TECHNOLOGY

15.950 NATIONAL WATER RESEARCH AND DEVELOPMENT PROGRAM
(Focused Research and Development Program)

FEDERAL AGENCY: OFFICE OF WATER RESEARCH AND TECH-NOLOGY, DEPARTMENT OF THE INTERIOR

AUTHORIZATION: Title I, Section 105(b), and Title II of . . .

OBJECTIVES: To support needed research and development into any aspects of water-related problems deemed desirable . . .

TYPES OF ASSISTANCE: Project Grants (Contracts).

USES AND USE RESTRICTIONS: To meet the necessary expenses of specific water resources R and D projects. JOINT FUNDING: This program is considered suitable for joint funding . . . For programs that are not identified as suitable for joint funding, the applicant may . . .

ELIGIBILITY REQUIREMENTS:

Applicant Eligibility: Educational institutions, private foundations or other institutions . . . whose training, experience, and qualifications are adequate for the conduct of water research . . .

Beneficiary Eligibility: Same as Applicant Eligibility.

Credentials/Documentation: Proponent must furnish evidence of applicant's qualifications . . .

APPLICATION AND AWARD PROCESS:

Preapplication Coordination: State and local governments submitting proposals are required to use standard application forms as furnished . . .

Application Procedure: OWRT distributes general guidelines as to research and development areas of interest along with proposal submittal instructions to potential applicants. Applicants submit unsolicited pre-proposals or proposals to OWRT for review and evaluation. Proposals from the academic community are to be transmitted to OWRT through the appropriate State Water Research and Development In-

---

FIGURE 12-1. PAGE FROM *CATALOGUE OF FEDERAL DOMESTIC ASSISTANCE*
(CONT.)

---

stitute. Each proposal should state (1) the nature of the project to be undertaken, (2) the period for which it will be pursued, (3) the objectives expected to be attained, (4) the qualifications of the personnel who will conduct and direct the project, (5) the importance of the project to water economy of the nation, (6) its relation to other known research or development projects currently pursued, and (7) an appropriate budget. . . .

Award Procedure: OWRT advises successful and unsuccessful applicants, and negotiates . . .

Deadlines: Unsolicited proposals may be submitted at any time unless specific deadlines . . .

Range of Approval/Disapproval Time: 150 to 180 days.

Appeals: None.

Renewals: Renewals are considered by submitting . . .

ASSISTANCE CONSIDERATIONS:

Formula and Matching Requirements: No cost sharing is required by statute; however, some cost sharing . . .

Length and Time Phasing of Assistance: Length of time for research project accomplishment varies. Usually, projects . . .

POST ASSISTANCE REQUIREMENTS:

Reports: Quarterly and annual project progress reports. Final completion reports, setting forth project accomplishments . . .

Audits: Audits of contracts and grants are conducted . . .

Records: Books and records must be maintained reflecting . . .

FINANCIAL INFORMATION:

Account Identification: 14-0115-0-1-301.

Obligations: (Grants and contracts) FY 81 $13,740,000; FY 82 . . .

Range and Average of Financial Assistance: $25,000 to $250,000; $90,000.

PROGRAM ACCOMPLISHMENTS: Copies of Research and Development Project Completion Reports can normally be purchased from . . . An estimated 45 projects will be funded during fiscal year 1982.

REGULATIONS, GUIDELINES, AND LITERATURE: OWRT Annual Reports, OWRT Procedures Memo 80-2, July, 1980 . . .

INFORMATION CONTACTS:

Regional or Local Office: None.

Headquarters Office: Office of Water Research and Technology, Department of the Interior . . .

RELATED PROGRAMS: 15.804, Water Resources Investigations; 15.951, Water Resources Research and Technology . . .

EXAMPLES OF FUNDED PROJECTS: Effects of Centrifuge Acceleration and Glow on the boundary layer during reverse osmosis. . . . Impact Upon Water Conservation in Tucson, Arizona, of Incentives, Disincentives, and Pricing. Water Recycling in the Food Processing Industry. . . .

CRITERIA FOR SELECTING PROPOSALS: Proposals are submitted in response to periodically published research and development areas of priority interest. Proposals are selected for funding on the basis of responsiveness to priority needs, soundness of technical approach, experience and reputation of proposer, uniqueness of approach, adaptability of project results to the solution of specific water problems, probability of success, and comparative cost.

The Federal Register, available in most libraries, offers daily help to grant writers. This newsletter, published when Congress is in session, specifies the rules and regulations of proposed grant programs and changes in existing ones. Everything that finally appears in the *CFDA* appears first in *The Register.*

Finally, private special-interest groups publish weekly reviews of grant opportunities. For instance, every Tuesday, Capitol Publications puts out *The Federal Grants & Contracts Weekly: Selected Project Opportunities for the Education Community.* Check your professional organization for a similar service.

Private Foundations

About twenty-five thousand private foundations exist across the country, though few are as well known as the Rockefeller or Ford Foundations. Fort Smith, Arkansas, a city of less than two-hundred thousand, claims twenty foundations, including the Automotive Foundation, the Ed Ballman Foundation, the Elizabeth H. and Stanley E. Evans Foundation, and the First Lutheran School Endowment. Not all of these foundations will respond to unsolicited grants, but all must award a certain percentage of their funds each year to retain their tax-exempt status.

Before you begin to write your proposal, find out as much as you can about your potential funding source. The Foundation Center at 888 Seventh Avenue, New York, NY, 10019, a private nonprofit organization, acts as a clearinghouse for information about the nation's philanthropic organizations. *The Foundation Directory,* available in most libraries, lists and describes almost three thousand of the largest U.S. foundations. Figure 12-2 illustrates the kind of information you find there.

Figure 12-2. Sample Entries from the Foundation Directory*

THE FOUNDATION DIRECTORY

1591

Kaufman (Louis G.) Endowment Fund
c/o The First National Bank and Trust
 Company
P.O. Drawer 178
Marquette 49855   (906) 228-7900
Trust established in 1927 in Michigan.
Donor(s): L.G. Kaufman Trust.

Purpose and Activities: Primarily local giving, with emphasis on secondary education, community development, youth agencies, and recreation.

Financial Data (yr. ended 12/31/81): Assets, $1,468,745 (M); expenditures, $154,140, including $129,878 for 13 grants (high: $43,500; low: $300).

Trustee: First National Bank and Trust Company (Harold N. Herlich, Jr., Vice-President).

Write: Howard D. Herlich, Vice-President, First National Bank and Trust Company.

Grant Application Information: Initial approach by full proposal in 5 copies; board meets as required.

Employer Identification No.: 386048505

1592

Kellogg Company 25-Year Employees
 Fund, Inc. ▼
235 Porter Street
Battle Creek 49016   (616) 966-2000
Established in 1944 in Michigan.
Donor(s): W.K. Kellogg.†

Purpose and Activities: Grants primarily for assistance to Company employees. After 1982, the foundation will make grants only to individuals; no grants to organizations. Report issued annually.

Financial Data (yr. ended 12/31/81): Assets, $7,528,316 (M); expenditures, $600,561, including $548,845 for 85 grants.

Officers and Trustees: Patrick S. Hirzel, President; D.E. Kinnisten, Vice-President and Treasurer; Clark Maddox, Secretary; C.B. Hookway, P.A. Humiston, W.T. Redmond, J.M. Stewart.

Write: Patrick S. Hirzel, President.

Grant Application Information: Initial approach by letter; submit 1 copy of proposal, preferably in April; application deadline June; board meets quarterly in January, April, July, and October.

Employer Identification No.: 386039770

1593

Kellogg (W.K.) Foundation ▼
400 North Avenue
Battle Creek 49016   (616) 968-1611
Incorporated in 1930 in Michigan.
Donor(s): W.K. Kellogg.†

Purpose and Activities: "To receive and administer funds for educational and charitable purposes." Aid limited to programs concerned with application of existing knowledge rather than research. Grants to institutions and agencies in the United States and Latin America, including the Caribbean. Supports pilot projects which if successful can be continued by initiating organization and emulated by other communities or organizations with similar problems. Current funding priorities include projects designed to improve human well-being through: adult continuing education; health promotion and disease prevention; coordinated, cost-effective health services; a wholesome food supply; broadened leadership capacity; economic development in Michigan and opportunities for youth in Michigan. No grants to individuals, for building or endowment funds, research, conferences, development campaigns, films, publications, equipment, religious purposes, or operating budgets. Report published annually.

Financial Data (yr. ended 8/31/82): Assets, $1,046,224,366 (M); expenditures, $57,238,941, including $51,373,248 for 607 grants (high: $2,190,400; low: $425) and $1,020,780 for 18 programs.

Officers: Robert D. Sparks,* President; Joanne M. Drewno, Vice-President– Administration and Corporate Secretary; Lloyd E. Holt, Vice-President–Finance and Treasurer; Robert E. Kinsinger, James M. Richmond, Vice-Presidents.

Trustees: *Russell G. Mawby, Chairman; A.H. Aymond, William N. Hubbard, Jr., Dorothy A. Johnson, Fred Sherriff, Howard F. Sims, Durwood B. Varner, Jonathan T. Walton.

Write: Robert D. Sparks, President and Chief Programming Officer.

Grant Application Information: Program policy statement and grant application guidelines available; initial approach by letter; submit 1 copy of proposal; board meets monthly.

Employer Identification No.: 381359264

1594
Kennedy (Elizabeth E.) Fund
c/o John Dobson
500 City Center Building
Ann Arbor 48104
Incorporated in 1954 in Michigan.
Donor(s): Elizabeth E. Kennedy.

Purpose and Activities: Broad purposes; primarily local giving, with emphasis on higher education and cultural programs.

Financial Data (yr. ended 12/31/81): Assets, $1,009,840 (M); gifts received, $50,000; expenditures, $56,844, including $49,242 for 21 grants (high: $6,100; low: $50).

Officers and Trustees: Elizabeth E. Kennedy, President; John S. Dobson, Secretary; Ann K. Irish, Joan K. Slocum.

Employer Identification No.: 386063463

1595
Kresge Foundation, The ▼
P.O. Box 3151
2401 West Big Beaver Road
Troy 48007   (313) 643-9630
Incorporated in 1924 in Michigan.
Donor(s): Sebastian S. Kresge.†

Purpose and Activities: Broad purposes; challenge grants only for building construction or renovation projects, major, movable capital equipment having a unit cost of not less than $75,000, and purchase of real estate; grants generally to well-established, financially sound, and fully accredited institutions involved in higher (four-year) and graduate education, hospitals and health-related services, social services, youth care and care of the aged, science and conservation, and the arts and humanities. Initial funds considered essential and support not given for total project costs; grants on a challenge basis for a portion of the

---

FIGURE 12-2. SAMPLE ENTRIES FROM THE FOUNDATION DIRECTORY*
(CONT.)

---

funds remaining to be raised. No support for operating or special project budgets, conferences or seminars, loans, endowment, student aid, research, church-building programs, debt retirement, completed projects, or general purposes. No grants to individuals. Report published annually.

* © 1983 The Foundation Center. Reprinted with permission of the publisher from *The Foundation Directory,* 9th ed. (New York: The Foundation Center, 1983).

In addition to this directory, the Foundation Center publishes other helpful guides. The *Foundation Grants Index* annually lists all grants reported to them of $5,000 or more. *Foundation Grants to Individuals* lists the more than one thousand foundations that allow individuals to compete for grants. And the two-volume *Foundation Center National Data Book* lists names and addresses of all IRS-certified private foundations.

Corporations

In spite of encouraging tax laws, corporate grants fall far short of their potential. The Filer Commission Report in 1976, *Giving in America,* notes the dismal record of corporate grants and concludes, "The record of giving by the corporate world as a whole in the mid-70's is an unimpressive and inadequate one" (p. 157). Corporations are not yet taking all the grant deductions allowed by the IRS.

The Conference Board at 845 Third Avenue, New York, NY, 10022, publishes the *Annual Survey of Corporate Contributions.* A glance through the *Survey* indicates that corporations continue to emphasize high-visibility, low-risk projects aimed at enhancing their image among consumers: Exxon's public broadcasting, for instance, and Pepsi-Cola's regional jogging events.

If you have a sound project but can't find a funding source, consider approaching a profit-making corporation. Familiarize yourself with the prevailing federal and state tax laws governing corporate giving and educate corporate officers to win their support.

Federal versus *Private Grants*

Significant differences exist between government and private (foundation and corporation) funding practices. Most of these differences result from the public accountability of government agencies; private sources have only to answer to their directors or stockholders. Before you write your grant application, consider the differences between funding sources.

Federal Grants. The main attraction of federal grants is their diversity and their large budgets. The evaluation procedure is another asset of these grants; proposals are likely to be judged by experts in the field and receive an evenhanded consideration. Also, the government must provide the grant writer with the scoring system by which the grant will be judged. Figure 12-3 illustrates the kind of

---

FIGURE 12-3. EXCERPT FROM TYPICAL FEDERAL GRANT EVALUATION CRITERIA

(e) <u>Supervision of students.</u> (4 points)
The Secretary reviews each application for information that shows the extent and quality of the supervision students will receive from the grantee or employer during the work experiences.

(f) <u>Recordkeeping.</u> (3 points)
The Secretary reviews each application for information that shows the extent to which the applicant has developed or will develop a recordkeeping system that documents each student's status, while enrolled in the Cooperative Education project.

(g) <u>Quality of key personnel.</u> (7 points)
(1) The Secretary reviews each application for information that shows the quality of the key personnel the applicant plans to use on the project.
(2) The Secretary looks for information that shows—
(i) The qualifications of the project director or principal investigator;
(ii) The qualifications of each of the other key personnel to be used in the project;

(iii) The time that each person referred to in paragraphs (b) (2) (i) and (ii) of this section will commit to the project; and

(iv) The extent to which the applicant, as part of its nondiscriminatory employment practices, encourages applications for employment from persons who are members of groups that have been traditionally underrepresented, such as members of racial or ethnic minority groups, women, handicapped persons, and the elderly.

(3) To determine personnel qualifications, the Secretary considers evidence of past experience and training, in fields related to the objectives of the project, as well as other information that the applicant provides.

(h) Budget and cost effectiveness. (5 points)

(1) The Secretary reviews each application for information that shows that the project has an adequate budget and is cost effective.

(2) The Secretary looks for information that shows—

(i) The budget for the project is adequate to support the project activities; and

(ii) Costs are reasonable in relation to the objectives of the project.

(i) Evaluation plan. (5 points)

(1) The Secretary reviews each application for information that shows the quality of the evaluation plan for the project. (See 34 CFR 75.590— Evaluation by the grantee.)

(2) The Secretary looks for information that shows methods of evaluation that are appropriate for the project and, to the extent possible, are objective and produce data that are quantifiable.

---

scoring system the government uses. If your request fails, you have a legal right to review the decision as well as to see the scores and written comments of the evaluators.

But submitting a grant application to the federal government is complicated and time-consuming. The guidelines are long, detailed, and confusing. You must fill out a multitude of cover sheets, prove compliance with various federal regulations, adhere to detailed (often torturous) proposal forms, and provide a precise and legally binding budget. Finally, the deadlines for submitting grant requests to the federal government are rigid and often very close to the announcement of availability. Still, competition for those big federal dollars is intense.

Private Grants. Applying for a private grant is a more relaxed process: deadlines frequently don't exist, guidelines are short, and contacts between you and the granting authorities are personal and frequent. A private foundation or corporation has more flexibility, more freedom in its grant-making decisions because it isn't the agent of the general public. (A foundation or corporation isn't completely autonomous, however. To retain its tax-exempt status, it must abide by many government regulations.)

The relative freedom private sources enjoy allows them greater flexibility to fund unorthodox projects; they can take greater risks. Private sources will give the grant writer more help and advice than will the federal representatives. But best of all, the private source grant proposal is shorter. Often a two- or three-page letter is all you need submit to be considered.

Of course, private funding also has disadvantages. A private foundation or corporation is not compelled by law to consider all applications equally. Also, private grant organizations provide few if any guidelines for preparing proposals, and they usually give no explanation for refusing requests.

Early Chores

After you think you have found a funding source for your idea, contact a representative of that group. When talking to the funding source, ask some specific questions, questions that will help you decide whether and how to proceed. You need to learn your source's practices, including its

—current goals,
—eligibility requirements,
—requirements for preliminary proposals,
—deadline dates,
—smallest and largest awards,
—previous grants,

—evaluation process,

—guidelines for writing the grant.

Decide if your project meets the criteria of the funding body—if your subject complements the group's current goals, whether you can meet the deadlines, and if your budget fits the range of previous grants. If you conclude that your idea and the granting body match, then discuss your project in greater detail with the representative of the granting organization.

Before your project is fully designed, get some informal suggestions from this representative. Usually these professionals have considerable experience and excellent ideas; many are eager to help mold an effective project that will meet the funding goals of their organization—if you give them the chance. Listen to their preferences; enlist them in your project design; ask them to contribute their expertise. (It is not unusual for small foundations to fund only those projects they have had a hand in shaping.)

The Preliminary Proposal

Almost all public granting bodies and some private ones ask for a short preliminary proposal or concept paper a month or so before the final proposal is due. This preliminary proposal seldom exceeds one page. Before you spend a lot of time writing the final grant proposal, the funding agency wants to make sure that your project qualifies for consideration. If the preliminary proposal presents an idea that interests the funding body, they will ask you for a complete proposal. At this stage, a representative of the funding agency may suggest ways to strengthen your idea.

Plan the Proposal

After you get the go-ahead from the funding agency to submit a proposal, organize a campaign to win the grant. First, study the granting organization; then design your proposal to match its preferences.

Project Requirements. Read carefully—and then go back and read again—all the material the funder sends you. Examine most carefully the grant guidelines and any evaluation criteria. Look for clues as to what the granting body expects.

Evaluation Procedures. Find out who will evaluate your grant proposal. As in all writing, the audience influences what and how you write. If you are putting together a grant request that deals with African art, it makes a big difference whether connoisseurs of African art or lay members of the foundation evaluate your proposal.

Style Preferences. If you can, study proposals previously funded by your source. See if your funder prefers a particular style: discursiveness, formality, or jargon. If you can't get hold of grants funded by your source, look at other winning grants. Get a feel for the style, the length, and the detail that make a grant successful.

Three Key Issues

After you know what the granting body expects, concentrate on the three issues every grant proposal addresses:
1. the need for the project,
2. the soundness of the idea,
3. the ability of your organization to complete the project.

Need for the Project. A good grant proposal includes a complete needs assessment. This takes effort and organization. You may have to review pertinent literature, create and distribute questionnaires, study existing systems, and consult experts in the field.

Soundness of the Idea. To demonstrate the soundness of your idea, search out authorities and solicit letters of support. (It is a good idea for you to draft letters of support for your experts. Then they'll know what details you want them to discuss.) Get as many people involved in the planning of the project as you can: members of your organization, participants in the program, citizens affected by the project, and officials outside your organization who may play a role. From these contacts, establish a board of advisers, respected specialists who will vouch for the soundness of your program, guide its progress, and later help evaluate its success. Hold meetings, poll people, ask for suggestions. In the grant proposal itself, document everything you do.

Ability of the Organization. Demonstrate the support and viability of your organization. The highest officials of your organization should write letters of support. Begin to collect the credentials of all key personnel in the project. Corroborate your organization's strengths: its track record with other grants, financial viability, management systems, and record-keeping skill.

Writing a winning grant takes more than an idea, a funding source, and time. Winning grant writers create, organize, manage, and administer. Winning grant writers are also patient, dealing with unpredictable personalities, details, and events.

Writing the Grant Proposal

In writing your grant, you will include the same material whether you are applying to a foundation or to the federal government, but the structure of this material will differ depending on its destination.

Proposal Form: Foundations and Corporations

Most foundations and corporations don't require a specific proposal form. The Kellogg Foundation's statement makes this clear: "The Foundation does not have grant application forms. To be considered for Foundation aid, an institution or organization should write a proposal letter or memorandum briefly describing the basic problem and the plan for its solution. The plan should include project objectives, operational procedures, time schedule, and personnel and financial resources available and needed." The lack of a proposal form may make things harder for you instead of easier. Sometimes, filling in a form is less formidable than facing a blank sheet of paper.

Proposal Form: Federal Agencies

Federal agencies must (by regulation) create elaborate guidelines for all major grant competitions. For instance, there is an eighty-six-page document titled "Application for Grants Under the Law-Related Education Program." One part of this document, shown in figure 12.4, details some of the information required in the proposal.

FIGURE 12-4. EXCERPT FROM FEDERAL GRANT APPLICATION FORM

Federal Register / Vol. 45, No. 66 / Thursday, April 3, 1980 / Rules and Regulations **22503**

§ 100a.113   Describe the key personnel.

An application must include the name and qualifications of each key person in the proposed project. The following information must be included:

(a) The name and qualifications of the project director . . .

(b) The name and qualifications of each of any other key personnel . . .

(c) The time that each person referred to in paragraphs (a) and (b) of this section plans to commit to the proposed project.

(d) If the name of the project director or any other key person is not known to the applicant when it submits the application, the application must specify the minimum qualifications for that person. . . .

§ 100a.114   Describe the resources.

An application must describe the resources the applicant plans to devote to the project, including—

(a) Facilities; and

(b) Equipment and supplies.

§ 100a.115   Describe the evaluation plan.

An application must include a description of the applicant's plan to evaluate the project under § 100a.590 . . .

---

§ 100a.116   Demonstrate capability; include evaluation of completed project.

(a) An application must include information to demonstrate the applicant's capability to—

(1) Conduct the project; and

(2) Meet the needs of the persons (if any) that the applicant plans to serve with the project.

(b) If an applicant wants a grant for a new project that furthers the objectives of a project already completed by the applicant, the applicant shall include any existing evaluation of the completed project.

§ 100a.117   Information needed for a multi-year project.

An applicant that proposes a multi-year project shall include in its application—

(a) Information that shows why a multi-year project is needed;

(b) A budget for the first budget period of the project; and

(c) An estimate of the Federal funds needed for each budget period . . .

§ 100a.118   Application for a continuation award.

(a) An applicant shall comply with paragraph (b) of this section if—

(1) The applicant wants funds to continue a project already approved on a multi-year basis;

(2) The applicant is about to complete one or more of the budget periods; and

(3) The budget period for which the applicant wants a continuation award is within the approved project period.

(b) An applicant for a continuation award shall submit the following:

(1) A revised face page (standard form 424) and revisions to any other affected pages of the approved application.

(2) A budget that covers the next budget period, and an estimate of the amount of funds that will remain unobligated at the end of the current budget period.

(3) An estimate of the Federal funds needed for each budget period that comes after the next budget period.

(c) The appropriate official of the Education Division may also require the applicant to submit a report of project accomplishments to date.

Structure your proposal using the required guidelines or the evaluation criteria (formatted for that purpose) as an outline, whichever the agency designates. For instance, in figure 12-4 under "§ 100a.116 Demonstrate Capability" appear two headings (*a* and *b*) and two subheads (*1*) and (*2*). Your grant proposal should contain the same two main headings and two subheadings, even the same formatting system. For instance, after you have described the evaluation plan (§ 100a.115), begin a new paragraph as follows:

§ 100a.116 Demonstrate Capability.

a1. Our organization is fully capable of conducting the proposed project. To demonstrate this ability, here are . . .

a2. Our organization is fully capable of meeting the needs of the applicants this proposed project will serve. As proof of this ability, here are . . .

b. Our proposed project continues the work begun September 30, 1978, when the Transportation Department awarded us funds to survey the need (grant #339-886-4839). Following the evaluation of the completed project . . .

Often the sponsoring agency creates a recommended outline for the proposal that combines the subjects to be covered and the evaluation criteria. The guidelines for "Grants Under the Cooperative Education Program" begin with the admonition: "The narrative for all applicants should be structured as follows for applications. Do not deviate from this sequence of content as it will be identical to that used to evaluate the application." A four-page outline follows, part of which we reproduce in figure 12-5.

FIGURE 12-5. EXCERPT FROM FEDERAL GRANT SELECTION CRITERIA

---

2. <u>SELECTION CRITERIA FOR ADMINISTRATION PROPOSALS</u>
(To be addressed in the following sequence)

632.30 <u>Selection criteria the Secretary uses.</u>
The Secretary uses the following criteria in evaluating applications for grants under this part.
(a) <u>Plan of operation.</u> (10 points)

FIGURE 12-5. EXCERPT FROM FEDERAL GRANT SELECTION CRITERIA
(CONT.)

---

(1) The Secretary reviews each application for information that shows the quality of the plan of operation for the project.

(2) The Secretary looks for information that shows—

(i) High quality in the design of the project;

(ii) An effective plan of management that ensures proper and efficient administration of the project;

(iii) A clear description of how the objectives of the project relate to the purpose of the program;

(iv) The way the applicant plans to use its resources and personnel to achieve each objective; and

(v) A clear description of how the applicant will provide equal access and treatment for eligible project participants who are members of groups that have been traditionally underrepresented, such as—

(A) Members of racial or ethnic minority groups;

(B) Women;

(C) Handicapped persons; and

(D) The elderly.

(b) <u>Involvement in planning and implementation.</u> (4 points)

The Secretary reviews each application for information that shows the extent to which and the manner in which the applicant has involved administrators, faculty, students, employers, and Cooperative Education specialists in planning and—if a Cooperative Education project is already in existence—in carrying out the project for which funds are requested.

(c) <u>Expansion of Cooperative Education.</u> (10 points)

The Secretary reviews each application for information that shows the extent to which and the manner in which the applicant has used or will use its own resources to increase the size, scope, and quality of its Cooperative Education project during the period of Federal support.

When the guidelines for the grant structure and the grant evaluation criteria are the same, you have extra writing help. Let the point value assigned to each section be a guide to its length. Within the page limit dictated by the grant, a section worth ten points should be about twice as long as one worth five points.

Writing the federal grant is easy compared to deciphering the guidelines. Honest. Plan to spend hours reading and studying the guidelines. After you thoroughly study them, call the agency and ask about unclear points.

We repeat the most important advice we can give to anyone responding to a federal grant request: *Follow the outline for the proposal given in the guidelines. Respond to every statement.* The most frequent reason for losing a federal grant is "nonresponsiveness," ignoring or overlooking some information the government is required to have in order to award a grant.

Proposal Content

Whether you are writing for a private or a public agency, whether your form is prescribed for you or not, you will include similar information. Let's discuss the various parts of a proposal, working our way from beginning to end.

Title. Choose your title carefully. It will appear at the beginning of your proposal and in all reports and publicity from the granting body. Make the title substantive, reflecting the essence of the project. The title should be short, familiar, pointed—and catchy. Keep away from a clumsy double title strung together with a colon—"Conceptualization and Praxis: Transference Patterns Among Young Adults." Experts and the public alike prefer "How Johnny Reads."

Since competition is stiff, take time choosing a title; it's important. An excellent title may help a mediocre proposal.

Summary. If you aren't required to follow a set form, always begin your proposal with a summary of your project. On that blank piece of paper, center the title on the page, follow it with several empty lines, then type "Summary" at the left-hand margin and give one.

If you attach a cover letter to your proposal, include a short summary in it too.

The summary should be clear, specific, and persuasive. In less than a page, it should explain who you are, the need for the project, the scope of the project, and its estimated cost. Write the summary last so you are sure it accurately reflects the proposal.

Your summary is important for two reasons. First, representatives of a granting organization use the summary to make sure your proposal meets the group's purposes and goals. Second, some grants go through a multilevel system of evaluation. On the first round, evaluators consider only a project summary. You want *your* summary to be circulated, not one written by an indifferent staff member.

Introduction. The introduction begins your hard sell, the promotion of your grant request. Here you introduce your organization: show connections between your organization's goals and the goals of the foundation, establish the viability of your group, prove your commitment to the project, argue that your organization should be the one to direct the project, and offer testimony of past successes.

To accomplish this hard sell, use your imagination. You might include quotations from your charter or policy directives (add the charter to the Appendix); mention of successful grant projects in the past (include a copy of such grants in the Appendix); references to financial statements, testimonials, honors (add the documentation to the Appendix); quotations from letters of support submitted by your organization's directors (the letters go in the Appendix); details of the money and time your organization will contribute to the project; and proof of your group's commitment to the project after the grant ends.

Each organization is unique. Use the introduction to convince your readers that your group is uniquely qualified to direct the project you propose.

Needs Assessment. Having shown the qualifications of your organization, document the need for your project. This section is crucial; make it specific and fill it with facts and figures. Evaluators don't want abstract statements of universal need. Precise and concrete data are convincing. Take surveys, mail out questionnaires, hold meetings, review literature, make projections, prove failure, and convince people of the need. No matter how brilliant your project, if you can't establish need, it won't get funded.

Goals. The project's goals relate directly to your analysis of the need. Explain in detail how your project will solve the need you establish. Be specific. In many proposals, this section is filled with generalizations, but here, too, generalizations are unacceptable. Not "The Indiana Arts Council expects these programs of classical music in our state prisons will benefit all concerned," but concrete goals:

> The Indiana Arts Council expects the following results from these programs of classical music in our state prisons:
> 1. the enhanced appreciation of classical music on the part of the prisoners involved,
> 2. the introduction to this nontraditional audience of a new means for their emotional release and expression,
> 3. the lessening of tension within the prison and between the prisoners and their jailers,
> 4. the awareness by the men and women in our prisons that they have not been discarded or forgotten,
> 5. the realization by prison authorities that we are both interested and involved in our criminal-justice system,
> 6. the opportunity for our musicians to see and experience our state's correctional facilities.

Tell precisely what outcome you expect from your project: how human behavior will change, what new process or product will come about, how your work will further knowledge or research or understanding.

Explain what happens to the project when the external funding ends. If continuing the project is desirable, discuss the likelihood of future funding. Even something as tentative as "The Indiana Department of Corrections has expressed an interest in continuing this project after the grant year ends" is better than ignoring the issue.

If the project ends when the grant runs out, discuss how any results or benefits of your project will be disseminated. Remember that from the granting organization's point of view, the project itself is not the primary concern. The results of the project are what count.

Methods. The methods section is the heart of the proposal; it will include a considerable amount of data. Create tables that list the beginning points and proposed end points of your project. Include a time line, showing the relative duration of various program components and their due dates. Include a flow chart that visually maps out the phases of the project. Visual representations of your project present precise information quickly and easily.

The methods section tells specifically how you plan to implement the project. Therefore, include a project organizational chart, showing the lines of authority for the project. Give important duties for all key personnel, and be concrete. Stating that the Indiana Arts Council will assign its publicist to make the program of classical music known to all possible audiences is not as convincing as writing that the publicist will 1) address the inmate council, the AA and JCC prison chapters, and the Wednesday morning chapel service; 2) write ads for the prison paper and circulars for the dormitories; 3) speak at the Prison Guards Union meeting; 4) write press releases for the state media.

We can't anticipate all the particulars you may include, but our point is clear: include specific details in your methods section, and present as much of it visually as you can.

Personnel and Facilities. Discuss your personnel resources. Detail the selection process for all participants in the project. Provide concrete and detailed job descriptions for each major position. Include at least a one-paragraph description of your key people, mentioning their qualifications: talents, training, background, and experience. In an appendix, attach résumés for each person.

Prove you have adequate financial resources and physical facilities to ensure the completion of the project and the grant. The project may take support staff, office space and equipment, or special technical tools. If you get the grant you will need to keep records of money and activities. Assure the granting body that you can maintain these.

Appraisal. Every project that receives a grant-in-aid undergoes close scrutiny. Granting organizations expect proof that you have administered the project according to the terms of the grant, that you spent their money appropriately, and that you disseminated the final results (when possible). Your grant proposal will fully detail all the ways the project will be appraised. Four different procedures are customary:

1. ongoing appraisals by project personnel,

2. ongoing appraisals by outside parties,
3. end appraisal by project personnel,
4. end appraisal by outside parties.

Appraisals are made during the life of the project by internal personnel—people directing the program and its board of advisors —and by external personnel—people the program affects and outside evaluators chosen for their expertise. These ongoing appraisals help keep the program on target, and they catch any design flaws that might jeopardize the work.

When the project is over, both the internal and external evaluators conduct a comprehensive review and submit reports, which are added to the final report to the funding agency.

Design the appraisal procedures thoroughly before you write the grant. Set progress and final report dates; create appropriate questionnaires for the appraisal; arrive at means to evaluate the success of your project—polling devices or before-and-after systems. Include all these in the proposal.

Without effective and thorough appraisal procedures no grant will receive funding. Appraisers function as counselors and watchdogs for the project while it is under way; they are also the means for assessing the end results of the project.

Budget. The budget is the trickiest part of any proposal because it does much more than just show how you'll spend the money. A budget offers a different perspective on your project. It must complement your narrative description.

Many foundations require matching funds for their gift. Find out if you need matching funds, and if the matching funds must be real money or may be "in kind" (contributions other than money: prorated salaries and hypothetical rent for facilities, for example).

Your budget should always appear in ledger-sheet form, and it should be meticulously prepared. (The budget section of the grant may be reviewed by accountants.) If a foundation or agency awards the grant, you must perform the services you propose at the price you submit. So don't skimp on the budget, and figure for inflation if the project is an extended one. Include any indirect costs which your organization will have to bear (secretarial expenses, insurance fees). Be reasonable, but err on the side of generosity. Unexpected costs always seem to come up after grants are awarded.

Appendix. For many grants, the Appendix is longer than the proposal itself. This is especially true when the length of the proposal is dictated by the guidelines. Include in the appendices a glossary of technical terms (when appropriate), documents to support the responsibility and competence of your organization, letters of support, lists and titles of advisory personnel, data from the needs assessment (including copies of questionnaires and responses), résumés of key participants, and examples of proposed appraisal materials (questionnaires, surveys, empirical evidence). The appendices should be carefully prepared and organized so readers can make their way through the mass of supplementary materials.

Proposal Style

Foundations and Corporations

Proposals written for private foundations and corporations usually use good business style (*see* Unit VIII). Refrain from jargon and technical terms whenever possible. (If technical terms can't be avoided, include a glossary.) Be clear, concise, and coherent. Don't try to impress your audience by using pretentious diction and convoluted sentences. Write simply and precisely.

Federal Agencies

We wish it weren't true, but many government agents expect bureaucratic jargon. Furthermore, since outside experts in the field often referee federal grant requests, technical argot is more acceptable in government grants than in submissions to private sources. If after careful study and thought, you decide you must satisfy your audience with jargon and verbal puffery, do it.

Some Style Pointers

When writing your proposal, echo the wording in the guidelines. When the guidelines require you to respond to "the characteristics of intended project participants and beneficiaries, including the extent that members of groups traditionally underrepresented have been reached," your response may begin, "The characteristics of the intended project participants and beneficiaries are. . . ." Follow this with, "Members of groups that have been traditionally underrepresented are included in all phases. . . ." Using key words and phrases shows that you know the guidelines, and it tells your reader exactly which item you are answering. Evaluators get lost sometimes, too. (Figure 12-6 in response to the guidelines in figure 12-3 illustrates this further.)

FIGURE 12-6. GRANT EXCERPT: RESPONSE TO GUIDELINES OF FIGURE 12-3.

(e) Supervision of Students

The extent of the supervision of students from the grantee and the employer during the work experience will be great. Supervision will be shared by faculty, employer, and Cooperative Education Specialist. The student's initial contact will be with the faculty member directing the project.

Supervision by the employer is also assured. During the field experience, the employer will supervise the on-job performance. The employer, who is paying the student's salary, has an intrinsic interest in the student's success. The employer will make weekly reports to the Cooperative Education Specialist.

The Cooperative Education Specialist will first supervise the student during the orientation session preceding the assignment of a Cooperative Education experience. . . .

The quality of supervision of the students from the grantee or the employer during the work experience will be excellent. Quality of faculty supervision is guaranteed by the faculty's responsibility for assigning grades.

Both the employer and the Cooperative Education Specialist will provide quality supervision. . . .

(f) Recordkeeping

A recordkeeping system developed specifically for this project by the Cooperative Education Specialist will document each student's status,

---

FIGURE 12-6. GRANT EXCERPT: RESPONSE TO GUIDELINES OF FIGURE 12-3. (CONT.)

---

while enrolled in the Cooperative Education project. This recordkeeping system will work as follows. . . .

(g) Quality of Key Personnel

(1) The quality of this project's key personnel appears in Appendix F. The vitas of the following demonstrate their quality and capability:
—Departmental Cooperative Education Advisers;
—College Liaisons;
—Project Director;
—Job Development Officer;
—Career Planning and Placement Director.

(2i) The qualifications of the Project Director are considerable. Ms. White has worked on previous Cooperative Education programs in North Carolina and Texas. She has earned a Master's Degree at the University of Wisconsin, where she wrote a thesis that detailed the recordkeeping problems inherent in Cooperative Education projects—and the solutions to such problems. . . .

(2ii) The qualifications of the Job Development Officer are many. Mr. Rooney has considerable experience with the job market in this area. The retired owner of a large placement service, Mr. Rooney is perfectly qualified to develop . . .

Maintain a positive tone. Don't say "we hope" or "maybe" or "if things work out all right." Instead write "we are sure," "certainly," and "undoubtedly." Both attitudes are hypothetical, so you might as well be optimistic.

But don't get carried away with excessive optimism, flag-waving, or apple-pie-mongering. Grant proposals are often idealistic. But to win the grant, you'll have to show that you can manage the grantor's money. The foundation, corporation, or agency expects to see evidence of your pragmatism and common sense as well as of your idealism.

Finished Proposal

Your grant proposal—for foundations, corporations, or the government—should be error-free, businesslike, and attractive. The layout and design should be pleasing to the eye, with sufficient white space (25–30 percent), consistent spacing, and careful underlining. The tables and illustrations should look professional. The proposal becomes an example of your work; its quality reflects your ability.

Your master copy of the proposal should be typed on quality bond paper, using a carbon ribbon to ensure clean and clear typeface. If you attach a cover letter, use the same typeface.

If your proposal is long, you may want it bound professionally. Use a simple and neat binder. If the proposal is short, use only a paper clip or a single paper clamp. Keep away from complicated methods of holding papers together and never use staples.

You Won!

Of course, if you win the grant your work only begins—work on the project and more work writing. Most funding agencies expect you to submit progress reports. We discuss these in Chapter 18.

13
Sales Proposals

WE HAVE DISCUSSED two of the most frequent reasons to write a proposal: to provide a product or service to the government and to apply for a grant-in-aid. But many other kinds of proposals occur. We can't anticipate all the sorts you may want to write, but a common kind is a sales proposal.

People write sales proposals because they want their product, service, or idea adopted. But that's not all. Usually, they want to be the person to implement what they propose. Figure 13-1 (at the end of the chapter) is a short sales proposal for a series of income-tax seminars. Helen Jamison, a certified public accountant, sent this proposal to L&A Associates, a small, professional organization. Helen wanted L&A to underwrite a series of tax workshops. But she also wanted to be the one to conduct them, so she added her résumé to the proposal.

The Buyer

Sometimes proposals are designed for a non-specific audience: the sales package you receive after you respond to an ad about a Caribbean cruise or the unsolicited life insurance promotion that comes in the mail. These proposals are usually produced by a professional advertisement agency; we're interested in those that aren't. We're interested in proposals whose writers know their audiences. Jamison had already talked to L&A Associates. She knew, however, that her proposal would have to be accepted by the senior partners, not just by her contact. As in all persuasion, audience identification and definition are important (*see* Chapter 1).

Aware of her multiple audience, Jamison included in her proposal all the essential details, even those she had already covered with her contact. And she kept the tone formal. The buyers were investing money in her workshop; they deserved to be treated with respect.

The Form

Like all business and government writing, a proposal tries to conserve the reader's time. Begin with a concise purpose statement, format appropriately, and use subject headings where suitable (*see* Chapter 2).

The content of a sales proposal is ordered like that of almost any proposal. Following the purpose statement, begin with an analysis of the customer's needs, and then point out the desirable results that will accrue from your program. Next detail your program, breaking the discussion into suitable segments, which might include project, work schedule, duties, and materials. Having shown that your proposal will meet the needs you initially identified, demonstrate your ability to perform the work or provide the product (sometimes this discussion opens the proposal). Finally, give a budget breakdown.

Figure 13-1 illustrates that this arrangement is flexible, not limiting. The needs analysis, for instance, is rather short and the discussion of the project more complete. Jamison assumed L&A recognized the need; she decided to sell her solution rather than recapitulate the need.

The Content

A proposal must be concrete and detailed. People want to know what they are buying, what they will get for their money. Proposals don't exist in the abstract; they deal with real problems and real solutions.

Many sales proposals begin with a "hook" or "grabber" that gets the reader's attention. Grabbers usually occur in unsolicited sales proposals. Helen Jamison didn't use one, deciding that conciseness was more important. She had the attention of her audience already. She decided her best persuasive strategy was to be businesslike— to get to the point. She began with a purpose statement.

Creating a need for your product or service is often a difficult chore. The methods people use to try to get us to say Yes prove how difficult a task this is: they appeal to our loyalty or make us feel guilty; they flatter us, threaten us, and scare us; they sometimes make us laugh, more often they try to make us cry.

When you get to the description of the project, you must be specific. The more facts you give and the greater detail, the stronger your presentation. Jamison discloses the structure of her classes, their logistics, and even their content.

The sales proposal itself is perhaps the best evidence of your skill and care, but include other proof. List repeat customers or satisfied clients. Tell what other major projects you have completed. Include honors or high offices or awards that are pertinent to your proposal. In short, do whatever you can to make yourself look qualified and responsible.

Close your proposal on a positive note, "This will benefit us both." "Thank you" will do as well as anything for your closing words.

The Style

Style, too, is a function of audience. In selling mink coats to wholesale jobbers you would use different words, different kinds of sentences, and different paragraph lengths than you would use in selling a series of tax seminars to professionals. The mink buyers would expect technical terms, mink-business jargon, and abbreviations common to their business from the mink wholesalers. In Helen Jamison's situation, the L&A professionals were not tax experts. They demanded clean, concise, and coherent business prose. Jamison wrote what they expected.

Proposals should be persuasive. Word choice, tone, and stance are important. Persuasive ends dictate that you neither patronize your audience nor show off your own erudition. Assume your audience is intelligent, frank, and well meaning. You won't go too far wrong.

Length

Many sales proposals are only one page, on letterhead, and follow the form we discussed above. Jamison's proposal, though slightly longer, is an example of this short type.

A long proposal may have a cover letter, a table of contents, an introductory summary, a statement of need, a full discussion of the product for sale, a review of costs, and a presentation of the credentials of the seller, a glossary, and an appendix.

FIGURE 13-1. SHORT SALES PROPOSAL

Helen Jamison, C.P.A.
Financial Advisor

May 18, 198–

Mr. George Aldridge
19th & Mission Sts
Kaysville, UT 84043

Dear Mr. Aldridge:

Thank you for the opportunity to present this proposal for a series of tax seminars at L&A Associates. I believe a series of workshops over a five-week period would be of personal benefit to your staff.

The following proposal presents the background for such seminars, their logistics, the weekly schedule, and the timetable. The budget reflects my fee of $1,000 for the five weekly seminars.

L&A'S NEEDS

I understand that your professional staff of forty-seven along with four summer interns will be invited to attend a series of tax seminars to introduce them to tax laws and recent changes.

FIGURE 13-1. SHORT SALES PROPOSAL (CONT.)

I am aware that these professionals already have a layman's understanding of the tax code, and that they are interested in the more refined areas of partnerships, tax shelters, and depreciation of rental properties.

While not a tax lawyer, I can provide insights into the tax code and teach useful personal-tax procedures.

THE SEMINARS

I propose to conduct five seminars lasting two hours each on consecutive Mondays from noon to 2:00 p.m. I will provide ten hours of instruction for approximately thirty professionals. (I assume some of your staff will be unable to attend.)

The sessions, held in your classroom on the fourth floor, will have two emphases. The first half of each seminar will be used to introduce concepts and theories. I will provide the class with relevant summaries and examples of the topics.

The second half of the seminar will practice the concepts introduced in the first half. I welcome individual tax problems from any of the participants. If there are none, I will provide examples from my own experience.

There will be no need for anyone to do work outside the seminars. However, I will be happy to comment on any specific problems outside of class as long as they don't involve preparing anyone's tax return.

SESSIONS

The five weekly seminars will consider the following topics:

- Week 1: The Current Theory of Income Tax: Increase Investment and Reward Saving
- Week 2: Common Deductions Made Easy: Depreciation, Capital Gain, Investment Credit

Week 3: Businesses, Partnerships, and Corporations: How, Why, and What
Week 4: Tax Shelters and Real Estate: Which Is Best for What Income
Week 5: Doing Your Own Return: Common Errors, Playing the Odds to Win

TIMETABLE

The timetable will depend upon the dates of your annual trade show, the beginning date of the seminars, and the July 4th holiday.

The earliest the classes could begin is June 6.

MATERIALS

I will generate all materials—outlines, summaries, examples, and practices. I understand L&A will provide typing and duplicating services.

QUALIFICATIONS

Attached is my résumé and a list of other successful workshops I have conducted.

BUDGET

I propose a fee of $1,000 for the ten hours of class for thirty people.

I appreciate the opportunity to present this proposal. I look forward to meeting with you to discuss in greater detail the structure and content of these seminars.

Sincerely,

Helen Jamison

UNIT V

Reports

14

Report Writing Overview

IN THE LATE 1950s, experts predicted the death of written communication. The spoken word would once again be supreme. New technology would make literacy obsolete, they said. But the opposite has occurred. As our organizations have grown larger and more complex, the need for effective written communication has increased.

The village shoemaker needed few if any reporting systems. He looked around and saw what materials he had on hand; he remembered who had ordered what shoes and when he had promised the job. But Florsheim or Endicott-Johnson needs an elaborate communication network to coordinate supplies, production, distribution, and sales; labor, management, and accounting; corporate headquarters, production plants, and distribution centers. Reports help the company keep track of itself.

Of course, effective reporting systems do not guarantee an organization's success. Without them, however, a business or agency will surely fail. Information must flow within an organization, between organizations, and from an organization to the public. This information flow often takes the form of reports.

Report Features

Written reports vary considerably. They may be a page or a volume long; they may look like memos, letters, or formal reports; they may report information, processes, or experiments; they may inform, investigate, evaluate, or persuade; they may be technical or conversational. You may write a report to a supervisor, to a department, to an entire organization, to existing or potential investors, to a group of consumers, or to the general public.

Reports demand the same care as other business and government writing. To be effective, a report must be accurate and correct; it must meet the needs of its audience.

But report writing is slightly different from other organizational writing. A report exists to communicate specific information to an identifiable audience from an identifiable source. To do this reports share several defining characteristics.

Single Subject

Reports usually discuss a single problem or subject. Because they report this single subject "for the record," reports invariably find their way into a file. Since you can't file a single report in two different places, each report must discuss only one problem or subject. If you wish to report two unrelated laboratory experiments, you must write two different reports.

Facts

Reports present factual material. They seldom theorize, speculate, hypothesize, or dream. Even when dealing with long-range plans, reports focus on facts, plausibilities, and specific goals.

A report is not the place for impressions or subjectivity. For instance, your trip report does not record "an unbelievable hotel" or "an outrageously expensive room" but "a luxury hotel with twenty-four-hour maid service, indoor tennis courts, and gourmet dining" or "a $175-a-night room." If the quality of the hotel or the expense of the room has nothing to do with the seminar you attended, omit that information, no matter how impressed or angered you were.

The information in a report is tightly packed, detailed, and concrete. Reports include everything pertinent and nothing more. They avoid general, abstract, or vague discussion. They present data in figures and tables.

Structure

Reports are structured. They have an introduction, a middle, and a close. The introduction is usually a detailed purpose statement, the middle a discussion of the problem or subject of the report, and the close a summary, conclusion, or recommendation.

Introduction. The introduction of a report often enlarges on the parts of the purpose statement—subject, task, purpose, and conclusion —in separate paragraphs or sections (*see* pages 19–21). Each section has a subhead.

Body. The body or middle of the report develops and structures your subject. A report must have an organizational scheme firmly in place and clearly signaled to the reader. The more kinds of organizing structures you are familiar with, the greater likelihood you will choose one suitable to the subject. Many possibilities exist; here are four.

1. *Physical Aspects.* A common way to organize material is around the physical aspects of the subject: time, space, or climax. Use time or process to organize the report—first A, next B, then C, and finally D. Use space—from top to bottom, from east to west, from point A around to point B. Devise a climax scheme—most to least, best to worst.

2. *Logic.* Another way to organize material derives from logic. Develop assertions that lead to a conclusion, or present a claim, some evidence, and a conclusion. These parts of an argument can form the structure of a report.

In a report dealing with a confrontational situation, it is useful to establish common ground between the two parties, restate the other party's view, then present your position in terms of the common ground and the opposing view.

Many letter reports from government agencies can use this structure to advantage. Suppose your agency has received a complaint from an angry taxpayer; the complaint, however, is not justified. Although you know the citizen will be displeased, you must report the facts. Structure your report to maintain as much goodwill as possible by setting out the points of agreement and the taxpayer's complaint, before presenting your response.

3. *Subject/Writer/Audience*. Every piece of organizational writing has a subject, a writer, and an audience. Each of these may determine the organization of the writing.

To report the success of Pleasantvale: New Town, the subject itself can organize the writing. Group your discussion into categories that arise from the subject and are pertinent: population, religious atmosphere, real-estate values, sewage-disposal plant, Standard & Poor's rating. An organization based upon the subject matter of a report is the least successful of these three because it provides few controls on the material.

To report the same subject from the writer's point of view gives a surer structure. You present the report as you investigated it or as you thought about it. This perspective sparks report categories and a developmental scheme.

Using the audience to shape your report is the most effective of the three. If you are reporting the success of Pleasantvale: New Town to city directors, concentrate on its public works and tax base, to potential residents stress amenities and resale value, and to merchants emphasize accessibility and household income.

4. *Implicit Structure*. Some subjects have an inherent structure. If you want to compare two things, you have a comparison structure. If your discussion shows cause and effect, you develop the cause first, then its effect.

Close. Reports close with summaries, conclusions, and recommendations. Not every report has all three, but many do.

1. *Summary*. A summary is a quick overview of the important information in the report. "We have reviewed all the applicable state and federal regulations that apply to this request for unemployment compensation."

2. *Conclusion*. A conclusion contains the deductions that can be drawn from the information or data of the report. "We conclude that Mr. Hamilton is not eligible for compensation under the standard guidelines, but he is eligible under the recent Supplementary Employment Compensation Acts just passed by Congress."

3. *Recommendation*. A recommendation outlines suggested action. "We recommend that Mr. Hamilton complete a Supplementary Compensation Form from his local Employment Security Office and apply for support under that new program."

Formatting

Unlike a persuasive document, a report writer is not obliged to engage the reader. The report must present all the necessary information; if someone needs or wants to read it, good. If not, okay.

This practical end encourages the use of subheads and other formatting devices (*see* pages 24–29). Readers should be able to spot whether the report is important to them by glancing over the headings and subheadings. Mildly interested readers should get the gist of the report without having to read the whole thing. Headings simplify the reading task for interested readers.

Style

Some report writers think that a style that reads like a telegram sounds impressive. "Went to meeting. Began at 9:03. Ended at 11:33. Much discussion. Nothing settled." This style is a parody of what good report style should be: clear, complete, and no-nonsense. Develop your paragraphs, write complete sentences, and include all necessary words.

Some report writers err in the opposite direction. They reach for pretentious words and bloated sentence structures to impress their readers with their stunning vocabulary and nimble sentence play. Instead, use familiar words and ordinary sentences.

Figure 14-1 is a short test to determine if your report style is simple. Go to your files and take out a report you have recently written. Glance through it and see if you are guilty of using any of these pretentious or wordy constructions. (We discuss general issues of style in Unit VIII.)

Documentation

Reports present information and often document their sources. Many reports have footnotes (or end notes) and a bibliography. They also may have an appendix with lengthy examples, illustrations, proofs, or supporting evidence for the content of the report.

FIGURE 14-1. STYLE TEST

pretentious	*better*
delineate	draw *or* outline
facilitate	help
multitudinous	many
optimum	best
terminate	end, stop, *or* dismiss
utilize	use

wordy	*better*
at this point in time	now
came to the conclusion	concluded
effect a change in	change
in view of the fact that	because
prior to the time that	before
provide information about	inform
to be in agreement with	agree
to have a preference for	prefer

Physical Appearance

A report should present a pleasing appearance. When you pick it up, it should feel and look good whether it's one page or two hundred pages. A report is typed, carefully proofread (*see* pages 313–317), clean, and (if more than a couple of pages long) has a cover. It has a meaningful title on the cover page or at the top of a single sheet that identifies its content immediately.

Overall, a report reflects the professional and businesslike attitude of the writer. It exhibits authority, competence, and industry.

Writing the Report

Report writing, because it is objective and often relatively lengthy, has some problems all its own.

Outlining

Many business and government professionals begin to write before they are fully ready. The step they frequently omit is outlining.

Outlining! The instant you saw the word you probably frowned, sighed, moaned, or even shivered a little. We all remember our fifth-grade teacher, forcing us to create tidy and elaborate outlines: scaffolds of roman numerals, arabic numbers, big and little letters.

But we're not talking about that sort of outlining. The outlining we mean may be elaborate or it may be a series of personal jottings on napkins with crayon. What's important is not the neatness of your outline but the organization of your ideas.

Outlining can save you considerable time and trouble. An outline may reveal holes in your logic or content, or it may show where you have too much information for a well-balanced presentation. An outline lets you examine the sequence of your ideas and inspect their progress. An effective outline will help you create a finished report in less time, because you will do less rearranging and redrafting.

First Draft

Plan to do at least three complete drafts of the body of your report, with a number of minor drafts in between. The first draft shapes the body of your report, organizes the material, fills in your ideas with words—not necessarily correct or good words yet, just words. The first draft puts flesh on the bones of your outline.

When writing the first draft, don't try for perfection. Write quickly and easily. Use the words that come to mind and keep a dictionary or thesaurus closed. Don't worry about correct punctuation, correct grammar, or neatness. Just write.

While composing the first draft from your outline, keep a pad of paper nearby. If any good ideas come to mind while you are writing (and they invariably do because the act of writing generates thoughts), jot them down on a blank page, but stick to your outline. When your draft is finished, when the heat of inspiration has cooled and your judgment is more sure, you can decide whether to include the new ideas in the report. To include new ideas in the draft when you think of them might change the direction of the draft and damage the whole report.

When you finish the rough draft, put it aside and work on tables or illustrations for the report. Don't try to do too much writing at once, and don't put off to the last minute creating your illustrations.

Second Draft

After you are satisfied with the structure, content, development, and logic of the first draft, it's time to work on the second draft. The second draft tackles more subtle issues: tone and coherence. (For other matters of style, *see* Unit VIII.)

Tone. Finding the right tone for the report—one that is appropriate to your audience, the occasion, and the subject—is difficult but important. Sometimes you will want a formal tone and sometimes an informal one. For instance, a report to an insurance company about an injured client's rehabilitation prospects might nicely be couched in the first-person-singular point of view. "I have visited Mrs. Jones five times and talked to three of her doctors. Here are my findings about the prospects of her recovery and rehabilitation."

Three factors contribute to the tone of reports: the speaker, tense, and voice.

1. *Speaker*. A common error among report writers is the misuse of the pronoun *you*. Even in informal reports, the use of *you* may be annoying: "In order to understand the consequences of her illness, you have to see how this problem affects every aspect of her

life." The *you* is either an abstract second person or a reference to the reader. In either case, its use in reports is troubling.

As irritating as *you* is the use of *one, person,* or *the subject* to stand for the writer of a report: "One gathers and analyzes the facts. Then one selects a random sampling and one maintains a representative sampling." Instead of the stilted tone this sort of reference creates, find a comfortable subject. Write in the first-person singular or plural (*I, we*) if the tone of the report is informal. If it is formal, find an appropriate subject (*the survey team/they* or *the directors/ they*) to use throughout the report.

2. *Tense.* Many writers have difficulty deciding what tense to use, when to use past and when to use present tense. In the example above, the writer interviewed Mrs. Jones and her doctors weeks ago, so shouldn't the report about those interviews be in the past tense? "The doctor reported that . . ." But what happens when the writer discovers differences between two interviews: "I saw a difference of opinion" or "I see a difference of opinion"?

For the sake of your sanity and the reader's ease, put verbs in the present tense. "Doctor Howe reports"—even if he did it three weeks ago. And the report writer "sees a difference of opinion." Keep the past tense for things that happened a long time ago. Once before, in 1954, Mrs. Jones "suffered an accident and collected insurance." This time, however, she "suffers and collects."

3. *Voice.* The writer of a report should sound objective and disinterested. You probably won't be tempted to include "I believe" or "it seems to me"—except in your recommendations—but judgmental words may create an equally subjective tone without your being aware of it.

Three statements marred by subjective language illustrate this problem. Following each is an improved version.

Subjective: The ethnic voters of New York City have been trained to vote mindlessly for the political party.
Objective: The ethnic voters of New York City vote the party ticket.

Subjective: America's timber companies are the guardians of our glorious forests in the Northwest.
Objective: America's timber companies own most of the forestland in the Northwest.

Subjective: Mrs. Jones claims she wants to return to work. She claims she hates sitting home watching soap operas.

Objective: Mrs. Jones wishes to return to work.

Coherence. Each section in the body of the report is, to a degree, self-contained, but no section is isolated. Too often report writers forget to tie together their ideas and the sections of their report. A report should flow; the reader should be able to move smoothly from paragraph to paragraph and section to section. This doesn't happen automatically. It happens when the writer has built links into the prose.

There are several easy ways to make your prose flow smoothly. Signal the continuity of your thought from paragraph to paragraph within a section. Use transition words like *next, for example, on the contrary,* and *besides.* Use parallel constructions and repeat important words and pronouns to create links. Sections of a report should be linked together, too. For instance, when you finish the section that reports on the interviews you had with Mrs. Jones and begin the section that reports the doctors' positions, make clear what you're doing. The new section begins, "Mrs. Jones thinks that rehabilitation will prove useless. Doctor Howe agrees, with some reservations."

This writer bridges the two sections of the report by a quick summary of the previous section—Mrs. Jones's views—and an overview of the discussion to come—Dr. Howe's beliefs. Notice the use of *Mrs. Jones.* When you start a new section, you must repeat the name and not use the pronoun *she.*

Third Draft

The third draft is the clean-up stage. Make sure your grammar is correct (get a grammar handbook if you aren't certain; we make some suggestions in the Bibliography). Check your possessives, punctuation, capitalization, and spelling. (For issues of correctness, *see* Chapter 28.)

This is the time to make your formatting consistent. If you capitalize a heading on page 3, be sure to capitalize the equivalent heading on page 6. If you put a colon after a heading, do the same whenever an equivalent situation occurs.

Organize your illustrations and figures. A visual never precedes its first mention in the text, and once mentioned it should appear on the same or following page.

When you think the third draft is finished, put it aside for as long as possible but at least for three days. Then copy edit your report one last time (*see* Chapter 25).

15

Short Reports

THIS CHAPTER will consider three common types of short reports: 1) those written on printed forms, 2) those that follow required outlines, and 3) informal reports.

Reporting on a Form

We have all filed reports on forms, a page (or pages) with printed questions and space for answers. However, most of us have never considered their usefulness. The closest we have come to thinking about such forms is to growl, "Another form to fill out in triplicate!"

But forms are excellent tools. They save us time and effort, help us furnish complete information, and make organizing that information easy. Form reports also make it easy to compare information between similar forms.

The secretary of state in our home state of Arkansas keeps the records of the businesses incorporated here. Each year the office receives thousands of questions about these corporations. Until several years ago, it took a staff of ten people to answer the inquiries. Then the secretary began to design forms to report frequently sought information. After considerable trial and error, the office has produced five forms which answer nearly 90 percent of all questions. In spite of increasing requests for information, the secretary now has a staff of three to answer the mail. Moral: forms save money.

Form Design

Figure 15-1 illustrates the importance—perhaps the difficulty—of good form design. This form doesn't help the writer select or arrange the information, nor does it help the reader collate information from other "Officer's Reports."

The form in figure 15-2 asks for precise information, but it doesn't allow much space to respond. The category "Info. (Location of Weapon, Etc.)" under "Subj's Class" has only one line on which to answer. Having seen some of these forms completed, we know that there is not enough space; the form is poorly designed.

Completing a Form Report

Even in a form report, you may be asked to supply information labeled "Discussion," "Comments," "Narrative," "Remarks," "Observations," or "Details of Information." If you have to write more than a word or two in response to a question, here are some helpful hints.

1. *Write complete sentences unless otherwise instructed.* Answering a question with a label or phrase can lead to misinterpretation.

2. *Limit your response to what is asked.* If you are responding to a "discussion" category, stick to the topic. In a police report, the officer should report only one event, such as the apprehension of Smith. A simultaneous but unrelated theft of the officer's squad car would be reported on another form.

3. *Structure your observations.* Begin your statement with a sentence that sets out the purpose and subject matter of what follows. The easiest way is to tell things in the order they occurred: "First I saw Smith run, then I apprehended him, then questioned him, and then booked him." End your discussion with a short conclusion or summary.

4. *Clearly indicate what is fact and what opinion.* Smith may be

FIGURE 15-1. INEFFECTIVE FORM REPORT

OFFICER'S REPORT

DATE_____ SUBJECT_____

TO:_____

FROM:_____

_____

_____

_____

_____

_____

_____

_____

_____

_____

                                        SIGNATURE_____

NOTE: Use this form for all written reports to your Supervisor. Use
Additional paper of the same size if needed.

FIGURE 15-2. DETAILED FORM REPORT

LITTLE ROCK POLICE
INFORMATION REPORT   LRN _____

INCIDENT # _____

Type _____ Inc. _____ Inc. _____ Type _____
Incident _____ Date _____ Time _____ Call _____
Call _____ Unit _____ Geo. _____ District _____
Date _____ Time _____ Assign. _____ Prem _____ Code _____ Occurred _____

ADDRESS OF INCIDENT _____ Apt. _____

Victim Business Name _____ Phone _____

1. Subj's Class: (Check One) **Person Reporting** ☐ **Victim** ☐ **Suspect** ☐ **Witness** ☐ **Owner** ☐ **Contact** ☐ **Missing** ☐ **Runaway** ☐ **ATL** ☐
Wanted ☐

Name: last _____ first _____ middle _____

Race _____ Sex _____ DOB _____ HGT _____ ft _____ ins Wgt _____ Hair Color _____ Eye Color _____

Address _____ Type _____ City _____ State _____

Phone _____ Type _____ Driver's Lic. # _____ State _____ Social Sec. # _____

Place of Employment _____ Phone _____ Scars; Marks; Aliases _____

Info. (Location of Weapon, Etc.) _____

Clothing Desc: Hat _____ Coat _____ Shirt/Bls _____ Pants/Dress _____ Shoes _____

(continued on following page)

FIGURE 15-2. DETAILED FORM REPORT (CONT.)

2. Subj's Class: (Check One) **Person Reporting** ☐ **Victim** ☐ **Suspect** ☐ **Witness** ☐ **Owner** ☐ **Contact** ☐ **Missing** ☐ **Runaway** ☐ **ATL** ☐
Wanted ☐

Name: last _____ first _____ middle _____

Race _____ Sex _____ DOB _____ HGT _____ ft _____ ins Wgt _____ Hair Color _____ Eye Color _____

Address _____ Type _____ City _____ State _____

Phone _____ Type _____ Driver's Lic. # _____ State _____ Social Sec. # _____

Place of Employment _____ Phone _____ Scars; Marks; Aliases _____

Info. (Location of Weapon, Etc.) _____

Clothing Desc: Hat _____ Coat _____ Shirt/Bls _____ Pants/Dress _____ Shoes _____

3. Subj's Class: (Check One) **Person Reporting** ☐ **Victim** ☐ **Suspect** ☐ **Witness** ☐ **Owner** ☐ **Contact** ☐ **Missing** ☐ **Runaway** ☐ **ATL** ☐
Wanted ☐

Name: last _____ first _____ middle _____

Race _____ Sex _____ DOB _____ HGT _____ ft _____ ins Wgt _____ Hair Color _____ Eye Color _____

Address _____ Type _____ City _____ State _____

Phone _____ Type _____ Driver's Lic. # _____ State _____ Social Sec. # _____

Place of Employment _____ Phone _____ Scars; Marks; Aliases _____

Info. (Location of Weapon, Etc.) _____

Clothing Desc: Hat _____ Coat _____ Shirt/Bls _____ Pants/Dress _____ Shoes _____

1. Veh. Class: (Check One) Wntd ☐ Suspect ☐ Subj of Reprt ☐ Stolen ☐ Abandoned ☐ Stored ☐ Other ☐ Hold Auth.

Clr: _____ / _____
Lic. _____ Lic. _____ Veh. Year _____ Veh. Make _____ Veh. Mdl. _____ Vh. Style _____
Lic. State _____ Plt # _____ Type _____ VIN _____
Special Marking _____
Remarks _____ SRN # _____ NIC # _____

1. Veh. Class: (Check One) Wntd ☐ Suspect ☐ Subj of Reprt ☐ Stolen ☐ Abandoned ☐ Stored ☐ Other ☐ Hold Auth.

Clr: _____ / _____
Lic. _____ Lic. _____ Veh. Year _____ Veh. Make _____ Veh. Mdl. _____ Vh. Style _____
Lic. State _____ Plt # _____ Type _____ VIN _____
Special Marking _____
Remarks _____ SRN # _____ NIC # _____

Officer Signature & Employee #	Date	Time	Supervisor
Investigator Assigned & Employee #	Supervisor		Case Status: Active Arrest
			Exceptionally Cleared Unfounded

213

the night marauder plaguing the neighborhood. Mention the possibility, but say "may be" or "I believe" to signal speculation.

5. *Unless told otherwise, avoid jargon and technical language.* Don't refer to Smith's apprehension as a "328"; call it the capture of a fleeing suspect.

Following Required Outlines

If you have ever had to write the same sort of report month after month, you probably used a previous one as a model for your latest effort. If so, you have used a report outline. By following and perhaps modifying the shape of the old report, you have created an outline that serves your need whenever you write a similar report (*see* figure 15-3).

An outline is not a form but a guide that report writers use to structure and organize their work. You do not write your report on the same paper that gives the format design.

A good outline elicits only necessary information. Avoid generating information whose only virtue is that it might be interesting. Otherwise you waste your reader's time, which reflects poorly upon your judgment.

An outline will simplify your reporting task in two circumstances. First, when the reporting situation repeats itself but the amount of information varies so that a form is ruled out. Second, when you want to give your report writer flexibility but retain a standard overall structure.

Outline Design

Your outline will vary according to the information you need to report. Figure 15-3, used by a district supervisor of an automobile-parts chain, illustrates one possible design. Some information is fairly standard; other information is added as needed.

Outlines should be flexible. They are not form reports but structuring devices. Allowing for changing circumstances and special situations will increase the usefulness of your outline. Including a

FIGURE 15-3. OUTLINE FOR FIELD INSPECTION REPORT

AUTO PARTS INTERNATIONAL
Dallas, TX

Inspection Report Outline

(Include all starred headings in report; include other needed headings.)

*Store # Visited	*Date of Visit
*Name of Store Mgr	*Time of Visit
*Name of Accountant	*Date of Report
*Reason for Visit	

Condition of Store
Attitude of Personnel

Current Stock Value
Sales This Year to Date
Sales Last Year to Same Date

Accomplishments
Problems
Future Outlook

Conclusions
*Recommendations   *Supervisor's Name

''Comment,'' ''Observation'' or ''Special Circumstances'' section will also add flexibility. Try to anticipate contingencies and include more topics in your outline than any finished report would use.

Outlines should reflect their subject matter. The one in figure 15-3 asks for much information that is irrelevant to, for instance, an insurance adjuster.

Informal Reports

Shorter than a formal report (discussed in Chapter 16), an informal report has fewer conventional parts (no need for a letter of transmittal, title page, abstract, or appendix). But it is not as short or unvarying as a report that simply requires a form or follows an outline.

If you must report a brief topic but aren't given a form or outline, write an informal report. If your topic doesn't take months to investigate or chapters to detail, you will write an informal report. You can present your informal report in a letter or memo, or you can write a report and clip on a title page. Whichever you do, keep the report simple and relaxed.

Informal Report Structure

An informal report usually begins with a purpose statement, including and emphasizing any conclusions or recommendations. Following this overview, provide whatever introductory or background information your audience needs: a history of your problem or the cause of your investigation, for instance.

Then report your information or results: an explanation of your subordinate's error, the findings of your comparison of epoxies, the benefits and problems with flextime, or the cost of the new employee lounge. You may want to represent complex data or elaborate relationships in figures or tables, which may appear in informal reports although they are more frequent in formal reports.

After you have reported your findings, conclude with a summary, a conclusion, or (when appropriate) a recommendation.

Informal reports use formatting devices, short paragraphs, simple sentences, and familiar words. Don't try to sound erudite.

Figure 15-4 illustrates an ineffective informal report. A quick glance reveals one conspicuous shortcoming: it can't be skimmed because there are no formatting devices. Every reader must read every word.

FIGURE 15-4. INEFFECTIVE TRIP REPORT

                                        2020 Judson St.
                                        Dallas, TX
                                        27 February 198–

Dear William Lee:

San Antonio Church of Peace is alive and well.

Their only problem (besides the usual Sunday school problem—
not enough children, consistently) is that these members are such
individualists "doing their own thing" that they scarcely have time for
church. And individually they do marvelous things for the community of
San Antonio. John Brandon does . . . The Clines spread their love by . . .
Ruth Ling is in school and can't find the time, right now, to make a
contribution.

The current lay leader is Dave Ramsey, 1005 Tully Road, San Antonio,
Texas.

The group is considering having a retreat/picnic that we might want to
send a representative to. I have the date if you are interested.

In regard to the foreign student in Louisiana that I have heard about, I
think someone should contact him and try to make him welcome. My
schedule is really full or I would do it.

These visitations are going quite well. But they are not for me! With all
the people out of work, someone needs to take this on who needs the
money. Please accept my resignation any time you find someone, but
definitely by August 31.

I will go back to San Antonio during the summer months.

                                        Sincerely yours,

                                        Pat Relker

Another error appears as you read the report. It isn't limited to a single subject. In addition to reporting the visit, the author buries her resignation at the close of the letter. No one could blame a reader for thinking this a standard visitation report and filing it away unread. The writer's resignation should be submitted separately.

Finally, this trip report needs structuring. Begin with a short purpose statement, detail the important facts of the visit, offer a summation or conclusion, and close.

Figure 15-5 is a reworking of the trip report, making it more effective. You can't model every report upon this rewrite, but it exemplifies good report form. It has a short purpose statement, good formatting devices, orderly content, and effective closing sections. This informal report remembers its audience and its purpose.

FIGURE 15-5. REWRITTEN TRIP REPORT

To: Director William Lee
From: Pat Relker
Re: Quarterly Visitation to San Antonio Church of Peace
Date: February 27, 198–

Date of Visit
    February 13, 198–

Purpose of Visit
    I visited the San Antonio church as part of my quarterly tour among the congregations in my area. Following is my report of their current state and my observation that they are a healthy congregation.

Findings
    I found a healthy congregation, but two matters need mention:
    1. Poor Church Attendance
        Many of the members of this congregation are so involved in community work that they have little time to devote to church affairs. I was told about some of the community work being done by members:
            —John Brandon continues to . . .
            —The Clines spread their love . . .

2. Coming Events

On April 1, the group plans a retreat/picnic from 9 a.m. to 10 p.m. at the City Park Lodge. Arrangements are handled by Paul Wolfe, who can be reached at the church office.

Lay Leader

The current lay leader is Dave Ramsey of 1005 Tully Road, San Antonio, TX.

Next Visitation

I will stop by this congregation again during my summer tour, probably the second week in July.

Conclusion and Observation

While attendance is a problem, it does not indicate lack of interest in the church. To the contrary, a strong commitment to the ideals of the church is the cause of the poor attendance.

Recommendation

You have no need to worry about the health of this group. We should consider sending a representative to the picnic.

16
Formal Reports

THE TERM *formal report* covers many possibilities. A formal report may be a feasibility study produced by a research and development group, a slick annual report turned out by the public relations department, or a labor relations evaluation circulated among upper-level management.

The term *formal report* has nothing to do with stiffness or correctness in the usual sense of the word *formal,* as in *formal evening dress*. It is called *formal* because it has greater *form*—greater prescribed structure—than an informal report.

Usually, this more elaborate structure occurs because of the length and complexity of the report. A long report, for instance, needs a table of contents. Sometimes, however, the importance of your subject (reorganizing the management structure) calls for a more structured approach. Or the existence of various audiences argues for a more elaborate structure to make the report itself easy to follow.

Theoretically, any report may be presented as a formal report. But in practice, choosing to write a formal report instead of an informal report means several things:

1. the information has taken longer to generate,

2. the subject matter is more complex and will take longer to detail,

3. the production of the report will take more time and cost the organization more money,

4. the report will have wider and more diverse audiences,

5. the report will more likely influence major decisions, or

6. the report will more likely have lasting significance either as a technical record or as a reference document.

Many major corporations and government agencies have their own preferred formal report structure, complete with a manual or instructions. Some organizations demand a specific length for formal reports, some require flow charts, others forbid flow charts. If you are beginning a formal report, check to see if your company has established guidelines for writing one.

Although in-house preferences exist, many organizations expect writers to follow conventional practice. If you understand the traditional structure of a formal report, you will more easily understand in-house guidelines or be able to duplicate conventional practice when there are no guidelines. Commonly, formal reports have preliminary materials, a body, and back materials.

Preliminary Materials

Preliminary materials—cover, title page, letter of transmittal, table of contents, abstract, and highlights page—indicate in different ways what the formal report is about. Readers who need few details may have to read nothing more than these preliminary materials. This front material also reveals how the ensuing report is organized. Readers may glance over these sections and discover the report's structure.

Cover

The cover is the first opportunity you have to tell potential readers about the report. Some readers will be able to decide from the cover alone whether they want to or need to read any further.

Use a substantive title. A cover should tell the reader what is going on inside. Not "Report to the Chairman" but "A Comparison of Three Duplicating Systems." When possible, a title should reveal your findings as well as your subject matter—for instance, "The Advantages of the X Duplicating System."

Your cover should also list the date of the report and your name and job title. Be sure to include your title. In five years, your name may not even be a memory. But your reader will recognize "Data Control Supervisor."

Title Page

The Title Page is the first page of the report. Center the title on the sheet (*see* figure 16-1). Also include on this page your name and title, the name and title of the primary audience, and the date of the report. Space this information attractively. An informational abstract of the report (discussed below), if it is short, may appear at the bottom of the title page. Center a long abstract on a following sheet.

Letter of Transmittal

The Letter of Transmittal (sometimes called the Cover Letter) contains important information that appears nowhere else in your report. Include it immediately following the Title Page. (Some people think the letter should not be included in the report itself. Therefore, you may at times find the letter separate.)

The Letter of Transmittal (*see* figure 16-2) prefaces the report. The first paragraph gives the report title, explains its origin, and includes any important dates. Subsequent paragraphs call attention to important features of the report and credit anyone whose help you want to acknowledge.

The Letter of Transmittal mentions relevant information not suited to the report itself. For instance, the annual report from a manufacturer of medical equipment consists of a list of new products put on the market during the previous year and a lengthy financial statement, all standard information in an annual report. The report begins, however, with a letter from the President addressed "To our shareholders." This letter details the progress of current research, patent applications, and future expansion, all of which may pay off in years to come, but this information is out of place in the report itself.

The Letter of Transmittal also offers the writer a subjective forum, a place to personalize what is otherwise an impersonal and

FIGURE 16-1. FORMAL REPORT: TITLE PAGE

A Study of the Flextime Method
of Improving Employee Morale and Productivity

Prepared by
Carole Nolte, President
Nolte Efficiency Consultants

for
Mr. Henry Vogel
Production Supervisor
Jantz Bedding, Inc.
August 198–

Abstract

A study of flextime as a management technique for dealing with employee
dissatisfaction, work alienation, and low productivity, including a
discussion of the traditional approach to employment. The report presents
physical and psychological effects of work on employees, the
consequences to organizations, and the influence of flextime. Positive and
negative aspects are studied through data gathered at flextime locations.

Figure 16-2. Formal Report: Letter of Transmittal

NOLTE EFFICIENCY CONSULTANTS

August 20, 198–

Mr. Henry Vogel
Production Supervisor
Jantz Bedding, Inc.
Morristown, NJ 07960

Dear Mr. Vogel:

Here is the report, "A Study of the Flextime Method of Improving
Employee Morale and Productivity," you asked for on May 28. Attached
to the report are relevant documents, including a short discussion of ways
in which flextime might work at Jantz Bedding.

The report presents flextime as an easy, inexpensive method of improving
employee morale and productivity. I discuss the negative effects of
conventional work schedules on employees and organizations, and I
present data from research studies done at flextime sites. I have also listed
some major problem areas that must be overcome by your organization
before adopting flexible working hours.

I want to thank the Accounting Department for their cooperation in
arriving at cost estimates for implementing flextime at Jantz. Also, Mr.
Reed in Personnel was a big help in supplying me with names and
addresses of key people to interview.

I hope this report will help you to see the feasibility of using flextime at
Jantz. I will be happy to answer any questions this report may raise.

Sincerely,

Carole Nolte, President

---

objective document. The president of the medical company closes his letter: "Our company is healthy, our board of directors enthusiastic, and our technical staff the best money can buy. Our future is one of the brightest in the field. So sure am I of that future, I will again exercise every stock option this firm makes available to me." This sort of endorsement is irrelevant to the body of the annual report, but it may be more persuasive than any financial statement.

Table of Contents

The Table of Contents, besides listing page numbers, provides a shorthand view of the report, an outline for what follows. Consequently, when you construct your table, don't limit yourself to such broad and meaningless headings as "Introduction," "Discussion," "Conclusion," and "Recommendations." Instead, be detailed and precise in your headings. For instance, rather than "Discussion" write, "Criteria for Duplicating System Selection." Then break down the larger heading into more detailed subheadings: "Accessibility," "Features," "Warranty," "Cost." And "Features," for example, could be detailed further: "Quantity," "Speed," and "Collation."

Don't worry if one, two, or even more of these headings have the same page number.

Since the Table of Contents is an outline, always use the same headings in the table as in the report. If the headings in the report include numbers and are capitalized, duplicate the system on the contents page. For instance, if the body of the report discusses the "Features" of three duplicating systems under the headings A. Versatility, B. Speed, and C. Collation, then the features should appear the same way on the contents page:

III. Features
    A. Versatility 7
    B. Speed 9
    C. Collation 9

Table of Illustrations

The Table of Illustrations lists all major tables and figures. You design it the same as the Table of Contents. Since readers often learn more from a glance at a table or graph than from hundreds of words of prose, make such illustrations quickly accessible.

Abstract

An abstract may accompany any report; technical reports almost always begin with one. Abstracts—difficult to write—take one of two forms: informational or descriptive.

Informational Abstract. An informational abstract tells what is in the report and contains information from the report. It is an overview; its length depends upon the length of the report. For instance, a five-page report may be abstracted in half a page, whereas a fifty-page report may take from three to five pages to abstract. An informational abstract is usually 5 to 10 percent as long as the report itself. The trouble with informational abstracts is deciding what to include.

Suppose, for instance, you are reporting on the demographics of a national election for a presidential candidate. Among the data in your report is one fact showing that an ethnic group on the East Coast—where most of this group lives—tends to vote by party. Members of the same ethnic group in the Midwest are more likely to vote for a specific candidate, regardless of party label. Does all this go into the abstract? Probably not. The abstract would state, "Most members of this ethnic group still vote according to party lines." The qualification you include—"most"—is sufficient to warn that the report may contain greater specificity.

An informational abstract isn't the report. But it contains sufficient information so that the overworked or merely curious reader can learn all that is essential in the report without reading it.

Descriptive Abstract. A descriptive abstract is not a résumé of the report nor can it stand in place of the report. Rather, the descriptive abstract states what the report does. It does not give any information from the report. Whether the report is 3 pages or 100 pages, the descriptive abstract will always be 50 to 150 words long. The style of descriptive abstracts is succinct, sometimes even terse: "Describes national voting trends by state and by voter blocks."

Highlights Page

If a formal abstract isn't appropriate—if your audience is general and your subject not technical—then provide either a highlights page or a summary paragraph before the report begins (*see* figure 16-3). A summary, more casual than a highlights page, details the report's purpose, scope, methodology, findings or data, conclusions, and recommendations.

A highlights section is an outline of the report. Some possible headings include "Title of Report," "Objectives of Report," "Methodology of Report," "Findings" (or "Data"), "Conclusions," and "Recommendations." A short discussion follows each.

Report Body

If your report is well designed, many of your readers will never look beyond the preliminary materials. But some readers will need (or want) to know more about the subject and read the report. For them, the report begins with an introduction.

Introduction

The Introduction is the purpose statement (*see* pages 19–21) of a formal report. Because the formal report is long and complex, the Introduction usually has a distinct section for each part of the purpose statement: "Subject," "Task," "Purpose," and "Conclusion."

FIGURE 16-3. FORMAL REPORT: HIGHLIGHTS

Report Highlights

Title of Report:
A Study of the Flextime Method of Improving Employee Morale and Productivity

Objectives of Report:
To discuss flexible working hours as a way to improve employee morale, labor relations, and productivity

Findings:
1) Employees favor flextime over fixed working schedules.
2) Flextime improves satisfaction with work and increases morale.
3) Tardiness is drastically reduced on flextime schedules.
4) Flextime can ease transportation problems.
5) Flextime schedules may not be possible in assembly-line and shift operations.
6) Productivity increases in some cases as a result of flextime.

Conclusions:
1) Flextime is an easy, inexpensive management technique.
2) Where possible, organizations should consider beginning a flextime schedule.

Methodology and Scope of Study:
The study includes data from private and public organizations in the United States and Western Europe.

Background

Following the Introduction is a section that provides any background information necessary to understand the content of the report. This section begins the presentation of the report subject.

The background section is a grab bag of possibilities in which you may present any information relevant to the report. Choose what to include with care and with an eye to your audience and your purpose. For instance, suppose you manage a car-rental outlet; your report to the home office concerning rental-car sales figures need not give background about the quality of your product. The boss knows the quality. But a similar report submitted to a local airport authority for the right to continue business might very well discuss the quality of your product.

To decide what to include, ask yourself if your reader will more fully and more easily understand your report after having read the background section. If you answer Yes, include the information in the background. If your answer is No, leave it out.

When possible, use headings that signal your reader. Not "Background" but "Foundation Policy History" followed by "Foundation Policy and Philosophy."

Body

The body is the most important part of the report, yet the least read. It presents specifics and discusses details most readers don't need or want (*see* figure 16-4). Nevertheless, the body must exist and be correct. Some readers will want to check your accuracy, thoroughness, and judgment.

Organizing Your Material. The biggest problem for most report writers is getting all their information into a logical order. You can organize material many different ways. Chapter 14 discusses four possibilities (*see* pages 199–200).

Whatever organizing principle you choose, clearly signal it to your readers. If you tell them how you are organizing, they can concentrate on the content of your writing and not be distracted searching for the ordering pattern.

Emphasizing Material. Report writers too often rely upon weak qualifiers—*very, really, great, many,* and *much*—to emphasize importance. Not only are these words overused but they give a subjective tone to what should be objective reporting.

Emphasize material by the organization of your report.

1. *Position.* Put important material at the beginning of any discussion, where even a busy reader will see it.

2. *Repetition.* Repeat important information; repeat but don't rename. Repeating key terms stresses importance.

3. *Proportion.* Give essential information greater discussion than less important material.

4. *Separation.* Use your format to separate and spotlight important information.

5. *Headings.* Include headings with key terms to signal importance.

Developing Material. Failing to develop your ideas fully can be a problem in the body of your report. You know what the report has to say, so you tend to forget that your readers do not know. A single unclear detail may confuse your reader for pages. Written reports can't answer readers' questions. Nor can written reports use facial expressions, voice inflections, or body language. All your reader has is the report.

Writers fail to develop their material adequately for many reasons: they assume readers know the subject when they don't; they fail to consider what information readers need; they overlook important information themselves.

Each of these pitfalls can be avoided if you examine your report for logical unity and coherence. For instance, a report on duplicating systems methodically informs the reader about the organization of the report: "The systems—A, B, and C—are discussed in order of increasing complexity." Unfortunately, the author fails to discuss how these three systems were chosen for the study. The author's logic is faulty.

In another report, the writer observes, "I have not met with Dr. X and do not know the results of those tests." Not only has this reporter overlooked important information, but the report calls attention to the oversight.

Read your report and look for gaps in logic. If you can't find any, give your report to colleagues or friends and ask them to look for holes. Complete development is essential—and difficult to achieve.

Documenting Material. Formal reports often include notes and a bibliography. If you choose to place your notes at the bottom of the page, they are footnotes. If you put them all at the close of the report, label them end notes.

Creating footnotes and bibliographical entries is a part of technical writing; use a style sheet to get the form correct (*see* the Bibliography).

FIGURE 16-4. FORMAL REPORT: BODY EXCERPT

. . . traditional practice of having all employees start and finish work at fixed times, *Gleitzeit* (or flextime, as it is called in the United States) divides the day into four parts, two optional and two mandatory. Employees may vary their arrival and departure times within the optional periods as long as they are present for the core period of time each day. Here is an example of a flextime schedule set up for an 8.5-hour day with a thirty-minute lunch period:

A.M. Option	Mandatory	P.M. Option
7:00 to 9:00	9:00 a.m. to 3:30 p.m.	3:30 to 5:30

Employees may report to work anytime during the two-hour morning period and may leave anytime during the afternoon period after they have completed a full workday. All employees work the same number of hours; they do so at different times. Response to the system has been favorable. Workers report feeling more in control of their own lives and less resentful of work. More freedom seems to compensate for lack of interest in the job itself.

Data

General

Flextime has spread rapidly through Western Europe since its beginning. In 1978, 50 percent of the West German white-collar force,

---

FIGURE 16-4. FORMAL REPORT: BODY EXCERPT (CONT.)

---

40 percent of the Swiss, and 30 percent of the French were on flextime schedules. More than eighty private firms and 500,000 civil servants in Britain were also using the system. Since the early 1970s, flextime has grown in popularity in the United States also. Appendix A lists some of the major U.S. corporations and agencies on flextime.

British Civil Service

A great deal of research was conducted on employee and organization reactions when the British Civil Service introduced flexible working hours. The results were highly favorable. Those interviewed gave the following responses:

Like and do not want to return to fixed hours	96%
Improves satisfaction with work	28%
Increases amount of work accomplished	25%

When asked specific features they liked best, interviewees listed:

a. feeling of freedom
b. time to shop
c. can keep appointments
d. traveling is easier to and from work
e. being late for work is not possible
f. can take advantage of good weather
g. able to store up leave
h. adjust hours if not feeling well
i. more time for hobbies
j. more time for social life
k. able to vary hours according to whether or not busy at work
l. sense of responsibility
m. increase in work amount or quality
n. less conflict between work and family life

Flextime was quite successful with employees, and by choosing to continue it, the British Civil Service showed its satisfaction as well.

Social Security Administration

The U.S. Social Security Administration (SSA), which employs about 78,000 persons, decided to experiment with flexible working hours on the assumption that the process would yield positive returns for both the employees and the agency. The SSA chose a representative mix of jobs and office environments to test their assumption, so the results could be generalized to the whole agency. Specific characteristics of the study sites are presented in Appendix B. Here are general findings of the research by categories:

Employee Responses and Morale
Employee reaction was overwhelmingly favorable and satisfaction grew. Supervisors were also positive, but somewhat less enthusiastic than employees. The impact of flextime on morale and job satisfaction was more pronounced in operational settings than administrative or staff functions.

Leaves and Attendance
In two sites annual and sick-leave use were reduced. . . .

Report Endings

Three conventional endings may close reports: Summary, Conclusion, and Recommendations (*see* page 200). The ending of the report must be concise and complete. Some readers will turn to the end first; make sure that someone can get a good idea of your report by reading nothing more than your summary, conclusion, or recommendation.

End notes are part of the report and not part of the back materials. Place end notes at the end of the report.

Back Materials

Important supplementary materials follow the body of the report: a bibliography, a glossary, and appendices containing information too detailed or too long for the body; reference materials that must be included but are not important enough for the body; and documents relevant to the methodology of the report.

Bibliography

You may choose to include a section titled "Bibliography" or "Works Consulted" or "Works Cited." Recognize the difference among the terms. The term "Bibliography" (or "Selected Bibliography") means that the list contains works pertinent to the report subject. "Works Consulted" means that you read all the works that appear but did not use them all in the writing of the report. "Works Cited," the most limiting of these labels, means that you used and footnoted in the report every title in the list.

Bibliographical entries are extremely difficult to structure correctly. This section must be done with great care. A knowledgeable reader, discovering errors in your citation form, may question your reliability in the other parts of the formal report. No matter how experienced a writer you are, use a style sheet (*see* the Bibliography) when you create your bibliography.

Glossary

The Glossary defines technical terms or difficult concepts. It can also inform the reader how the report writer wants familiar terms understood. In a report on forests, for instance, the Glossary may define "rotten trees" as "live trees of commercial species that do not contain at least one twelve-foot sawlog, now or prospectively, primarily because of rot." That's not the weekend gardener's idea of "rotten trees."

If you add only a glossary to your report, you don't need to label it as an appendix; "Glossary" is sufficient. Otherwise, you include the Glossary as part of the Appendix.

Appendix

The Appendix is a catch-all section for documents that readers may want to consult but don't absolutely have to look at. For instance, the results of a survey depend greatly upon the surveying instrument. The actual questionnaire you designed for your survey of voting trends belongs in the Appendix. In the example of the auto rental report, you would include in the Appendix the letters of praise you received that month.

What goes into the Appendix is up to the writer, but you needn't be overly selective. There is no reason to limit this section. If you have an inkling that someone may want to see a document, add it to the Appendix.

In structuring this section, you have two choices. One is to give each document a different letter:

Appendix A: Bibliography
Appendix B: Glossary
Appendix C: Duplicating System Warranties
Appendix D: Duplicating System Service Contracts
Appendix E: Duplicating System Price Lists

Including one cover sheet titled "Appendix" is more common. Following this appendix title page, the title of each document is typed either near the top of the page on which the document begins or on a separate sheet preceding the document.

Bibliography
Glossary
Duplicating System Warranties
Duplicating System Service Contracts
Duplicating System Price Lists

Either format is acceptable, depending on your preference.

Writing the Formal Report

Formal report writing has much in common with other report writing (*see* Chapter 14). Its more elaborate structure creates one peculiar problem, however. You write a formal report from the inside out. First, write the narrative—the body of the report—then the conclusion. Next write the Appendix, the Introduction, the Letter of Transmittal, the Abstract, the Title Page, and, last, the Table of Contents (to get your pagination correct).

When you have finished writing a formal report, choose an effective binding. If it is relatively short, the report may be held together by a paper clip. If long, it may better be bound by a professional printer. By definition, the formal report is important. Its appearance should reflect that importance.

17

Progress Reports

BUSINESSES AND GOVERNMENT agencies often require progress reports. Most funding agencies expect periodic reports on how their money is being spent. Recipients of government contracts or grants-in-aid, consequently, must submit progress reports. Progress reports may also be internal instruments, with the employee turning in a summary of activities every quarter.

Progress reports (*see* figure 17-1) are sometimes called status reports. The difference between the two is one of emphasis, not substance. A progress report stresses what has happened since the previous report, what change has occurred. A status report emphasizes the current condition of the project, detailing what exists rather than what has transpired.

The period covered by a progress report may vary. For instance, suppose you work for the city and your department is coordinating a booster campaign, including TV spots, special promotions, billboard advertisements, and projects developed by each of seven city departments. The mayor may ask you for a progress report each month, or six weeks, or three months. In turn, you will request a report from each department head detailing the ways that department is implementing the campaign.

Or you may break the campaign into three stages—start-up, blitz, and repeat—giving reports after each phase rather than according to some set time period. Or maybe the mayor doesn't ask for any reports. In that case, submit progress reports anyway. The progress report will protect you from going too far astray. After you submit it, you share responsibility for the project with the person who received the report.

Both the mayor and you profit by progress reports. They allow the mayor to check on your handling of her campaign, and they allow you to find out if all the department heads are supporting it. Both of you find out if the campaign is on time, on budget, and on target. Progress reports encourage the report writer (usually the project director) to stand back from the project and review its progress. Too often the everyday routine of problem solving interferes with long-range analysis and thought. Progress reports ensure periodic, comprehensive analyses.

Progress reports may be routine and unimportant, if everything is running smoothly. The mayor will glance at details, note that the campaign is on track, and file the report. But if something unexpected occurs, the progress report may become the means of correcting the problem and of determining responsibility. Progress reports may even figure in legal situations and should be treated seriously.

Audience

The audience for a progress report is often a limited one. In our example, it would be the mayor. If all is well, even the mayor will do little more than glance over it. Sometimes, progress reports are distributed to managers, customers, and co-workers. For instance, if the mayor wants to make sure she has support for her campaign, she may take your report to the city council and make sure the council agrees with the direction of the program. If a problem occurs or if someone complains, you can be sure the progress report will get attention. The local newspapers may get hold of your report and question specific campaign strategies and expenses.

Form

Progress reports can be either formal or informal, though most are informal: letters if the reports are going outside the organization and memos if the reports are internal. Because of the transitory nature of the progress report, we prefer informal ones. Writing a letter or memo report also saves you the trouble of producing a cover letter.

Structure

Progress reports have five distinct sections.

1. The introduction includes the name of the project, its number (if it has one), the director, and a short review of the project's goals. A purpose statement may follow (*see* pages 19–21).

2. The next part summarizes the previous progress report. Remind your reader of what went before.

3. The third part reports what progress has been made in the present reporting period and comments on problems or notable features. A budget report ends this section.

4. The fourth part predicts what progress is expected during the next report period.

5. The conclusion presents an appraisal of the overall project.

The first project report will omit part two, the summary of previous reports. After the first report, much of parts one, two, and five will be "boilerplate" (repeated verbatim from previous progress reports)—unless the project changes direction or goals.

Organizing the Progress Report

Progress reports are comparatively easy to write. The only difficulty is in deciding how to organize your discussion of the completed work. Three possible methods of organizing exist, called the 3 Ts: time, task, and topic.

Time. The common way to organize the discussion of a progress report is around time. First A happened, then B, then C. Use this "T" for a simple project or one of limited scope.

Task. A project with several activities going on at the same time may not lend itself to a time organization. If, for instance, your agency is sponsoring a booster jingle contest, the police department is organizing a city beautification campaign, and the water department is handing out booster T-shirts—all at the same time—organizing around time is not efficient. In this case, organize your report

---

FIGURE 17-1. PROGRESS REPORT EXCERPTS

December 15, 198–

Mayor Barbara J. Barr
Room 343
City Hall
Binghamton, NY 13902

Dear Mayor Barr:

On June 1, 1980, the City Council, upon your recommendation, approved
funds for the Binghamton Alive Booster Campaign. At that time I was
designated project director.

Purpose
Complying with my appointment and the agreement that I would submit
bimonthly progress reports, here is the second such report, due by
December 15.

Scope
Following is a short summary of the last progress report, the work
completed during this period, the status of the budget, and the work
remaining.

PREVIOUS REPORT

Previously I reported that all budget heads had agreed to participate in the
Binghamton Alive project. Six of the seven had submitted the ways in
which their department would carry out the campaign. I also reported the
progress we had made in choosing a logo and a slogan.

WORK COMPLETED

Since the progress report of October 15, considerable progress—detailed
below—has been made in planning and organizing the campaign. We are
ready to kick off the campaign January 1.

Project Director

My office has supervised the design of a logo for the campaign (Appendix A)
which has been approved by all budget heads. The slogan is not yet

settled. We have narrowed the choice to two. Since there is no unanimous opinion, we plan to let the citizens of Binghamton vote for the slogan they prefer over a special radio program donated by Station WWWW. That will occur December 22.

The slogans are . . .

Fire Department

The fire department has agreed to open the firehouses for a kickoff celebration January 2 . . .

Parks and Tourism

The head of Parks and Tourism is excited about the campaign. In the last eight weeks, she has . . .

PROBLEM AREAS

Everything is running smoothly and according to plan. In fact, we are ahead of the schedule we set for ourselves. Only the Water Department has yet to submit a plan for their involvement in the project. The director can't think of any way to participate. (We decided that coloring the water was not appropriate!)

BUDGET STATUS

The budget remains unchanged from the previous report since no money has been spent. $2,250 remains in the salary line, $5,000 in the materials line, and $3,570 in the outside consultant line. We expect most of our expenditures to occur in the coming report period.

WORK REMAINING

The planning of this project is about to draw to a close. The next phase will begin with the radio contest December 22, when the public learns of our Binghamton Alive campaign. Then we will get everything off to a brisk start January 1.

Specifically, the work remaining includes . . .

FIGURE 17-1. PROGRESS REPORT EXCERPTS (CONT.)

SUMMARY

The initial phase of the Binghamton Alive Booster Campaign is nearly completed to the satisfaction of almost everyone involved. The success of this phase will be reflected in the success of the campaign itself. We are looking forward to the beginning of the campaign.

Sincerely,

David Richards

---

around a task concept: "Jingle," "Beautification," and "T-Shirts." Using different tasks to organize the content of your report works well if you have several projects within a larger program.

Topic. Instead of organizing by a specific job to be done, topic organization uses a subject breakdown from the project. In our example of the booster campaign, we might organize the report around the progress made by each department: "Personnel," "Police," "Water." The Water Department isn't a task; it performs several tasks for the good of the booster campaign.

Progress reports often blend more than one of the Ts in a single report. For instance, you may report on the progress made by each department toward the success of the booster campaign, and within the discussion of each department organize the material around time or task.

Content

Like all reports, progress reports should be detailed and specific. Generalizations and vague concepts are no help to the report writer or the person responsible for the project. The mayor wants to know exactly how many TV spots you have purchased, not that you bought "some."

One pitfall in writing progress reports is stressing procedures over facts. Project directors are closely in touch with tactics, strategies, methods, and policy. Much of a project director's time is spent establishing guidelines or making procedural decisions. But usually, as important as such logistical concerns are to the success of the project, they are not important to the mayor. The mayor wants to know about procedural concerns only when they influence the project. Focus on results, facts, and consequences—not what makes them possible.

Everyone likes to be pleasantly surprised; we all like to have our expectations exceeded. When possible, set up the goals of your progress report so that your next report will meet or exceed the goals you set. One way to do this is to set lower goals than you know you can meet. This is a standard practice. Remember, you generally set the goals you are to meet for each period of the report. Don't make them impossible.

Tone

The tone of a progress report is similar to that of any report. But remember, confidence is catching. A strong, vigorous, and optimistic tone creates the same feeling in your reader. If you want the mayor to have confidence in your handling of her booster campaign, begin by couching your report in a positive and assured tone. Write "This campaign will surely increase our convention business," not "We believe the campaign may influence convention business."

18
Position Papers

POSITION PAPERS are—in theory—disinterested statements announcing the position of a person or group on a public problem or issue. Congress considers passing a law to ban cigarette smoking on airplanes. The American Lung Association expresses its opinion; the American Tobacco Institute does the same; the airlines give their position.

While position papers aren't new, they have achieved importance since World War II. In an economy increasingly dominated by public and nonprofit private agencies, many groups try to mold public opinion and influence attitudes and legislation. These positions are expressed in position papers.

Many—though not all—positions are first articulated in speeches, either by the policy maker to an appropriate audience or as testimony given to a legislative body. If the position paper you are writing is first to be given orally, it must work as an oral presentation.

1. *Begin and close your presentation by acknowledging your audience.* Thank them for inviting you; then thank them for their attention.

2. *Work to hold the attention of the audience.* Oral presentations use personal anecdotes, interesting quotations, and concrete illustrations to keep the audience involved.

3. *Charts and graphs are effective, but oral presentations can't include detailed data.* A complicated figure can't be seen by a wide audience. Even if it could be, there isn't time to study it.

4. *Keep it simple.* Members of an audience who miss an essential point can't go back and reread your argument. They must understand everything important the first time.

244

5. *Practice reading your paper beforehand.* Discover where difficulties lie and what needs emphasis. Know the paper so well that you can make eye contact with your audience while you read.

A live audience has a special impact upon position papers. It takes a unique politician, for instance, to present a position paper attacking Social Security in Florida and to denounce unemployment compensation in West Virginia. U.S. presidents often wait until the annual American Legion convention to announce an increase in the defense budget.

If you must attack Social Security in Florida, be prepared for greater resistance to your position than you would get from a group in California called Teens for Tomorrow. If you have a hostile audience, your position paper must be more persuasive. Carefully identify and define your audience (*see* pages 8–14).

Persuasion

As our example about cigarette smoking on airplanes suggests, self-interest is often an integral part of what poses as a "disinterested" position paper. Position papers strive to seem objective when, in truth, they are often highly persuasive. The most difficult task in writing a position paper may be to appear evenhanded while working strenuously to persuade your audience to agree with you.

From this conflict between appearing disinterested and being persuasive come three guidelines.

1. *To maintain an objective tone, seldom include overt emotion.* Rather, position papers rely on reason and data.

2. *To create a sense of fairness, address the issue of self-interest head-on, pointing out areas of potential subjectivity.* Of course, you should do this in ways that advance your own interests. If you create an aura of frankness and goodwill, your audience will be more likely to accept your most self-serving positions.

3. *To persuade an audience of the merits of your position, demonstrate how your stance is, in fact, in their best interest.* Most, though not all, position papers work hard to prove that the position

advances the general good (or at least the good of the audience at hand) and is not self-serving.

(Figure 18-1, at the end of the chapter, presents the testimony of United Brands Co. on the Panama Canal Treaties.)

Content

A position paper has two parts: a review of the issue and a presentation of your specific position. Your thinking must not be divided.

The Issue. Define the issue in ways that will help develop your position. For instance, in testimony about the 1978 Panama Canal Treaties before the U.S. Senate Committee on Foreign Relations, the chairman of a transportation trade association narrowed his focus: "My statement will deal with the Panama Canal as an artery of commerce and the economic impact of the proposed treaty on the users of the canal. . . . I will not deal with any geopolitical or military aspect of the canal." This narrowing gives the speaker's position greater credibility; it implies that he is addressing only those areas he knows. It also prepares the way for his perspective in the second part of his presentation, where he details his group's position.

During the same hearings, a critic of the Canal Treaties defined the issue differently. Representative Eldon Rudd said the only question was whether or not the canal was Panamanian territory. "This is the whole treaty. All the rest is window-dressing." Having defined the issue this way, Congressman Rudd argued that the canal was legally U.S. territory—not Panamanian—thus the treaties were pointless. Another witness stated, "Our interest in the canal . . . is in its use, not its ownership." This testimony was fundamentally different than Rudd's. Defining the issue is often the key to a persuasive analysis.

The Position. Having defined the issue in terms amenable to your position, thoroughly detail your organization's stand. Include data, facts, and reasoning that support your stand. The more concrete and detailed a position paper, the better.

Complex or lengthy data—"for the record"—may appear in an appendix.

Structure

Position papers, because of their formal nature, have a fairly standard structure. Outlining the structure clarifies the writing task facing you.

Identify Yourself

Identify yourself and your organization, your interest and your credentials in regard to the issue. Congressman Rudd's opening statement to the Panama Canal hearing sought to establish his expertise in the area: "Let me note by way of background that I am very familiar with the countries and people of Latin America, having spent several years on diplomatic assignment in many countries throughout Latin America."

The Ripon Society also testified on the Canal Treaties. Their representative offered this identification: "Founded in 1962, the Ripon Society is a national Republican research and policy organization. . . . The society works to formulate the kind of sound programs that will enable our Party to better fulfill its potential for constructive political leadership. . . ."

Because Republicans led the attempt to defeat the Canal Treaties and because the Ripon Society supported those treaties, the representative wanted to emphasize the Republican affiliation. As Republicans who supported the treaties, the society hoped its testimony would carry added weight and its views be treated as thoughtful commentary. The mention of "sound programs" anticipates the disagreement with many Republicans. Nowhere in the statement did its representative reveal that some Republicans disavow the Ripon Society as ultraliberal.

State Your Organization's Position

Some writers of position papers hold off signaling their position until they have marshaled all their evidence. We think this is self-defeating. You gain little by surprise, while you stand to lose the confidence of your audience, which feels manipulated. State your position, briefly, at the outset. You will be thought honest and forthright.

Define the Issue

Define the issue in ways that will advance your position. The Ripon Society, for instance, focused upon the history of our involvement in the canal. It was not an economic or geopolitical analysis but a historical one that focused on the morality of the American protectorate.

Appropriate here is a review of your group's previous analysis and previous position on the issue. Many issues have a long history that can be used to strengthen your present argument.

Support Your Position

The support for your position is the heart of your paper. Establishing a credible stance, identifying your interests with the general good, creating a concerned voice—all are wasted if you fail to argue convincingly for your position.

To argue convincingly use all the tools available: inductive and deductive logic, testimony, authority, semantics, data, and facts. Keep in mind that an argument has three steps. You start with a claim, corroborate it with evidence, and reach a conclusion. For instance, the Panama Canal Treaties will create chaos in the Western Hemisphere. Here are the economic proofs. Conclusion: Don't sign the treaties. If you skip any step, you lay yourself open to charges of faulty reasoning.

In an emotionally charged situation—the kind many position papers deal with—the Rogerian approach often proves effective. Carl

Rogers, a psychologist, observed that traditional forms of argumentation don't work when passions run high. No one is listening closely enough to make all the rational connections. Rogers recommended a different approach, one that tries to defuse emotion, to get opposing parties to listen to each other, and to encourage people of goodwill to reach an agreement. (The method also works as a way to arrange the body of your position paper.)

Rogers advises a three-step approach:

1. *State fully some common ground between you and your opposition.* Demonstrate that you have common interests or even a common end.

2. *Fully articulate your opposition's views.* Don't agree with them. Rather, show that you understand them and have considered them.

3. *State your position in terms of the common ground you established and in terms of your opponent's arguments.*

Refute Your Opposition

Anticipate objections to your position and answer them without harming your own case. Of course, only include objections that you can effectively counter. This strategy works two ways: it answers objections your audience might be thinking of and it furthers your image as an evenhanded spokesperson.

The Ripon Society, in its testimony on the Canal Treaties, titled a long section "Arguments Against the Treaties." The section began: "Treaty opponents have raised numerous objections to ratification of the new agreements. Some of these arguments have merit. . . ." Having established an evenhanded tone, the Society then selected arguments against the treaty and answered them.

Common Fallacies. Some common fallacies often appear during refutations. Watch for them in your opposition's work and spot them in your own.

1. *The argument-to-the-personality-of-the-speaker fallacy.* Judging an issue by the personality of its proponent and not on its own merits. "If Senator X is in favor of the treaty, it can't be worth anything."

2. *The after-X-therefore-because-of-X fallacy.* "The treaty ne-

gotiations began after the change in administrations, therefore, they must have been caused by the change in administrations.''

3. *The red-herring fallacy.* Switching topics in the middle of the discussion, bringing in an emotional ploy that displaces the original argument. "How can you support the Canal Treaties, don't you love your country?''

Close Optimistically

Position papers restate the position at their close and often predict a bright future if their recommendation becomes policy. Congressman Rudd's closing statement: "The treaties that Wall Street wrote must be rejected. We cannot gamble with an installation so vital to the economic well-being and to the peace of the Western hemisphere.''

A spokesman for the Panamanian people concluded this way: "The Panama Canal was and is a great achievement for which our people are justly proud. What we have now is a chance to make it a showplace not only for the genius and courage of our engineers and doctors and workmen, but also of our people and our foreign policy and our political institutions. We can make it a showplace . . . that will make the United States the strong and admired world leader we all want it to be.''

Date

Always date your position papers. You may find yourself taking a different position next year and referring to previous statements.

Style

In order to project an image of sound judgment and good reason, position papers should sound sober without being ponderous or pretentious. Most position papers maintain a conversational but formal tone in an effort to be both accessible and serious. If the

paper is first given as a speech, it might contain well-chosen entertainment. The Ripon Society's statement to the Committee on Foreign Relations included the following anecdote: "Last fall the *New
Yorker* published a cartoon in which one of the patrons of a local
drinking establishment exclaimed to his friend, the bartender, 'For
thirty years I never thought about the Panama Canal. Now I can't
live without it!' "

Perhaps the most distinctive stylistic feature of position papers is
their often ingratiating tone. This can become heavy-handed and
sound insincere, or it can further the end of the position paper. An
example of good tone occurs in the purpose statement of a position
paper from a religious lobby, the Friends Committee on National
Legislation:

> This statement is the attempt of a broadly representative group of
> Friends to declare what should be the objectives of government
> decisions and public policy. We claim neither omniscience nor
> infallibility in a world of cruel dilemmas and difficult choices. . . . We
> are aware of possible consequences and repercussions of the changes
> we are advocating. We expect to share in the costs and burdens of
> these changes as well as in their benefits.

Many attempts at a similar judicious tone are much less effective.

Good position papers are hard to write. You must persuade without sounding persuasive. You must ingratiate yourself with your
audience without slipping into syrupy and unctuous prose. You
must include concrete details to corroborate your argument. You
must refute your opposition without sounding contentious. Though
difficult, writing position papers is crucial for many organizations.

FIGURE 18-1. EXCERPT FROM CANAL TREATIES TESTIMONY

STATEMENT OF ROBERT F. CORRIGAN FOR SEYMOUR
MILSTEIN, PRESIDENT AND CHIEF EXECUTIVE OFFICER,
UNITED BRANDS CO., WASHINGTON, D.C.

Mr. Corrigan. Mr. Chairman and members of the committee, I speak for
Mr. Seymour Milstein, president and chief executive officer of the United
Brands Co. This is his statement.

He very much appreciates this opportunity to express to you our

FIGURE 18-1. EXCERPT FROM CANAL TREATIES TESTIMONY (CONT.)

reasons for urging ratification of the Panama Canal Treaties which are before this committee for consideration.

United Brands Co. is the largest single user of the Panama Canal. During 1977, our vessels transited the canal nearly 400 times, an average of 33 trips per month, and we paid approximately $3 million in canal tolls and transit-related charges. The company also acted as agents for vessels that made an additional 513 transits last year. In addition, we maintain offices and have operations in the Canal Zone.

UNITED BRANDS SUPPORT FOR TREATIES

We are convinced that ratification of the Panama Canal Treaties is the only fair conclusion to the good-faith negotiations conducted by our two countries over the last several years. In our judgment, these treaties represent the best evidence yet of this Nation's commitment to fair treatment for Panama and the other developing nations. Fulfilling this commitment, in our view, is particularly important if our Nation is to continue good and mutually beneficial relations in Latin America.

CONFIDENCE IN PANAMANIAN CAPABILITY TO MANAGE CANAL

We are equally certain that the Panamanian Government and the Panamanian people are fully capable of assuming the responsibility for managing the canal over the period of time set forth in the treaty documents. Our position reflects our confidence in General Torrijos and the present Government of Panama, based on our first-hand experience with that Government over the past several years.

Our company has a long history in Panama. Our United Fruit Co. division, which is engaged in the production and distribution of tropical agricultural products, principally bananas, has operated in Panama for nearly 90 years. United Brands' overall contribution to the Panamanian economy is substantial and we employ more than 10,000 people in Panama, 98 percent of whom are Panamanian. During this period, we have made repeated and large commitments of personnel, capital, and other resources in that nation, and we have seen our business grow and prosper there. . . .

IT IS THE RIGHT THING TO DO

Our most important reason for urging ratification of the treaties can be stated simply and succinctly: We believe it is the right thing to do. As a company actively involved with Panamanian affairs throughout this century, we are convinced that the time has come for a reassessment of the Panama Canal arrangement. Our sense of fairness and justice persuades us that the Panamanian people's interest in achieving control of the canal is a legitimate one. We can say forthrightly that as a company, Panama has been good to us, and we believe it has been a good neighbor to our country as well. Today these treaties present the best opportunity to reciprocate this good will.

SIGN TO LATIN AMERICA

Ratification of the treaties will be a sign to Panama and all of Latin America that the United States recognizes the growth and maturity of its neighbors to the south. In an interdependent world, how we treat our smaller and less developed friends in this hemisphere is a measure of our commitment to the goal of mutual respect. It will be a sign that we have come to appreciate the need for cooperation and accommodation in dealing with our neighbors and that the day has passed when smaller, less developed countries will tolerate anything less than the controlling voice in their own destinies.

As users of the canal—its largest single user as I mentioned before—no one can have a greater interest in its efficient and safe operation. Were we to believe that the Government of Panama would provide anything less than the highest standards in the way of maintenance and efficient and safe operation of the canal we could not endorse these treaties as warmly and completely as we do. . . .

In addition, there should be no better motivation for the efficient and responsible operations of the canal than the concept of self-interest embodied in these treaties. Twenty years ago, United Fruit paid $4.6 million in taxes and payments for the use of 30,000 acres, or approximately 47 square miles of land in the Republic of Panama. In comparison, the U.S. Government paid $2 million for the use of 500 square miles of land in the Canal Zone. Today, we pay in excess of $15 million, while the U.S. Government pays only $2.5 million. The new arrangements called for in the treaties should remedy such an imbalance in the share of taxation and are all the more reason for Panama to operate the canal on a sound and economically viable basis.

FIGURE 18-1. EXCERPT FROM CANAL TREATIES TESTIMONY (CONT.)

STRATEGIC IMPORTANCE OF CANAL

In urging upon you ratification of the Panama Canal Treaties, I do not minimize for a moment the strategic importance of the canal for the United States. Certainly the United States has a vital stake in the future security of the waterway.

However, we are persuaded by the arguments set forth by the Joint Chiefs of Staff and others in the Departments of Defense and State that the treaties now under construction provide adequate protection to us in this regard.

In our own dealings with the Panamanians over many years, we have found that while bargaining is hard, an agreement, once reached, is meticulously observed and this, we think, is an important point for the Members of the Senate to bear in mind.

PROMPT RATIFICATION SUPPORTED

Mr. Chairman, we welcome this opportunity to share with this committee our support for prompt ratification of the Panama Canal Treaties.

Thank you for your kind attention. . . .

UNIT VI

Other Formats

19. Manuals
20. Minutes
21. Policies and Procedures
22. Informal Surveys and Questionnaires
23. Press Releases

19
Manuals

ALL OF US have tried to put together something with a screw-driver and a badly written manual. Recently, a friend bought a video cassette recorder, and we rushed over to help play with it. First, however, it had to be hooked up. The manual was an impressive document—glossy paper with color photographs and detailed diagrams. It covered everything anyone needed to know about installing, operating, and maintaining the VCR . . . we thought.

Then we tried to use it. After two hours of annoyance, exaspera-tion, and anger, we sat in the middle of the floor surrounded by packing materials, parts that didn't seem to fit anywhere, a dead VCR, and an impressive-looking—but useless—manual. We boxed up the machine and headed back to the dealer.

The manual for our friend's VCR failed in several significant ways:

1. *The authors incorrectly defined their audience*. They assumed a level of electronic expertise far beyond ours. They chatted know-ingly about "300 ohm transformers," "75 ohm coaxial cables," and "F connectors." They weren't talking to us.

2. *The diagrams didn't look like the parts they were supposed to represent*. We even had one part that didn't appear in any diagram.

3. *The instructions didn't cover all contingencies*. The manual assumed the owner's TV had an outside antenna. Our friend's set had rabbit ears, and that totally changed the installation procedure.

4. *The instructions were badly arranged and incomplete*. One task was presented out of its proper sequence; some others were not mentioned at all.

Poorly written manuals can turn an expensive VCR or a Christmas bicycle or a multimillion-dollar weapons system into useless metal and plastic.

Kinds of Manuals

According to a recent survey, the most frequent on-the-job writing task—next to correspondence—is producing manuals. This isn't surprising if you consider the many kinds of manuals that exist. Manuals tell us how to assemble, operate, maintain, and overhaul machinery of all sorts. They tell us how to train employees and then what procedures these employees are to follow. They describe jobs, provide information, and detail personnel matters.

Manuals explain how to evaluate a school system or manage a restaurant. They tell us how to use a word processor or maintain a crock-pot. They remind us when to have our car serviced, or they refer us to a support group or a resource center.

Whatever their content, manuals invariably contain instructions of some sort. What frustrated us about the VCR manual was its poor instructions.

Instructions

More than any other writing, a set of instructions must meet the needs of its audience. No other business writing is as closely involved and so directly responsible for human behavior. Identifying and defining the audience (*see* pages 8–14) for a set of instructions is the essential first step in their production.

Instructions usually begin with a purpose statement (*see* pages 19–21) followed by a list of tools needed for the job. The task is then broken into consecutive steps that describe, in sequence, what to do and how to do it. Sometimes the steps are numbered to make them easier to follow.

Each step contains only one task. If it is a complex task, it gets broken into sub-steps for the reader's convenience. Each step or sub-step must be precise and specific. There is no place for fuzziness or ambiguity in instructions.

Effective instructions anticipate every contingency, as difficult as this is. Our friend's VCR manual failed to consider the possibility of an indoor TV antenna, making the instructions useless in this instance.

Good instructions anticipate dangers or problems along the way. They use underlining, red ink, capital letters—whatever it takes to warn the reader of potential trouble.

The need to communicate clearly influences the style of instructions. Short paragraphs—each concerned with only one step—short sentences that cannot be misread, and direct and familiar language are the keystones of good instructions.

Instructions usually take the imperative voice. Commands, using active verbs, sound confident and certain. Here is an example.

> BAD: The plug should first be removed from the electric socket before the backplate is removed.
> BETTER: Remove plug from electric socket; unscrew backplate.

The first sentence, using passive verbs, establishes a weak and qualified tone. The rewritten sentence is firm and exact.

The design and layout of instructions help the reader understand the designated tasks. Detailed diagrams, short and clear labels, lots of white space, arrows, bullets, underlining, indentation, different-colored type—all can help direct the eye of an inattentive reader.

The final test for instructions is their usefulness. Have someone ignorant of the task try out your instructions when you finish them.

Manual Form

Manuals usually contain explicit instructions of some sort. In fact, one meaning of manual is "ease of handling," and manuals seek to make something easy to do. But manuals are more than instruction sheets; they present other information to help the reader enjoy a product, perform a job, or understand an organization. This diversity of information makes manuals different from other organizational writing, and it affects their form, layout, graphics, and style.

Suppose you are putting together a manual for the manager of a McBurger franchise. You will want to include information about product, inventory, personnel, advertising, maintenance, insurance, profit and loss. You will cover topics as different as how often to change the fat in the fryer and how to find potential sources of capital. You will write a very large manual; it may be several volumes long.

Sectioning

The variety of subjects in a manual calls for sections or chapters, partitioning of different kinds of information into different units. The VCR manual, for instance, has assembly instructions, of course. But it also has sections that offer maintenance advice, list repair centers, provide warranty information, and sell other company products. In producing a manual, you must first determine the items you will cover and the sections you need. Let each section have the format and length it requires.

Arrangement

Arrange the overall manual, as well as every section, according to the reader's needs. The design of the VCR manual, for instance, ignored the readers. It began with promotional material about other company products. Our friend had just bought a VCR; the manual should have begun by discussing it.

The manual had other problems. It separated "Installation Instructions" from "Operation Instructions" by five pages. But to test the correctness of the installation, the installer must operate the VCR. These two procedures are closely connected, and the sections should be adjoining. If the writer had tried the manual, this difficulty might have been anticipated.

Always use your own manual; test it out. Then arrange the contents to meet the reader's needs.

Details

A good manual is a series of specifics. Not "Get the fat hot" but "Don't fry until fat reaches 220 degrees." A manual is not a place for generalizations, abstractions, or theories. Manuals direct action and inform.

But not all details are necessary. You needn't explain—even to us—that the plug must be in the wall socket for the VCR to work (though you may want to include in a troubleshooting list to check the outlet and plug). You needn't explain to the owner of the Mc-Burger franchise that a profit is desirable. But you may have to explain to new employees how to operate the grill.

The amount of detail depends upon your audiences: their intelligence, knowledge, and interest. The most important decisions you will make in producing a manual concern the level of detail. Too little detail and the VCR manual is useless. Too much detail and you insult the reader.

Layout

Because manuals get handled and used—frequently and intensely —design yours so that it communicates clearly and emphasizes appropriately. And so that it appeals to the reader. These three ends —clarity, emphasis, and appeal—inspire a variety of layout gimmicks that don't occur in most other business and government documents.

Clarity

Enhance clarity by manipulating the layout of your manual.
1. *Divide your manual into sections, each focusing on a single*

activity or purpose. A computer manual we are looking at has three different sections:

    a) how to operate the system;
    b) how to use the system language;
    c) how to use BASIC.

2. *Within each section, divide the material into pieces and label each piece.* The label can be a heading—"BASIC Abbreviations" or "Examples." If you prefer not to use headings, you can keep extra wide margins and put labels in the left- or right-hand margin, alongside the discussion. This second method produces more white space and less print on the page. It is a pleasant alternative to headings.

3. *Use lines, boxes, or tinted areas to create divisions and separations to help clarify your discussion.*

4. *Indent to show the relationship between ideas.* Physically positioning one idea under another signals subordination.

5. *Whenever possible, turn information into series, lists, or parallel steps.* This signals the relationship between information while simplifying the reading. Format these series, lists, and steps on the page to increase their clarity. An example from our computer manual:

LINE INPUT is similar to INPUT, except:
• the computer will not screen an explanation sign;
• leading spaces are not ignored;
• end the string by typing in END.

6. *Whenever possible, use parallelism.* Entire sections should use parallel arrangement when possible. For instance, the computer manual section on operation and the section on using the system language reflect parallel form. Both begin with background information, followed by a brief discussion of theory, and then instructions.

Headings and subheadings should be parallel. Even sentences within a paragraph are easier to understand if they are parallel.

Emphasis

In a manual, not all information is equally important. In the computer manual, for instance, how to prevent losing data is more important than how to command the printer to type capital letters. The former is emphasized. Much of your "writing" time and attention will go into manipulating the layout for the sake of emphasis.

You can emphasize material in different ways:

—You can change type: size, style, and boldness.

—You can add things to the page: underlining, asterisks, bullets, exclamation points, and quotation marks.

—You can leave things off the page, emphasizing by white space or colored space.

—You can use drawings, pictures, or just abstract lines to focus the reader's attention.

But, you can't emphasize everything. We are reminded of a friend's textbook. He had used yellow highlighting pen to call attention to important material for the final exam. Half of the pages were nearly filled with yellow ink, while the rest were bare except for a yellow "WP" at the top. When we asked him what "WP" meant, he replied "Whole Page." He could have saved himself time and the price of a marking pen by just memorizing the entire book.

Reader Appeal

The layout of a page directly affects reader appeal. A page should contain wide margins with considerable white space within the writing; some experts think at least one-third of a page should be white. This means short paragraphs, formatted lists and series, and space between sections.

The page layout should be interesting. Even if no material needs emphasis, occasionally vary the type font, shift the margins, turn information into indented series, and add page breakers—lines, dashes, boxes, and bullets.

Finally, use the size and shape of the finished work to increase its effectiveness and its reader appeal. Our computer manual, for instance, is in a loose-leaf notebook, permitting additions as they become necessary and allowing us to remove pages we are using.

Odd-sized manuals are common. Some are magazine-sized to accommodate large print (easy to read while you're performing the job). Others are pocket-sized for easy carrying. Some are large squares; others brochure-sized. There is no standard manual size or shape.

Graphics

Manuals rely heavily on graphics to make clear and precise what the prose describes. If you choose to include drawings, make sure they look like what they depict. If the diagrams of the VCR components had been accurate, we might have been able to make the machine work. But they weren't and we couldn't. Drawings should clarify, not confuse the reader.

A drawing seldom substitutes for discussion; it augments it. Be sure to put the drawing next to or directly after the point it illustrates. Refer to your drawing in your discussion and label it clearly.

Occasionally, however, a drawing may be all you need. Remember how scouting manuals use diagrams to teach a square knot and a bowline. It's almost impossible to explain in prose how to tie the knot; the diagram is all. Be sure it's clear.

Some manuals use photographs. If you can't afford photographs, don't worry; they are hard to use and often confusing. Photographs present all details equally. Drawings exclude irrelevant details and highlight important ones.

In addition to increasing the clarity of a manual, graphics enhance the manual's reader appeal. The manual that came with our computer printer, for example, is filled with cartoon characters: talking computers, "bugs" that look like beetles, stick-figure people, and visual puns on the serious text. These cartoons break up the visual monotony of the text, and their position on the page varies. Sometimes an entire page will be a cartoon, sometimes a talking computer will interrupt a paragraph, other times a cartoon "bug" will crawl in the right-hand margin. The authors have tried to lighten and enliven a potentially dreary topic.

Style

General issues concerning style are discussed in Unit VIII. Manuals, however, have some distinctive stylistic features.

To facilitate communication:
1. *Keep verbs in the present tense.*
2. *Shun first person pronouns: "I" and "we."*
3. *Use the second-person "you" in its imperative voice to create a familiar and relaxed tone.*
4. *Slant your discussion to the reader's point of view.* "While you want to learn quickly, it will take you awhile."
5. *Keep sentences and paragraphs short.*
6. *Don't write in "telegraphese."* (That is, don't leave out all the words except the essential nouns and verbs.)
7. *When possible, express ideas positively, not negatively.* "Write positively," not "Do not write negatively."

To increase reader appeal, create a familiar and conversational tone:
1. *Use contractions whenever they feel right.*
2. *Include slang if it works.*
3. *Use idiomatic expressions.*
4. *Incorporate personal anecdotes and fictitious narratives.*
5. *Enliven your prose with wit and figurative language.* Use puns, allusions, similes, metaphors, and hyperbole—as long as you don't distract or confuse your reader.
6. *Play with unconventional constructions.* Creating sentence fragments. And beginning a sentence with "and" or "but" for the sake of familiarity and immediacy.
7. *Pop in a playful—nontraditional—verb now and again.*
8. *Relax your word choice and use conversational diction.*

FIGURE 19-1. PAGE FROM *MX PRINTER MANUAL**

_____ More Print Control Commands

Chapter 4
More Print Control Commands

That last chapter was a heavy one, but it gave us a good overview of the printer's major features. In this chapter we'll explore a few of them in more detail, plus learn additional features related to print size and quality.

As before, in BASIC, CHR$ is the magic wand, and we are using a popular version of Microsoft BASIC as our standard. Continue to refer to Appendix B as needed to help maintain perspective on where we're going and what we're doing.

A Cheap Buzz

Type:

```
LPRINT CHR$(7)
```
Microsoft "Standard" BASIC-type computers

```
PR#1
```

```
PRINT CHR$(7)
```
Apple-type computers

EXPENSIVE ALARM CLOCK

Sorry if that scared the dog! Just couldn't resist it. It really has nothing to do with printing, but is widely incorporated in programs as an alarm to indicate something. A built-in alarm is a standard feature on quality printers.

Sure . . . do it again. We'll wait.

If our computer has a real-time clock, we can use it as a time-is-up alarm. Just include LPRINT CHR$(7) in the program. It also makes a great audio prompter, telling the operator it's time to do something. The applications are virtually endless. Most expensive alarm clock in the place.

When you must write a manual, don't miss out on the fun. Give free rein to your imagination and produce an effective and appealing manual.

Figure 19-1, a page from the *MX Printer Manual,* well illustrates basic principles of this chapter: be clear, be playful, and create a readable layout.

20
Minutes

MINUTES RECORD what happened at your meeting; they are the chronological outline of the subjects discussed and the action taken. Minutes include all motions, amendments and procedural motions, the names of the people who proposed and seconded them, along with the disposition of each vote.

Any group may keep minutes. Even an informal *ad hoc* group may want a formal record of its actions. For instance, a committee that has been set up to review the workings of a personnel evaluation system may do well to keep a record of its proceedings. What the group discussed, concluded, and recommended may be important for future reference.

Minutes are more than a record, however. The existence of minutes sometimes spurs a group to reach decisions and conclusions. Because the recorder must write something down, side-stepping a tough issue is difficult. "What should I put in the minutes?" motivates group action.

Meeting Reports

Sometimes you don't want an outline of a meeting, and you may not want detailed information reported. Meeting reports, unlike minutes, are not comprehensive. They present only the conclusions of the meeting, recommendations, and perhaps a summary of the discussion. They seldom mention names. Meeting reports are often included in some other writing, such as a letter or final report (*see* figure 20-1).

FIGURE 20-1. MEETING REPORT

Summary of Meeting on Establishing Mini-Courses for Spring

A group of interested faculty and administrators gathered in the conference room of the Vice-Chancellor at 1:30, January 17, 198–. Present were: [list follows]. Absent were: [list follows].

The discussion focused on the 130-140 high-school students who enrolled this semester to secure Social Security benefits. While some of these students are eligible for Early Admission, the majority have come as Special Students; we have very little academic information about them. We need to pay special attention to these students, to help them complete high school and the university courses they are taking.

Registration will begin March 20; classes will begin March 30 and continue through May 15.

Dr. Jones will contact the deans and department heads to see what courses may be offered. The availability of space will be checked with existing classes. Dr. Brown will work out the financial arrangements for instructors through Continuing Education.

Summary prepared by Eve Steele, chair, on January 21 and distributed to those present, department heads, and deans.

Purpose

The primary function of minutes is to record—accurately and thoroughly—what happened at a meeting. But they may have other purposes. Minutes inform absent members what went on at the meeting. Also, the minutes may be used to circulate information about procedures or policies to members of the larger organization.

"Put that into the minutes, Bill, I want everyone to know about Sheila's new assignment. And be sure to pass the minutes around the office." Many large corporations circulate abbreviated minutes, using them as an internal public relations device to help create a sense of belonging.

Audience

People at the meeting (or who should have been at the meeting) are the immediate audience for any minutes. For this audience the minutes serve as a résumé of what transpired, and accuracy is essential. On receiving a copy of the minutes, members of this audience should read them carefully for accuracy.

Sometimes a secondary audience exists, members of the larger organization not privy to the meeting but in need of information. For this audience the boss may tack the minutes to the bulletin board.

Generally, minutes are written for the record, for an unknown future audience. They should be complete and self-contained with no unnecessary detail or irrelevant chatter.

You the Recorder

People often assume that taking minutes is the job of a professional secretary. More often, however, a member of the group gets assigned this task (and often a relative newcomer, since the chore is not desirable). If you are asked to take minutes, remember that your participation in the discussion may be affected. If you want to take part fully or if you expect to be directly involved in the proceedings, ask someone else to take the minutes. Minutes must be accurate, and accuracy demands your full attention. For the sake of accuracy, you must be willing to ask questions or seek clarification of unclear points. If you don't speak up at the meeting, you may be embarrassed to find your minutes incomplete or in error.

Here are five suggestions for creating accurate minutes:

1. *Write up your notes as soon as possible after the meeting*. The longer you wait, the greater your chance for error.

2. *Make sure that the dates and days in your minutes are accurate*. During meetings, dates and days get confused. Double-check their accuracy on a calendar in the quiet of your office.

3. *Ask someone else who was at the meeting to glance over your minutes before you have them typed, checking for completeness, accuracy, and coherence*.

4. *Keep a file copy for yourself and one for the permanent file*. If no permanent file exists, start one separate from your personal file.

5. *Proofread minutes carefully before you distribute them*.

Content

The arrangement of minutes varies with the tradition of the organization, the purpose of the minutes, and their audience. Here is a short list of what may appear and the usual order:

1. date and place of meeting,
2. name of person presiding and of person taking the minutes,
3. names of persons present,
4. names of persons absent,
5. disposition of the previous minutes and any corrections,
6. summaries of reports, unless you attach a copy of the report (if you do, note the attachment and record how the report was handled),
7. exact wording of all motions, with sponsors and seconds, and the disposition of each motion,
8. record of other action,
9. date the minutes were written, the name of the writer, and the title of the writer.

Minutes usually omit summarizing discussions and routine announcements. They never include personal comments, either complimentary or pejorative.

If attachments accompany your minutes, mention them within the minutes.

Style

Minutes report meetings, and like all reports they strive for objectivity, accuracy, and completeness. But the style of minutes varies from formal to conversational. If you are taking minutes, find copies of past minutes from your group and use them as guides.

Minutes may be either full or abbreviated (*see* figures 20-2 and 20-3). Full minutes attempt to summarize the reasoning of the group

---

FIGURE 20-2. EXCERPT FROM MINUTES

Minutes of September 23, 198–
Commission Members Present: [list follows]
Staff Members Present: [list follows]

The meeting of the state committee on Health Care Cost Effectiveness was called to order at 8:45 a.m. on September 23, 198–, in Room 195 of the Conference Center of the State Health Division Offices. Dr. Sarah McNally, presiding; David Hammond, staff member, recorder.

I. Old Business

1. The minutes of August 8, 198–, were reviewed and approved with the following addition: Robert Jackson, commission member, was present.
2. Dr. Cyril Drucker announced that the October 21st meeting will cover health insurance, reimbursement, and alternative delivery systems. The meeting will be held at 8:30 at the Conference Center.
3. At the suggestion of Barbara Branchard, it was agreed to postpone the November meeting to December 2, because several members will be attending a regional health care planning symposium.
4. The revised report "Physicians and Health Care Providers" was distributed (see attachment A). Discussion centered on the means used to gather the statistics and the trends foreseen in the report. The report was adopted (moved, Cyril Drucker, seconded Deborah Ebbon) by voice vote, and ordered distributed. . . .

FIGURE 20-3. ABBREVIATED MINUTES (#3 & #4, FIGURE 20-2)

---

3. It was agreed to postpone the November meeting to December 2.

4. The revised report "Physicians and Health Care Providers" (attachment A) was adopted (moved, Cyril Drucker, seconded Deborah Ebbon) by voice vote and ordered distributed. . . .

---

and give a sense of the discussion. They are difficult to write, requiring the recorder to thoroughly understand the dynamics of the group as well as the history of the subject matter.

Abbreviated minutes may be little more than a brief outline of the meeting, reporting only motions and actions, without any discussion. Easier to write, abbreviated minutes are poor reference documents compared to full minutes.

Whichever style you choose, refrain from subjectivity. It is appropriate to write "The Chair commended the committee for its work." But not "The committee did a good job." The first is reporting, the second a personal observation. Be sure you report; don't comment.

21

Policies and Procedures

POLICIES AND PROCEDURES are the rules and regulations that govern organizations, including their structure and methods; their employee duties, promotion, pay, and fringe benefits. Policies and procedures, though not identical, are usually so similar that the differences are inconsequential. Both normally appear together in a company handbook with no distinction made between them.

Policies are the laws of an organization: when you work, how long you work, when you get paid, how many vacation days you accumulate, and which washroom you use.

Procedures detail the process of an action: how you change your retirement benefits, what you must do to join the credit union, what you must do to appeal a demotion, how you change a company policy.

Policy statements and procedural guidelines are used inside organizations (between employer and employee) and between organizations, between management and a trade union. Most organizations have them. Even a two-person business may post a policy statement next to the door: Turn off the lights!

More often, however, these documents deal with crucial matters of employment, pay, and benefits—concerns that often have legal ramifications. The regulatory nature of these documents causes their special format, content, and style.

Format

Organizations change slowly, almost imperceptibly. One grievance procedure may change while all the rest remain the same. The formatting of policies and procedures statements permits individual rules or regulations to change without rewriting or republishing them all.

Treat each policy or procedure as a separate unit with its own page and sequential number. If the grievance procedure should change, you need revise only a single sheet. Gather the total collection of policies in a loose-leaf folder to simplify the replacement of individual policies or procedures.

Collect the policies and procedures into small chapters or sections, each dealing with a common topic and each with its own identifying title. Within a section, give an identifying tag—either a number or a letter—to every important point or procedure. This makes precise reference easy.

Suppose that an employee can take sick-leave days in four different circumstances. Let each circumstance stand in a separate paragraph and each paragraph have a different number. For instance, Part II discusses non-monetary employee benefits, section C of Part II presents leave time, number 3 concerns sick leave, and the four sick-leave discussions are lettered consecutively:

II.C.3.a. Sick Leave For Illness,
II.C.3.b. Sick Leave for Death in Family,
II.C.3.c. Sick Leave for Pregnancy,
II.C.3.d. Accumulated Sick Leave at Retirement.

When the company changes its policy concerning sick leave for pregnancy, a rewrite of that one policy is all that is necessary.

This sort of individual notation permits precise reference and easy recovery of detailed information. Injured workers consulting Part III—"Worker's Compensation"—learn that they will use up sick leave when receiving worker's comp. A parenthetical note refers readers back to the appropriate section on sick leave in Part II.

Because of the need to change individual policies or procedures, page each section separately. The section dealing with sick leave might be: SL-1, SL-2, SL-3, SL-3a, SL-4. If you later add or subtract a page, you only need change the page numbers of one section. Notice, too, that using "SL" (sick leave) instead of 3 or II allows you to reorganize sections without disturbing the overall numbering system. It also helps readers locate the section they need.

The existence of multiple units, the greater number of pages caused by putting individual policies and procedures into separate sections, and the unusual pagination make a table of contents essential.

Content

Background information about the policies and procedures usually introduces them: what they replace, when they take effect, who needs to know them, and who authorized and wrote them.

Following this background information often appears a section that defines terms. A "work week," for instance, can be many different things, and its exact definition is pertinent when discussing vacations, sick leave, leave without pay, and retirement benefits. Define "work week" and other important terms at the outset.

Title individual sections of the policies and procedures and begin each with a clear purpose statement (*see* pages 19–21). For example:

Worker's Compensation

This section discusses worker's compensation: what qualifies you for compensation, how long you are eligible for it, and how we calculate the benefits. The section closes by listing what you must do to prove your eligibility.

Because policies and procedures are practical and important tools for all employees, they should be as direct and clear as possible.

The policies and procedures of organizations that do business with the federal government must often meet federal standards. Many public agencies, too, have legal standards to meet. To ensure full and correct compliance with these regulations, get a copy of the regulations from the appropriate governmental unit and use its language in your policies and procedures.

The looseleaf format and convenient numbering lead to one pitfall. When you change or add to a section, you may have to change the numbering that follows. Also, scrutinize the entire document, revising all references to the old section number.

To avoid renumbering each time you delete or move an entry in the middle of a section, you can leave the section number empty. If you want, include a short note by the unused number, explaining where that section went or that it was deleted.

Style

Policy and procedure statements are, potentially, legal documents. They should be factual, detailed, and objective—free of personal observations, opinions, and prejudices. They include few adjectives and adverbs.

Although policy and procedure statements serve as rules, don't try to make them sound legal. Legal-sounding language is often less clear and more ambiguous than well-written English. Make your policies and procedures direct, simple, and easy to understand. After all, you are writing for employees, not for lawyers.

Policies and procedures may be formal, but they don't have to be. Even law briefs today are increasingly relaxed. If you are beginning a new set of company guidelines, we recommend using the pronouns *we* (the organization) and *you* (the employee). If you are adding to existing directives that don't use *we* or *you*, match their tone. But if the existing policies and procedures use bloated, pretentious, trying-to-sound-important language, make yours clear and concise.

Here is an example of an overwritten policy statement:

Inclement Weather Policy

When the Vice-President for Finance determines, based on data available, that the weather or other conditions have made roads impassable, the news media will be notified through the company news service that the plant is closed.

Why data "available"? (Would he "determine" anything on unavailable data?) Since this is a weather policy, what "other conditions" might occur here? Why all these needless qualifiers? Why one long, convoluted sentence even if all this detail *is* necessary? This opening sentence tries to sound official and legal for a policy that is local and, finally, not all that important. Here is our rewrite:

Bad Weather

When driving becomes dangerous, the Vice-President for Finance may close the plant. The company news service will notify the media.

The rewrite gives the same information in half the words. And it doesn't intimidate the reader. Policy and procedure statements should use familiar diction, active verbs, and short sentences.

22

Informal Surveys and Questionnaires

SURVEYS MAY BE sophisticated, scientific public-opinion polls or they may be little more than loaded questions in a scientific guise posed to selected audiences to ensure getting desired results. Between these two extremes lie the numerous informal surveys and questionnaires that we use in business and government to explore employee feelings and customer needs.

Although this chapter may help you understand scientific surveying a bit more, it deals only with *informal* surveys and questionnaires—the kind you might use to find out about your organization's phone needs as you get ready to buy a new system, the kind you might use to find out how to improve sales in the employee cafeteria.

As you begin thinking about your survey, recognize that you have two audiences, both of which you must understand thoroughly.

The first audience is whoever wants the survey done. You must understand the purpose of the survey and how the information will be used. The second crucial audience is the people you are surveying. Understanding the nature of that audience will help you decide how to conduct your survey.

Understand Your Purpose

Begin by finding out why you are taking a survey. What is the purpose of the survey?

The boss wants to know whether or not to get a WATS line—so

you need to know what kinds of long-distance calls are made and received, how often they are made, why they are made, and how long they last. You do not need to know about telephone habits in general or whether individuals think a WATS line is a good idea. You need to know whether or not the long-distance calls are useful to the boss. Do they lead to orders? To new customers? To happier customers? Do they simply provide information for people too lazy to get it elsewhere?

The boss wants to increase business in the employee cafeteria. The employees-benefits committee wants to expand the menu. Someone needs to take a survey. Would an enlarged menu increase business? But if you simply ask that question, everyone will say Yes, and you will know nothing. You probably need to know why people choose to eat in the cafeteria or, if they don't, why not. Do the same 20 percent eat there daily? Do 80 percent of the employees eat there twice a week? The answer makes a big difference in how to go about trying to increase business. You must find out how people behave. Then you need to know about expanding the menu. What kinds of entrées do people prefer? Do they prefer luncheon specials? Would they like a salad bar? Would adding more variety or lowering prices do more to increase business?

The questions can multiply endlessly. You must recognize that you are looking at two issues and how they interact—increasing business and possibly expanding the menu. Stay on target. Keep your questions focused.

Length

As you develop the survey, remember you are asking people to take their time and the organization's time to fill out your questionnaire. Make it useful, but keep it to the point. If it were someone else's questionnaire, would you fill it out?

Asking too many questions and splitting questions too finely may even give you more information than you can or want to use. Ask yourself if you are willing to tabulate and summarize all the information that your survey generates, including the comments. And if you have someone to do that drudge work for you, then ask yourself if you are willing to *use* all the information you will be accumulating.

Window Dressing

Don't waste your time creating a serious survey if all you want is window dressing. Getting a survey to come out the way you want is a matter of asking well-loaded questions or of surveying the right audience. Politicians send out phony surveys all the time, loading the questions so that the results support their points of view. Then they can honestly state, "Eighty-five percent of my constituents who cared enough to respond to my recent poll agreed with me."

Selecting a particular audience can also skew a survey. A recent catsup commercial announcing the results of an "impartial" taste test illustrates this. The survey found that about half of those who used the competition's catsup preferred the less expensive brand, the one doing the survey and the advertising. Since most of us can't tell much difference between catsups, it's not surprising that limiting the survey to the users of the competition's brand created this result. (If they had tested their brand, they probably would have found that about half the users preferred the more expensive brand.) But the result appears scientific enough for the commercial.

The Survey Medium

How you present the survey or questionnaire is important. If by telephone, then the questions must be easily understood—the questions short and clear, the answer format direct. If face-to-face, the questions may be a little longer and more involved, but the respondent must still be able to follow the questions and the answer choices easily. If the survey is printed, then individual questions can be more elaborate, but the questionnaire must look short. Over the telephone and even in person, a long questionnaire can be concealed with a pleasant "just a moment more," but with a printed questionnaire, the reader sees the two additional pages and puts the whole thing aside.

You must also define the audience you are surveying. Your understanding of them, their education, and their knowledge of the issue will determine how you phrase questions and how sophisticated the answering formats are. If the audience is ill-educated, for instance, you will probably use yes/no questions that require little reading—that is, if you want them to respond.

But since you are more likely to survey office workers about flextime or political constituents about name recognition, the controlling factor will probably be time. How much time are you expecting people to put into your survey? Surveys that ask yes/no questions can be filled out more quickly than questionnaires that ask for discussion.

Asking for discussion often seems attractive because it allows people to respond as they wish. They control the emphasis and the amount of detail. But dangers exist in the open-ended questionnaire. First, people do not necessarily respond to the points you want covered. Second, you will have many fewer questionnaires returned. Third, tallying or interpreting open-ended questions can be an endless task.

People may become exasperated with surveys full of "simpleminded" yes/no questions, but they answer them. When faced with a survey full of open-ended questions, people find other things to do, even when they care about the issues.

The way you present the questionnaire and the amount of time you are willing to spend tabulating or summarizing the results limit the possibilities for presenting questions. If you are interested in people's thoughts on a broad subject and do not need to tabulate the thoughts, then open-ended questions may be appropriate. If you are taking a poll on a specific group of issues, you want questions that can be easily tabulated.

In most questionnaires you will use two or three formats; be sure not to confuse readers by switching formats too often.

Yes/no questions are easily tabulated, but sometimes exasperating, particularly when the questions are broad.

Should the cafeteria menu be expanded?
    yes ——   no ——

True/false questions differ only slightly. The question is in statement form, either positive or negative.

The cafeteria menu should be expanded.
true ＿＿＿ false ＿＿＿

or

agree ＿＿＿ disagree ＿＿＿

The statement form invites use of an agreement scale.

Generally speaking, the cafeteria does a good job of food preparation.
strongly agree ＿＿＿ agree ＿＿＿ disagree ＿＿＿ strongly disagree ＿＿＿

With such a range of answers, you may feel that you should provide a neutral answer, usually *uncertain*. The names of these categories and the number of them may dramatically affect your results (*see* pp. 286–287).

A ten-point scale with only the end points labeled *seems* to provide a more sensitive scale for readers than the statement form.

On a scale of 1 to 10 (1 being outstanding and 10 being abysmal), rate the quality of the food in the cafeteria.

1   2   3   4   5   6   7   8   9   10
(outstanding)   (abysmal)

A ten-point scale is likely to yield precise-looking but meaningless numbers: you may have no idea how to interpret the difference between 3.7 and 4.7. And the labels you choose for the end points may alter the number score (*see* page 287).

Some questions are for background information: how often do you do something? why do you do something? In these questions be sure to give a good range of likely responses.

How often do you eat lunch out?
three or more times a week ＿＿＿ once or twice a week ＿＿＿
two or three times a month ＿＿＿ once a month or less ＿＿＿

Measuring Intensity

Most surveys report preferences well, at least within the outlined boundaries. But many surveys, especially informal ones, fail to gauge the intensity of people's feelings. The information you gather will probably be much more useful if you do.

> Of the issues we have discussed, is there any single one that would by itself lead you to favor or oppose a candidate?

or

> Rank these issues in order of their importance to you.

You can also ask people to select items from a list or to rank items in a list, either the two or three most important items or all of them.

> The list below contains some reasons people give for choosing where they eat lunch. Rank the items that affect where you eat lunch beginning with 1 (the most important). Please rank all the items.
> ____being with friends   ____ quiet   ____ price   ____ good coffee
> ____selection of entrées   ____ salad bar   ____ usual place

Some simple forced-choice questions (if carefully constructed) may help you understand the intensity of feelings:

> Is a salad bar or a no-smoking area more important to you?
> Would you rather have prices reduced by 10 percent or free refills on coffee and other beverages, except milk?
> Would you prefer linen tablecloths and napkins or larger portions?

Such questions do not tie actual choices together but will indicate, for instance, how strongly people are interested in improved atmosphere. After all, when simply asked, "Would improving the atmosphere of the cafeteria make a difference to you?" 95 percent might check yes. By asking people to make choices you have a feeling for how strongly they meant yes.

Critique the Questions

Before you write up the final questionnaire, critique the individual questions and possible answers. Try to anticipate the kinds of answers people will want to give. If the survey is important, you may want to try out questions on a few people from your survey group. Here are some common problems that people have with survey questions and answers.

Too Broad

In an effort to reduce the number of questions asked, surveyors often make questions too broad, leaving too much room for interpretation. "Should the cafeteria menu be expanded?" is not a useful question. Useful questions center on whether individuals will eat other entrées. Do they want larger portions? a salad bar? vegetarian main dishes?

Loaded Questions

The language of your questions should be neutral. For instance, a question about changing to flexible work schedules can be biased either for or against the issue:

Do you favor retaining the uniform starting time rule that allows for an orderly flow of business in the company?

or

Do you oppose retaining the uniform starting time rule that causes traffic jams twice daily in the parking lot and requires employees to use sick time or vacation time to take care of important personal business?

or

    Do you favor adopting flexible work schedules so that employees can integrate their work and their personal lives in ways that are individually meaningful?

The questions contain their own answers.

The Number of Choices

The number of choices you offer may be crucial. If you offer respondents only *agree, uncertain,* and *disagree,* you may lose all indications of intensity. Generally you will want at least four degrees in your scale. A scale with an odd number of points seems to encourage people toward the middle. Researchers feel that a scale without the neutral point—that is, with an even number of points—gives a more accurate picture of feelings, although many responses around the middle may be ''soft.''

When providing a scale or a range of answers, be certain that you have not left out a possibly significant category.

When, in the name of simplicity or in an effort to focus on the big picture, you reduce the options in the question

    How often do you eat in the cafeteria?

to

    daily ____ once a week ____ once or twice a month ____

you omit at least one significant group—those who eat in the cafeteria two or three times a week. Those people are forced to dramatically overstate or understate their activity. Your question forces them to misreport what they do.

The Names of the Choices

The labels you choose for the categories may affect the responses dramatically. If you ask someone to rate the cafeteria food on a three-point scale excellent _____   fair _____   poor _____

you force people who are moderately satisfied to choose between
fair and *excellent*. Your results will probably come out *fair*. Change
the scale to

excellent _____   good _____   poor _____

and your cafeteria, unless it is pitiful, will be rated *good* to *excellent*
by almost everyone you survey. That may be good PR, but it is not
very real information.

You can control the results even more forcefully. Give your respondents a four-point scale of

excellent _____   good _____   poor _____   abysmal _____

and you should be able to write that the food is "rated excellent or
good by 80 percent of those responding." (If you want to make
doubly sure of such a response, load the question with a phrase
such as "Given the problems the cafeteria staff has faced recently"
or "All things considered." Most people will remember how overworked they feel and sympathize with the overworked cafeteria
staff. The rating should go up several points.)

Try to evenly space the responses along a reasonable continuum
such as

excellent _____   good _____   fair _____   poor _____

The Question/Answer Fit

Be sure that your answer scale fits your question. Consider this
question which was put to school volunteers:

> Did the teacher with whom you worked provide sufficient continuing
> assistance or guidance?

That's a "yes/no" question, or an "always/sometimes/seldom/
never" question, but the choice of answers was "much/some/lit-
tle." The question was probably rephrased at the last minute, but

someone neglected to actually read the question and the answer together.

Writing up the Questionnaire

Although your purposes will affect how much you tell people about the survey when you send it out, you will generally follow this format.

Narrative Introduction

Introduce your survey and persuade people to fill it out. Sometimes this is done on the first sheet of the questionnaire, sometimes in a cover letter.

What is the purpose of the questionnaire? What are the rules for handling it?

Will responses be confidential or not? Should it be signed?

To whom should it be returned? How? By what date?

Are additional comments allowed, invited, or encouraged? Where are they put?

Political and product surveys often omit the names of the sponsors to avoid prejudicing the reader.

Background Subject Information

If you are supplying background information on the subject, do so here. Otherwise your first survey questions should ask if your respondent knows something about the subject: Have you heard of ____? Have you formed an impression about ____? Have you ever eaten in the company cafeteria? Have you eaten there in the past two weeks? How many times?

Find out if this person can give you useful answers about the current menu or about why people don't eat there.

Ordering Questions

Put the survey questions in a logical sequence, making certain that one does not prejudice a later one. Also make certain that you have enough different formats or responses (some statements phrased negatively, perhaps) so that someone cannot blindly mark "true," "frequently" or "always" without attending to the question.

Close

Close with a thank you and perhaps a reminder of what should be done with the survey. If the answers are potentially sensitive, remind people of your commitment to confidentiality.

Do People Do As They Say They Do?

Surveys are predicated on the assumption that people can and will report themselves and their behavior accurately.

Certainly, the general accuracy of sophisticated election polls suggests that in this case the assumptions are valid or that the errors are randomly distributed.

But these assumptions may not always be safe. For instance, college graduates may not be willing to report that they do not read the newspaper daily. Not reading the newspaper daily goes against what they believe the norm is; they may answer with wishes or expectation rather than facts. And there may be times that surveys make readers self-conscious enough to be unable to report their behavior accurately.

The Results—Statistics and Other Leading Indicators

Numbers, especially the crude ones you are likely to create with the instruments we are talking about, are dangerous. People pay attention to numbers, no matter how little the number actually means. The number itself receives more attention than the way the number was generated or than the possibly important narrative information.

Creating a misleading number is worse than not taking the survey. Better to use summaries and questions that cannot be easily tallied than to create numbers that, once created, can be misused.

In some situations, creating tallies and votes may give an impression that a group is of a particular mind when in fact there may be many "soft" positions within the group. If people talked, positions might change; people might create a consensus around an option that was not originally available.

23

Press Releases

PRESS OR NEWS releases are reports, written in news style, about a service, product, or event that has been, is being, or will be offered or sponsored. Press releases put information about your organization, its products or services, in front of the public.

Your goal in writing a release is to have it become a news story, a feature, or a portion of a new-products column. In general, you are more likely to get the release into a newspaper or magazine than onto radio or television, but don't ignore radio and TV.

In addition to creating stories, news releases keep editors informed of potentially important stories. Papers will seldom run a release about a conference being planned, but the release alerts editors to watch for other stories or to cover the event themselves. Then conference participants, main speakers, and distinguished guests may receive actual news coverage.

Radio and television coverage is relatively rare because of the limited time in those media. Your preliminary news releases should encourage editors to become interested enough to cover the event or to run a feature highlighting your new product or service. A news release about your company's new export might lead to a feature about local exports, highlighting your company.

Making News

Press releases are tied to news or potential news—new products, new services, conferences, speakers, promotions, and retirements.

Depending on your announcement and the publications you want to alert, you can send out press releases in a nearly continuous stream.

If your consulting firm is preparing a new records management system for grain elevators, you can send out numerous releases. When you begin the project, send out a release focusing on the improvements you plan to make in the present systems. When you have developed your system, your release explains what yours can do that the others can't. When you get a contract to install your first system, when you begin to install it, and later when it works, send out more releases. In short, send out a press release at each milestone.

The possible occasions are innumerable. Some organizations turn every holiday or Health Week into an occasion for a news release. And on slow news days, some of these releases will be printed and some turned into features.

Audience

Your audience is the reader of the newspaper or magazine; you need to define it. Is it a technical audience of a trade or professional journal, or is it one of the many audiences of the Sunday newspaper? It may be both and everyone in between.

But first you must convince an editor to use your release. You will do this by having a worthwhile item (one the editor thinks newsworthy) and by writing in news style.

News Style

Write your press release in news style. If you do a good job, you will have done much of the editor's work, saving rewriting and copy editing time. Editors appreciate that; they too are overworked.

News writing is not ordinary writing. It is as factual as possible, more factual even than reports. News writing focuses on the 5 Ws and an H: who, what, when, where, why, and how. The answers to these questions will compose most of your story. These are the facts, the news.

For writing press releases, you need to know how to write a news lead, how to write in the inverted pyramid, and how to avoid editorializing. While there is much more to news writing than these three concerns, being aware of these will allow you to write effective press releases.

The Lead

News stories do not have introductory sentences. They begin with the most important facts—generally, the who and what. Those facts are your lead.

Write your lead as a brisk, active sentence:

> The Community Symphony will hold auditions for second horn and for the violin and bass sections Tuesday evening, May 31, at 7:30 p.m. at City Auditorium.

It would be nice to have a hook or a grabber in the lead, something to get the reader's attention. But something like "Have you always wanted to blow your own horn?" or "Get down, come down and boogie with us" are cute, not catchy. Get a hook if you can, but better to have a straightforward businesslike lead than a cute come-on with out-of-date slang. Few papers will print it, and most editors will throw the release away without reading beyond it.

Because the product or service being announced is usually the most important item, writers too often begin in the passive voice:

> A new line of frozen-food gourmet entrées featuring Chicken Cordon Bleu and Coq au Vin was announced recently by Charles Jackson, Vice-President of Western Poultry Processors and manager of the newly formed Food Products Division.

Turn this lead into an active sentence without losing sight of the new dinners:

Western Poultry Processors today announced a line of gourmet frozen-food entrées featuring Chicken Cordon Bleu and Coq au Vin.
In making the announcement Vice-President Charles Jackson, manager of the new frozen-foods product line said that . . .

Much clearer and more forceful. Now it sounds like something you might read in a newspaper. Now that you have a decent lead, try putting a hook into it:

Coq au Vin in a TV dinner?
Not only Coq au Vin, but Chicken Cordon Bleu, also. That was the announcement from Western Poultry Processors today. Vice-President Charles Jackson, speaking for the company, said . . .

This may verge on the cute, but at least it won't get thrown out without a look.

Inverted Pyramid

Writing in the inverted pyramid means that you begin with the most important point in the lead, and close with the least important point. You are writing an information piece, not a feature. The news release has no introduction and no conclusion. When you run out of information, stop.

If you want to lengthen your press release in an effort to get a longer article published, add background material at the end of the story—the history of this service, the firm's position in the field, previous accomplishments, and so on.

Because the least important information is at the bottom, if your story must be shortened, it can be cut from the bottom like all news stories, paragraph by paragraph. No one needs to take time finding a paragraph that can go.

Editorializing

You are writing an objective news story. That means no editorializing, no self-aggrandizing comments, at least none that are un-attributed.

The event you are writing about is important and does have implications for your agency or company, perhaps for an industry or for society. Include these things in your release by quoting and paraphrasing freely.

If you are announcing the line of frozen gourmet chicken entrées, let people in the company explain. Let the company dietician talk about the quality of the food, the chef talk about the succulent aromas and pleasures to the palate. Let the vice-president in charge of the new product talk about the impact on the local economy. Taking ten minutes to make some phone calls around the company will get you plenty of quotations that you can use to add color and life to your story.

If one of your quotes is a dud—"The outstanding quality of these products will be created by our unique processing methods and the proximity of the plant to fresh ingredients"—and you feel obliged to use it, you have three choices. Use it, paraphrase it, or put words in the person's mouth—after talking with the person, of course. If you want or need the thoughts, get them into English before putting them in the release. Make each quotation sound like someone talking, not like someone pontificating.

Attribute all quotations and paraphrases, preferably to someone with a name and a title. An occasional "a representative for the company said" is all right, but not nearly as strong as "the vice-president for overseas marketing said." When you attribute the praise of your product, you are not editorializing, you are reporting.

If you, as writer, also happen to be vice-president in charge of sales, quote yourself by name as vice-president; ignore the fact that you, as publicist, are writing the release.

Physical Format

Editors expect press releases to follow a standard physical format.

The first page, on letterhead, includes a release date or the notation "For Immediate Release," the name and phone number of someone to contact for more information, and a subject line or title. Often the words "News Release" appear on the page. The arrangement of these items varies. Figure 23-1, which is a technical news release, illustrates a correct format.

Type double-spaced in a narrow column. Leave generous margins at the beginning of the release and throughout your copy so that there is room for copy editing, headline writing, and print notations.

FIGURE 23-1. PRESS RELEASE

ARKANSAS SYSTEMS INC.
8901 KANIS ROAD • SUITE 206 • LITTLE ROCK, ARKANSAS 72205
• (501) 227-8471

John Chamberlin
(501) 227-8471

FOR IMMEDIATE RELEASE   September 22, 1981—Little Rock, AR

On-Line CIF and ATM Modules for IBM System/34
Based On-Line Banking Environment

Arkansas Systems, Inc. (ASI) announces the availability of the On-Line Central Information File (CIF) module and On-Line Automatic Teller Machine (ATM) module of ASI's IBM System/34-based On-Line Banking Environment (OBE).

The program product initially includes provisions for a Diebold ATM system to be directly attached to the System/34 and a complete on-line Central Information File and Account Inquiry facility. The package performs memo posting of transactions from ATM's and administrative workstations. The On-Line Banking Environment can be customized to support teller terminals and on-line application file maintenance.

The On-Line Banking Environment (OBE) is interfaced to the financial institution's application processing, whether that is done in-house on the System/34, in-house on a mainframe, or remotely on a mainframe. The On-Line Banking Environment is designed to be largely independent of the application processing environment and thus provide great flexibility in processing options.

#   #   #

COMPUTER SOFTWARE • CONSULTING AND SUPPORT

End each page at a paragraph break. At the bottom of each page except the last, type a continuation mark such as "—MORE—" or "—continued—."

At the top of the second page, put an identifying label and the page number, usually in the upper left corner.

At the bottom of the last page of your release, type a traditional end mark such as "# # #" or "-30-."

Getting into Print

Finding out where to send releases can be troublesome at first.

Address press releases to appropriate editors. If you do not know names, address the New Products Editor, the Business Editor, Education Editor, Features Editor, or the editor of whatever column or section you hope to be included in. If your story warrants more attention, that editor will pass it on quickly.

For press releases of only local interest, the telephone directory may contain all the addresses you need.

For more extensive mailings, you will find useful lists through trade associations, educational associations, and chambers of commerce. Most public libraries, as well as college and university libraries, have directories of newspapers and magazines. These directories are organized geographically and by subject.

The following directories are particularly useful:

Editor and Publisher International Yearbook, New York: Editor and Publisher, annual—listing newspapers and their principal editors.

Standard Periodical Directory, New York: Oxbridge Communications, biennial—containing virtually complete listings of U.S. and Canadian periodicals, indexed by subject.

Ulrich's International Periodicals Directory, New York: R. R. Bowker, annual—listing world periodicals, by subject headings.

Especially if you are just beginning to write news releases, personal contact with an editor can help. Most editors are willing to spend some time talking about the problems of writing press releases for a specific project or meeting. Such a discussion may help get your story used when your press release lands on the editor's desk. But don't overstay your welcome; editors are busy. And never carry in your news release and ask about its being printed. The editor probably doesn't know right then. The only straight answer you are likely to get in such a situation is Maybe.

PART THREE

The Writer's Self-Help

UNIT VII

The Writing
and Editing Process

24

Writer's Block

ALL WRITERS get writer's block at times. You may understand the material, but the words simply won't go down on the page. You may be in a new situation, trying to write a presentation for a customer or for a city-council meeting after years of writing only field reports. You may be trying to write a letter of recommendation for a friend with whom you have just argued. Or you may be feeling uneasy about what you are expected to say or how you expect one of the audiences to respond. You put down one sentence and scratch out half of it. You put down three words and get out the dictionary to check the spelling of one. Then you worry about a comma or wonder about a synonym—all in a group of words you may edit out of the next draft.

Being Stuck

Sometimes you don't recognize that you are blocked; you simply wonder why a supposedly simple writing task is taking so long. Ideas spin around, but they don't go anywhere. Distractions pour in from every direction—from bosses, from friends and co-workers, in the mail and over the telephone. Being distracted is a kind of writer's block, even if you don't recognize it as such; by giving in to these distractions, you put off writing.

Most of us help keep our writing blocks intact because we believe some unhelpful notions about writing. When we were learning to write, our teachers told us that to write well we needed to think of what we were going to say, make an outline, and then write it up. They expected us to make a clean copy, correcting the misspellings and other errors in the first copy, then turn it in.

The Writing Process

Researchers know now that composing, the creation of sentences as well as of ideas, usually happens during the writing process. That's why, as students, few of us could follow the outlines we were told to make up. We outlined an idea we thought we understood, but as we wrote, the idea changed shape; it grew away from us. Sometimes we wrenched it back to the outline, sometimes not. If we had paid attention to the way we wrote, we would have discovered something that our teachers never told us: writing is a dynamic process. Putting words down on the page changes what we know and what we think. We have new insights and make new discoveries as we write. That's true for almost everyone. Thinking, outlining, then writing works sometimes—especially on the job when you understand the audiences, the task, and your purpose well—but when it doesn't work, you need a different approach.

To become a more efficient writer, discover the way that you write best. Do you usually write more effectively in the morning or in the afternoon? On a full or empty stomach? With or without a cup of coffee? Do you compose better when you use pen and paper for your first draft or when you write on the typewriter? Perhaps you work best talking into a dictaphone and then, after the rough draft is typed, reworking and editing extensively. Watch yourself work. Reproduce your ideal conditions when you can, but don't fret if you sometimes can't. Remember that you can work well in almost any situation if you will let yourself.

Recognizing Excuses

As you examine your composing process, watch for danger signals that may mean you are running into problems. Especially watch for the excuses that we all sometimes use to avoid writing.

Excuse #1. I don't know enough to write.

Maybe, maybe not. Seldom do we know everything that there is to know about anything. If we do understand something thoroughly, we usually know there is much more to know.

Perhaps you don't know enough to write; on the other hand, you may just be making excuses. If you have the slightest suspicion that you are using this as an excuse, assume that you are. Sit down and write, perhaps using some of the techniques we outline below. If you find you do need more information, trying to write will help you identify what that information is. The writing time will not be wasted.

Excuse #2. Just as soon as I get my desk cleared, I'll get started.

Offices, even small ones, are wonderfully cooperative; when we want distractions—mail to answer, phone calls to return, files to sort—we can find them. We look and feel busy, overwhelmed perhaps, and certainly overworked. There is no way that this could be an excuse for not writing, we think, but it often is.

Admittedly, a few people keep clean desks. These people may honestly say that they will begin writing when they have caught up on one or two tasks. But if you find a fresh, urgent, nonwriting task when you finish the current one, you are using these tasks to avoid writing.

Excuse #3. There are just a few minutes until lunch . . . or until an important meeting . . . or until quitting time.

Some of us spend our lives waiting for one thing and another. Use those five, ten, or twenty minutes until lunch or quitting time to write scattered sentences or make notes. For many people, the best time to start a troublesome project is during an otherwise wasted few minutes. Not expecting much, you will be ahead if anything at all happens.

Excuse #4. I do my best work under pressure.

Deadlines. Most of us say that we work best under pressure, but afterward we say we could have done better if we had had more time.

Deadlines help you get to work, even when you don't know everything you need to know, even when your desk isn't clear. But a deadline may slip up on you while you are dealing with distractions instead of writing. If you deal with the writing—getting words down—you can use the time far in front of the deadline almost as effectively as you use the last hours.

Excuse #5. I can't think of the right opening sentence . . . or paragraph

Many of us shackle ourselves by believing that we must start writing at the beginning, with the introduction, the first chapter, or the first word. We begin reading at the beginning, so we think we must begin writing at the beginning.

Begin writing wherever you have a clear idea of what you want to say. That may be the conclusion or somewhere in the middle—a key example or illustration or a central point. Begin where your thinking seems clear. When you come to the end of that section, start another one that seems clear. The opening paragraph may take care of itself.

Excuse #6. I deserve a break—besides I'm stuck.

This danger signal appears after we've been working for a while. After getting stuck, the first thing most of us do is to stand up, stretch, and walk over to the water fountain or vending machine. We take a break to think things over.

When you leave your desk stuck, you reinforce all the negative feelings you have about the writing—how poorly it's going, how tired you are, and what an ape the boss is. Don't leave the writing while you are stuck. Write yourself out of the problem by changing composing styles (writing by hand instead of at the typewriter, for instance), by simply putting down a few notes about your problem and bridging to the next part that you are prepared to write, or by using one of the tricks below.

Later, when you are writing well, when you know what comes next, take your break.

Excuse #7. I like to edit as I write . . . or . . . I only have time to write it once.

Editing is the process of cleaning up your writing, transforming rough drafts into final copy—arranging details, choosing more precise words, improving punctuation, correcting spelling, and so on.

These things must be done. But when you try to do them while you compose sentences, instead of afterward, they interfere with the flow of words and ideas. Very few people write best when they edit as they write.

Getting Started

Recognizing your own excuses is not always easy, but admitting that you are responsible for letting yourself become distracted or restless is the first step. The rest of this chapter suggests some ways that you may be able to get words down on the page when you are stuck. The techniques here are suggestions. Try any one that sounds useful, but discard it if it isn't helpful. Any one of these methods can be used to excess; when you are stuck, you may find that your best strategy is simply to use a different technique. You may even find that a technique that was worthless one time is helpful another time.

Composing with Notecards

Using notecards can help you start a difficult piece of writing. Working quickly and with little thought, begin making notes about the project, one note to a notecard. Make notes without worrying about the order or whether you will use all the ideas. The notes may be topics, brief sentences, assertions, questions, or even brief writeups.

With luck, you may find suddenly that you are able to sort and shuffle the notecards into a working outline. You will have to add things, of course, and you will discover still more things to add as you write. But you have a beginning.

Composing with Recorders

Some of the worst writing (garbled and vague) occurs because of dictating machines and microcassette recorders. Most of the people who use these machines attempt to skip the rough-draft stage; the resulting memos and letters are often unreadable.

But the same recording devices that often lead to disastrous results can help. For some people, talking into a recorder is less intimidating than trying to type or write. If using a recorder helps you to get started when nothing else will, by all means use it. But always assume that your material will need to be typed *at least* twice—once in a rough form and once for a signature. Only then will you see your work often enough to rework and edit it.

Freewriting

Many writers find that freewriting helps them on difficult projects. Freewriting allows writers to put words down on the page while ignoring the clutter in their minds. Freewriting does not produce finished writing—far from it—but it may produce new insights and possibilities.

To freewrite, simply write whatever comes into your mind, without hesitation or backtracking, without looking up spelling, without doing any of the things that might distract you. Just keep writing—using pen, pencil, typewriter, word processor, or whatever. When you run out of things to write about, keep writing. Write nonsense or, better, repeat the sentence you have just written. This may sound silly, but it works. The act of writing keeps your concentration narrowly focused on the words in front of you.

Begin writing for a set period of time, ten minutes or so, on your topic or problem. The time limit is important because it forces you to continue long enough to start something, and it also lets you know that there will be an end to this.

Don't look for finished prose or gems of wit and wisdom, no matter how good some of the words feel as they are going down on the page. Do look for possibilities, for beginnings of arguments and explanations, illustrations and examples or comparisons to be developed. Make notes as you reread. You may also find that other ideas seem to pop into your mind, perhaps ideas that are more important than the ones you have written down. Make note of these ideas too.

You may want to do a second or third freewriting, either following up on ideas in the first writing or making explicit ideas that were only hinted at there. Follow the words where they lead. Evaluate them later.

Freewriting can help writers who are stalled in the middle of a writing task. Begin freewriting with the words "I am stuck" and write—again with a time limit of ten minutes or so. At the end of the time, you should have some useful ideas; you may have written your way out of your problem.

Listmaking

Listmaking is another effective way to generate ideas, to start writing, or to get unstuck. Add anything about the topic that even nibbles around the corners of your mind. Listmaking allows you to put down many ideas quickly—much more quickly than with freewriting—but if you stall, listmaking does not force you to keep on as freewriting does.

Clustering

You can take listmaking a step further by physically clustering notes on the page. You do this naturally when you jot down notes and draw arrows from one item to another. When you cluster, identify the central ideas in your list and spread them out on the page around the topic or problem. Then quickly begin adding items that belong to or extend each group. The advantage of clustering is that it breaks the linear form of listmaking and encourages you to discover new relationships between ideas and new areas of interest.

Exploring Ideas Further

Sometimes writers seem to run out of things to say, though they know they're not finished. They know that there are arguments left to develop and objections left to anticipate, but they can't seem to spot them. Here are seven broad suggestions that provide dozens of possibilities for discovering or inventing new ideas or arguments.

Several of them will produce material that you can use directly; others are aimed at getting you to loosen up your thinking and to bring to the surface problems that you may be fighting.

1. *History*. Write the history of your subject—the company, the client, the dealings between the two.

2. *Future*. Write the history from five or ten years in the future. What has happened and why? What was done? What should have been done? The project you are proposing has been a great success, but some people were reluctant to go along with it. How has the project been successful? Who had to be sold? How was that done?

3. *Audience*. Write for a different audience. If your intended audience is your supervisor, write instead to a rival company, to a knowledgeable friend, or to a naive one.

4. *Biases*. Write about your bias in favor of or against your subject. Or write of your reservations about the position you are putting forward. If you have none, invent some. What kind of reservations might a person have about supporting this company or this person?

5. *Abstractions*. Explain the abstractions and summary words you have used. What does each mean in concrete terms?

6. *Viewpoints*. If you are writing about something that seems static, examine it as if it is part of a larger entity or process. What happens to this thing? How does it change or wear out? If you are writing about something that is dynamic—a process or a changing situation—write as if it is isolated and static. What are the parts of this thing? How do they interact?

7. *Journalism questions*. Focus exclusively on one of the traditional journalism questions: who, what, when, where, why, or how. Consider one question at a time and don't stop at the obvious. You might want to respond to the same question under different circumstances—before and after getting the sale, before and after the design has been altered or the defect corrected, for instance.

Pairing the traditional journalism questions makes a powerful tool for exploring all kinds of situations and ideas. For instance, ask how the What influences the Who. How can the new sales promotion be expected to influence the agents, the customers, the home office? How does the Who affect the What? How do the customers or the sales force influence what kind of promotion is likely to succeed? Or how does the When influence the Who? If the promotion is introduced earlier or later, what will be the effect on the agents, customers, or home office? On the suppliers and the service network? Will the promotion bolster Christmas sales or will the extra work of the promotion overburden the staff during an already busy season? How does changing the When of the promotion affect How the promotion should be done?

Final Thoughts

If you are a person who can sit quietly for a while, figure out what needs to be said, make a few notes, and write, perhaps correcting and editing as you go, then ignore everything that seems wrongheaded here. Count your blessings and get to work.

25
Copy Editing and Proofreading

YOUR READER EXPECTS polished, professional writing. That means error-free writing as well as accurate and readable writing. Producing an error-free product is not a matter of luck; it is a matter of work and knowing a few techniques of copy editing and proofreading. (To simplify this discussion, we will speak as if you are sending a report to the printer, but the issues and procedures described in this chapter obviously pertain to all kinds of writing whether it is printed or typed.)

Creating an error-free report begins with the copy that you send to the printer. The cleaner that copy, the better the printing should be and the easier accurate proofreading will be. Your task during copy editing is to get your copy right in all details.

We generally think of proofreading as finding and correcting the typos—the mistakes that the printer introduced into our copy. We may also find some other error or an inconsistency that needs correction. To proofread properly means to eliminate from the finished report all typos, inconsistencies and other mistakes.

But good proofreading begins with good copy editing. If the copy you send to the printer is wrong, you can expect that the printing will be wrong.

Copy Editing

Edit your manuscript one extra time before you send it to the printer. Once more, smooth out rough-reading sentences, find exact words for ones that have seemed "all right," and eliminate needless bits of jargon. Anything that strikes you as a bit rough now will strike you as very rough when the copy is printed.

The copy you send to the printer cannot be almost right or "good enough." It must be right, without reservation. This includes using capitals consistently, spelling out numbers when they should be spelled out, marking titles and names consistently, as well as being sure that indentation and formatting are consistent throughout the text. (Chapter 28 discusses dictionaries, style and usage guides, and other reference tools you will find helpful.)

It is easy to postpone these matters of style during the writing ("I'll fix that later") and then, in the rush to finish, forget them altogether. But before you turn the copy over to the typist or printer, you must get the little things right. On major projects, find time to read the final manuscript as carefully as if you were proofreading; read once for continuity, once for spelling, and once for format and mechanical details.

This extra copy editing may save you from having to choose later between sending out a faulty job and making extensive, perhaps expensive, corrections.

Proofreading

Proofread everything you send out—proposals, reports, letters, memos—everything. Printers make mistakes, sometimes lots of them. You are expected to find the errors, mark them, and then proofread the corrections.

Accurate proofreading is never a matter of chance. Some people may be more accurate proofreaders than others, and some projects may be easier to proofread than others, but you can proofread well by following the procedures we outline here, double-checking problem areas, and carefully marking changes.

If you use a word processor to check your spelling, you still need to proofread (*see* page 330).

Note on Author's Changes

While you are proofreading, you will be tempted to tinker with your language and style. Some of these changes will seem minor—spelling out a number instead of writing it in figures, taking out or putting in a comma, for instance. Other changes will be major, smoothing out a choppy paragraph, for instance. But whether your tinkering leads to large or small changes, you are no longer correcting typos; you are rewriting. These changes should have been made before the copy was sent to the printer.

Your changes cost money. Publishers and print shops often charge for them. Even if you do not pay for such changes, they cost time, slow down the job, and provide an opportunity for new errors to slip in.

Author's changes involve more than many writers realize. Adding a comma or changing a capital letter to lower case on a printed page may require resetting a full line. Adding a word may require resetting an entire paragraph. Some computer typesetting and printing systems "rerun"—that is, work through the entire program for any change, even a comma! Rerunning invariably changes word breaks and hyphenation. Every line that is reset, every page that is retyped, is another chance for errors to creep into the finished work.

Your copy should be right before it goes to the printer. Don't count on making changes during proofreading.

Proofreading Procedures

In addition to the report you are proofreading, you will need the reference tools you have used and the copy you sent to the printer (using earlier, or "foul," copy may cause confusion).

Use a Copy Reader. Major projects, as well as projects involving tables or numbers, should be proofread by two people working together—a copy reader, who reads aloud from the final copy, and a copy holder, who marks corrections and changes on the copy being proofread. The copy reader must read everything, including punctuation and capital letters.

Read from the Final Copy. Whether you are working alone or with someone else, be certain to read first from the final copy, *not* from the printed copy. Omitted words or sentences are more easily discovered when the final copy is read rather than the printed copy.

Take Breaks. Work in short, concentrated sessions. If you try to work too quickly or for too long, you will find yourself reading instead of proofreading, skimming paragraphs instead of proofreading words. You need frequent short breaks. When you come back from a break, however, reread the last few lines. Your mind may have gone on break shortly before you got up from your desk.

Reread Lines with Errors. Anytime you find an error, reread the line that the error is in. Errors cluster. When you find an error, you focus on it, and often overlook a second error nearby. Always find that second error and look for a third; then reread the sentence or line once more.

Proofread Corrections. After the printer has made all changes and corrections, proofread them. Read the corrections as diligently as you proofread the original copy. Especially in printed work, where entire lines and paragraphs are often reset, it seems that half the corrections introduce new errors. Make sure the old errors have been fixed; find the new errors and correct them.

Be Methodical. The larger and more involved the project, the more methodical you must be. Only then can you be certain you have checked each item. If someone is helping you proofread, you may be tempted to check everything at one time. Don't. An important piece of work deserves to be read *three* times—once for continuity and content, once for spelling, and once for format and routine matters.

Read for Continuity and Content. First, with the help of a second person, read straight through, reading from the final copy, reading everything: headlines, subheads, punctuation, capital letters, sentences, and paragraphs. This first reading is for sentence sense and continuity. This is the time that you must catch omitted words and substituted words (*there* for *their* or *you* in place of *your*). With word-processor copy, remember to check especially for doubled words and unbalanced quotation marks and parentheses.

Tables and sets of numbers should be read by two people, reading *from* the final copyedited text. Numbers in columns are easily misread. Prices and specifications must be checked carefully. If questions arise, if a number does not seem right, check against the original source.

At the end of this reading, *reread* all headlines, subheads, and caption material. A dropped headline is easily overlooked and particularly noticeable when the report is printed. Reread headlines and subheads *from the copy*. Double-check caption material, including identifications, if possible.

You may also want to reread the first and last lines of each paragraph; often your eye begins anticipating what is coming instead of proofreading what is there.

Double-check the places where the typeface changes size or style (from italic to roman, from regular to boldface, for instance). We often look at the change and fail to proofread the words.

Read for Spelling. Checking spelling is usually done by one person working without the final copy. You probably found many typos in your first reading. The goal now is to find the rest of them. Since, in your previous reading, you should have found the words that were mistaken—*affect/effect, you/your,* for instance—you are looking strictly for misspellings. The most accurate way to do this is to read the text *backward*. Reading backward forces your attention on the individual words. You are not distracted by the sentences, the style, or even the format.

If you are a poor speller, you may want to get help from a good speller. Every word you are unsure of should be checked. Poor spellers, who must look up many words, will find a spelling list easier to use than a dictionary (*see* Bibliography).

Read for Format and Routine Matters.   Finally, you must *read* the format of the finished report. You must check all "routine" matters from size of headlines to page numbers, including the layout and the spacing.

If you are proofreading with someone, you will be tempted to check the format when you read through the text for the first time. Don't. It is too easy to overlook a wrong heading or page number.

To "read" the format, you need to page through the entire final document, concentrating on a single item, such as size of headlines or page numbers. This is the only way to be certain (as certain as possible) that you have not overlooked an obvious error (obvious, that is, when people see it in print). Checking for one problem at a time is quicker and more accurate than trying to check for several at one time.

Check the running titles and page numbers. Turn through the document page by page and check each one of these. It takes only a minute to page through looking at one small thing. Now check the size and darkness of the headlines and subheadings; make sure they follow the pattern that you want.

Next turn to each cross-reference. Each "*see* Section X" and "*see* page Y" must be accurately keyed to the finished text. Check footnotes or end notes for correct numbering; see that the numbers in the text and the notes correspond. Don't trust the final copy, but check the printed report to see that the numbers match.

Continuations must be checked. Turn from one page to the next to make certain that your copy continues where you say it does and that it reads as it should.

Section and chapter titles must match the Table of Contents; page back and forth to see that they do. Titles of figures and tables must match the titles in the Table of Figures.

Finally, look over datelines and volume and issue numbers.

Marking Systems

You do not need to use traditional proofreading marks. In fact, using a simple marking system helps reduce errors. The system that we present in figure 25-1 should work for any project. If you need to mark something not included here, put a note in the margin. Circle any notes or commentary about the copy.

In a formal system, you will mark each correction and change twice—once in the margin nearest the change and again, usually with a caret, at the point of change in the copy. If you have room to write changed or added letters and words in the copy, do so; usually there will not be room in the text to write the additions. If you need

---

FIGURE 25-1. PROOFREADING MARKS

Here are all the proofreading marks that you probably need. We omit the symbols used to mark such things as broken and misaligned type. Problems that cannot be marked with these signs can be indicated with marginal comments.

This mark in margin	*Means*	*And turns this*	*Into this*
ᷰ	add letter	fin̩l	final
by	add word	run home	run on home
#	insert space	runaway	run away
ℐ	delete letter	argue̷ment	argument
ℐ	delete word	run b̷y home	run home
less #	less space	run ᷈ home	run home
ⓣⓡ	transpose letters	befoͬre	before
ⓣⓡ	transpose words	(often run)	run often
ⓣⓡ	transpose words	(beast or man)	man or beast
ⓣⓡ	transpose lines	words,	letters,
		letters,	words,
		or phrases	or phrases
᷎	close up	fol̫ks	folks
⁋	paragraph here	is easy. ⌐Now is the	is easy. Now is the
(no ⁋)	no paragraph	is easy. ⌐Now is the	is easy. Now is the

Use the following marks to indicate punctuation.

This mark in margin	*Means*	*And turns this*	*Into this*
⌃	comma	red white	red, white
⊙	period	ran home⊙	ran home.
⍮	semicolon	ran home⍮	ran home;
⊕	colon	as follows⊙	as follows:
|o|o|o|	ellipsis	but then|o|o|o|	but then . . .
( )	parenthesis	₤see page 6 ₣	(see page 6)
˅	apostrophe	mayor˅s	mayor's
˅ ˅	quotation marks	�667Help!�	"Help!"

Indicate subscript and superscript numbers and letters with a caret containing the number or letter to be added.

This mark in margin	*means*	*and turns this*	*Into this*
$\overset{23}{\vee}$	superscript	10	10^{23}
$\overset{23}{\wedge}$	subscript	H O	H_2O

Put comments about the text, such as *boldface, spell out,* or *caps,* in the margin; circle them.

This mark in margin	*means*	*And turns this*	*Into this*
(all caps)	set in caps	Report	REPORT
(lc)	set in lower case	REPORT	report
(clc)	set in caps and lower case	REPORT	Report
(ital)	set in italics	italics	*italics*
(bf)	set in boldface	boldface	**boldface**
(rom)	set in roman type	*roman*	roman
(stet)	set original copy above dots	to ignore changes	to ignore changes

---

to mark more than one correction per line, write them in the order they are found in the text and separate them by vertical lines; use both margins if you need to. The sample text (figure 25-2) illustrates the basic principles of marking a page of copy.

In handling typed copy, you don't need so elaborate a system as this. Most of your corrections will be for spelling, and if problems arise, you will usually be able to talk with your typist.

Whether or not you use the system we present, all corrections and notes must be legible. Print all corrections, notes, and comments. If the typist or printer must guess at your corrections and changes, you are not likely to get what you want.

FIGURE 25-2. SAMPLE PROOFREAD TEXT

ACCURATE PROOFREADING

Proofreading is a nuisance at times. Having sweat blood over over a project for a week, having fought just to get the figures you need, then having to fight to get the boss to agree with the implications of the report, and finally to have the boss nitpicking sentences (and being wrong!) tires a writer out.

When it goes to the printer, you are ready to go home. Fine. Just remember that you have to proof it when it comes back.

You can't get rid of it. If you wrote it, you must proof it. A unless you can con someone else into doing it. But even so, you remain responsible.

You may want to get someone else to work with you. As the writer of the report, you may be your own worst proofreader. You know what it should say, you may not read what is actually on the page. Also, you still mix up affect and effect, and you still have trouble spelling. You may want to make a deal with someone else to share proofreading chores on major projects.

Remember, too, that even if your copy has been computer proofread, you must still proofread for mistaken words, for format, for incorrect word breaks, and for residue from changes.

The tricks we present in this chapter will help you as you proofread. These tricks begin with good copy editing. This sample has so many many author's changes in it that it is impossible to feel how the finished copy will read.

Don't waste energy resenting copy editing and proofreading; instead of simply doing it.

Simply accepting proofreading as part of the job will, probably, help you most of all.

Take as much pride in your proofreading as you do in your writing.

26

Using Word Processors

IT WON'T HAPPEN on a Monday morning, at least not before ten a.m., and probably not before Tuesday noon, but one of these days in an otherwise uneventful week, the word processors will show up in your office . . . if they haven't already.

The boss will have talked about it for a month or more. There will have been vendors demonstrating and cajoling. Stories—some funny, some frightening—will have been bouncing around the office about the problems another company or another department had when their word processors arrived. Now it's here in your office, probably on your desk.

Some people consider word processors overblown, overadvertised gimmicks, certain to go the way of Esperanto, hula hoops, and Rubik's cubes. They may be overrated and they may be technological gimmicks, but they will be around for a while. The revolution is happening. The question is not whether you will need to be able to coexist with a word processor, but when.

This is a brief survival guide to the word processor. We point out the common misconceptions that many novices have about word processors and suggest ways to make friends with your own word processor. Finally, we deal with how word processors may change your working conditions and your writing and editing style.

Some Misconceptions

Let's get rid of some common misconceptions.

First, you don't have to know how the computer works or how to "talk" to it in computer language. All the programming has been done for you. You will talk to the computer in English or with a few simple coded commands.

You do not need to know how the computer works, any more than you needed to know how your typewriter worked or Jefferson needed to know what held the ink in his quill pen.

Second, computers are not delicate. People think about their touchy self-correcting typewriters, and they fear that these word processors, which cost several times as much, must be at least as touchy. Wrong.

Are you old enough to remember mechanical calculators? If you looked at them crossly, they jammed. Electronic calculators—more versatile, much faster, and infinitely cheaper—are much more reliable and much less delicate. Word processors are also much less delicate and sensitive than mechanical, self-correcting typewriters.

Don't be afraid of hurting the computer. Short of spilling something on the keyboard or dropping the whole thing, you are not likely to hurt the actual computer, the hardware. You may at some time have to retype something, you may waste some paper and time, but you won't hurt the computer.

Pound on the keyboard. You will put gibberish on the screen, but you won't jam or hurt the machine.

Finally, word processors are not difficult to use. You need some learning time, you need a sense of adventure, but you can learn to use one.

Your neighbor writes business reports on a word processor, but can't change the oil in a car; the beautician uses one to keep accounts; your bookie and your paper carrier both use them. "If they can do it, so can I!" you cry. And that's right. Not because you are mechanically minded and they are not, not because you are smart and they are not, but simply because anyone who can type can use a word processor.

The Dangerous Misconception

Your misconceptions about word processors may intimidate you and slow down your learning, but the most dangerous misconception belongs to your boss. If the boss thinks that the mere presence of the machine will double the productivity of every writer and typist in the office, you have trouble.

The word processor won't double productivity. It will cut down on retyping. It will help documents go out error-free. It will dramatically speed up some processes, but it may actually slow down some aspects of composing.

And before the word processor increases productivity at all, you must learn to use it, and that takes some time. It takes time to learn to use the machine and then to learn to do your work on it. For a day or two, very little "work" will get done.

Before the Word Processor Arrives

If you are invited to try out a word processor before it is brought into the office, do it. Don't plead ignorance. Try it out.

Ignore the demonstrations and the sales talks. Let the boss try to find the right word-processing programs (the programs can almost always be changed and are relatively inexpensive). If you are going to be making your living on the machine, you care only about two things at the moment: the monitor and the keyboard.

A good monitor and a comfortable keyboard are crucial to your working health. The best way to judge a monitor is to look at it for an hour or two and then to go look at another. This does not mean watching someone work for a while. This means sitting down and reading the screen—typing in numbers and words and reading them back.

The color of the screen (black and white, green on black, or black on amber) makes little difference if the letters are well-formed and the screen does not flicker. The *v, u, m,* and *w* are the most difficult letters to form. On some monitors the *u* and *v* are hard to distinguish. Also the monitor should have brightness and contrast controls so you can adjust the screen to changing room light.

If you discover you have a headache an hour after trying out a machine, something was probably wrong with the monitor or with the lighting around it. Investigate; make your boss try out other monitors. Ask friends in other offices what systems they have and how they like them.

Evaluate the keyboard, too. They range from spongy to firm, from hard-touch to no-touch, from silent to clickety-clack. Make your preferences known.

The feel of the keyboard and the quality of the monitor are crucial to your surviving with a word processor. Insist that any system being seriously considered be brought to *your* office for *you* to play on for a half-day.

Your Health

Many people report health problems when they begin using word processors—backaches, headaches, eyestrain, and sleeplessness, to name a few. These problems can almost always be corrected by paying attention to the way you work—to the place and pace of your work.

Let's get radiation out of the way immediately. In several studies (by the U.S. Department of Health and Human Services, for instance) scientists found the radiation of all the terminals to be much lower than current occupational standards, and some types of radiation in some terminals were too low to measure. Radiation, in spite of the closeness of the screen, does not seem significant. But health problems and hazards do exist.

From the moment you begin learning to use the word processor, pay attention to yourself. At the work station, pay specific attention to your posture and to the surrounding lighting.

Posture

If you are straining to reach the keys, hunched over to see the screen, or otherwise holding your body in an unusual position, you will be sore. If you sit at the screen for many hours a day, poor posture can lead to backaches, headaches, and numerous other aches and pains—sometimes ones that don't seem associated with the word processor. If after the word processor arrives you begin sleeping poorly or start waking up with a stiff back or a headache, check your posture.

Look at three things in particular: the height of the keyboard, the height and location of the monitor, and the firmness of your chair.

The best guide in all these things is your own comfort—what feels good. Even though you have been typing for years, you may need the keyboard a little lower or higher than your typewriter keyboard. The most comfortable location for the monitor seems usually to be further away and higher than your typewriter carriage was, often with the bottom of the screen about where the top of the carriage was.

If your monitor and keyboard are attached, you will probably have to make some compromises, but experiment with heights, with distance, and if possible, with the angle of the screen and keyboard. Reevaluate your comfort after you have been working with the word processor for a while.

We have found that most people underrate the importance of their chairs. A chair that was comfortable for typing, depending on how you hold yourself as you use the word processor, may be too low or too soft. Particularly if you have had back problems, be certain your chair supports you firmly, even if you must borrow an old library chair from a dank storeroom.

The Screen

Glare on the screen will quickly make word processing tiresome and uncomfortable. Turn off lights, adjust lights—do whatever you need to do to keep the screen free of glare. Adjust screen brightness and contrast if you can.

Eliminate backlighting around the screen. Sometimes this means closing drapes during part of the day or moving the monitor into a different position. If the screen glares or is backlit, you will get tired, you will make mistakes, you will contort your body trying to get away from the glare. Light the screen well.

If glare continues to be a problem, you may need to convince someone to invest in a polarizing screen to cover the monitor.

If you still seem to have tired eyes, you may want to get your eyes thoroughly examined. Word processing is often intense, and you can strain your eyes. Focusing your eyes away from the screen briefly every few minutes will help, but you need longer breaks than that.

Taking Breaks

Take frequent and regular breaks. This will give your eyes and back a chance to relax and let you work at peak efficiency. You don't have to take your break at the vending machine. Much of your daily work probably does not involve the word processor. But at frequent and regular intervals, get off the monitor for a while. One 1981 report, from the U.S. Department of Health and Human Services, recommends a fifteen-minute break after every one or two hours of work at the screen, depending on the intensity of the work: repetitive tasks and work involving "high visual demands" require more frequent breaks.

Get used to taking breaks from the beginning, while you are learning the machine, whether you are entering billing addresses, editing manuscripts, or playing games. Every ninety minutes or so take a break, a fifteen-minute break. Three two-minute breaks won't do the job. You must let your eyes and back relax. The machine, your boss, your own momentum—all these invite compulsiveness. Fight it. Take breaks before you are tired. Juggle your work schedule if necessary so that you can have a change of pace.

As you become more comfortable with the machine, your breaks may become a *bit* shorter and a *bit* less frequent. But keep taking them. Demand them if you must. When the work piles up, keep taking the breaks.

If you pay attention to yourself and your feelings—aches, pains, moods, and sleep patterns—you will know if you are taking enough breaks. But remember to connect that sore back in the morning with the chair you sat in the day before. Fix the chair and keep taking breaks.

Befriending the Word Processor

Word processors come in two distinct forms: souped-up typewriters and scaled-down computers. The souped-up typewriters have been around for a long time. They began as mag-card typewriters and have become memory typewriters and display writers. Generally, they look, sound, and behave like typewriters. A few have screens or monitors, but many display only a line or so of text. Changing from a self-correcting typewriter to a memory typewriter is about as much trouble as changing the water in a goldfish bowl.

If your office produces reports longer than a few pages, you will probably have a computer word processor or at least a "typewriter" with a display of twenty or more lines and some sort of permanent storage (disk drive or hard disk). Some include their own printers. Word processors can look intimidating, but you can learn to use them by approaching the machines step by step, by experimenting and playing before you try to work, and by following instructions.

The first word of warning is simple: If you are in the midst of a major project with a tight deadline, don't switch to a word processor. No matter what the dealers and vendors say, it will take you some time to learn to use the machine. It may not take you long, but if you are trying to finish a report while you are nervous about using the word processor and the boss is pacing around because the report is late, you will not have a happy time. Finish the report, then take a day or two to learn the machine.

Getting Started

Divide the task of learning the computer and learning the programs into small steps. Then take it step by step. Ask people when you have questions, but don't be afraid to try things out. To get started, you need to learn how to turn on your machine and begin working. Then before you begin trying to work on anything, you need to do some experimenting (playing around, actually, but we can't call it that in front of the boss).

1. *Have someone show you how to start up the machine, load the word-processor program, and how to shut down.* This may involve loading disks and pushing keys, or it may involve flipping a switch and typing in a passcode, depending on your office setup. Shutting down may involve doing "saves" or simply signing off. Whatever your system requires, practice doing it a half-dozen times in succession right at the beginning—before you have a chance to forget. Make this second nature to you. Learn how to start up and to find the document you were working on; learn how to stop and to save your morning's work.

Now load the word processor program, fill the screen with something—anything—and do a little experimenting. Don't try working yet; you are trying to become familiar with the machine.

2. *Find out how easily you can destroy what you are working on.* Sometimes a single wrong command will wipe out your morning's work. Find out. Is the plug for the machine where it can be easily kicked? Is the on-off switch accessible (which means you may switch off the machine inadvertently)?

The easier it is to wipe out your file, the more frequently you should save it or have the machine memorize it. You should get in the habit of saving your work whenever you leave the machine, even if you intend to be gone only a minute.

3. *Play with the cursor keys or cursor commands. Move the cursor around.* Learn to make it jump around the screen, from word to word, sentence to sentence, page to page. Learn to use the universal find.

Take the cursor to the end of a line and ask it to go to the next space; it will probably jump to the beginning of the next line. Take it to the beginning or end of your screen and ask it to go further; again, it will probably jump to the next word or space, making room on the screen for the new words.

Learn to set temporary text markers, and learn to find them. Temporary markers are useful when you are "cutting and pasting" copy; without them you are likely to lose your bearings halfway through your rearranging. Markers will speed up the cursor movement and help you keep your place.

Much of your word-processing life will be devoted to moving the cursor from one spot to another. Find out how to do it easily. Practice.

4. *Do the practice lessons in your word-processor manual.* Find

the training aids or tutorials. If there is not a "cheat sheet," a listing of the word-processor's commands, create one as you go. Now take time to do whatever practice lessons you can find. These will introduce you to the program without your worrying about trying to write something. If you wipe out a practice lesson, you should learn something about the machine; wiping out a morning of report writing is more upsetting.

Keep notes as you work. Note how you solved problems that came up; add explanations to the manual and index your additions.

Plan to take a day or two to learn the word processor before trying to write anything more serious than a letter to a friend.

Writing with the Word Processor

Having practiced (and perhaps mastered) the training aids, the canned lessons, you are ready to begin working. Begin with short projects and with projects that are as straightforward as possible. Add frills slowly.

For a while, type envelopes and forms on the leftover typewriter. Envelopes are hard to space on a word processor; complex forms are almost impossible to line up.

Finally, create format files. When you space a letter heading well, save the letter heading in a separate file, to use later. When you need another letter, type over the old heading. When you have a good-looking title page, make a file that you can call up when you need to do a new title page. Do the same with envelopes and address labels. Such files save you from having to count lines and guess at spacing from typed pages.

Write-It-Right Syndrome

As you grow comfortable with the word processor, you may become compulsive. It is so easy to make changes and corrections as you write that you may find you are doing too much editing as you write. You may find that when you should be developing ideas, you are editing sentences, sentences that may not even appear in your final draft. This is the write-it-right-the-first-time syndrome. Trying to polish sentences before ideas are understood and organized hurts most writers. The word processor encourages your doing this.

Proofreading

Proofreading will change if you use a word processor. You can search the text for a consistent misspelling and correct it. You can search format changes and have them changed automatically. You can try different formats and reprint with little inconvenience, without having a secretary complaining of the extra work, and with little need for new proofreading.

But the word processor is not omnipotent. It will check your spelling, if it has a dictionary, but it will not tell you that you have *your* instead of *you* or *paunch* instead of *punch*. It will not tell you that you spelled *cannot* as two words or that you used *its* instead of *it's* or *affect* instead of *effect*. You must catch those errors.

You will need to check word breaks and hyphenated words. Some word processors will not check the spelling of hyphenated words; others will rehyphenate the text every time you change the copy or format. (And the rules that some word processors follow to hyphenate words are strange indeed.)

Finally, because the word processor always gives you pristine copy, most people leave residues from changes in their texts. You make the subject of a sentence plural and forget to change the corresponding verbs. You edit one sentence into another and leave a double *the* or forget a closing quotation mark. Such things are easily caught in retyping or as you edit a dirty text. But you're not retyping, and you don't have a scratched-up text to alert you to places you changed an hour ago.

With the word processor, you must learn to hunt these problems out.

Hunting Perfection

The freedom that the word processor gives you to make a few more changes and print out, to try a slightly different format and print out, to get the copy perfect can distract you from the work itself. Although much less time is required to print out something than to retype it, it still takes time. The little changes you are making, the different formats you are trying—all these take time. Be certain that the changes you are making are important.

Minor editing changes are made quickly, especially when compared to retyping. However, major editing can be very time-consuming, and if you are a good typist it is often easier to retype than to make major changes. All editing changes will take longer than you expect them to.

Don't let your fascination with the technology distract you. Experiment, of course. Work for perfection, of course. But keep things in perspective. Don't forget about the next project you need to work on.

The Pleasure

Many people say that the word processor makes writing fun again. The gimmickry may be part of this, but there is joy in not having to retype everything in order to have clean copy at your fingertips.

Writing with the word processor does take much of the tedium out of writing. Minor corrections are made with ease; substitutions can be made quickly and easily. Form letters can be fabricated for individuals and typed out nearly painlessly. You will begin finding the pleasures of the word processor as soon as you are used to the machine.

From the beginning, however, you will probably appreciate the looking at your copy on the screen and the ability you have to try out different paragraph arrangements with little trouble.

You will also enjoy being able to add a forgotten point with a few keystrokes or to join paragraphs each containing a half-formed idea and then to rewrite and edit them together to make your point clearly.

Hard Copies

Finally, even though you see the words and pages on the screen, on any project longer than a few pages, print out hard (paper) copies as you work. Yes, you can flip from screenful to screenful of words, but this does not let you compare page 6 and page 23 very easily (although some word processors let you have portions of two pages on the screen at one time). Because the screen focuses your attention sharply on single pages and individual sentences, it may be difficult to gauge the overall proportions of your work. In hard copy, it is much easier to see that you have overdeveloped one section and left another underdeveloped.

As you read through your hard copy, you may be astounded at the number of typos you find. You will have corrected many as you worked, of course, but reading hard copy lets you find more. Because your text on the screen is always clean, you will forget where you made changes or where you were struggling with a sentence. This leads to leaving tracks, residues of changes in the text.

This leads to a final suggestion. If you are not satisfied with a sentence or paragraph as you rewrite and edit, mark it with asterisks or plus signs, something that you can easily find. Since the copy is always clean, you may forget tomorrow that you were struggling on page 6 today. Mark the spot so that you can come back to it, fix it, and make certain that you have cleaned up your tracks.

UNIT VIII

A Guide to Style

27

Understanding Style

HERE IS A fine example of the bad writing business and government writers must learn to avoid, with jargon strung together by prepositional phrases, and nouns and passive verbs trying to surround each other:

> If the operational personnel and dependents are also factored into this scenario, the peak population would obviously increase. From the standpoint of regional growth management, the magnitude of this development and the uncertainties inherent in the population growth scenarios pose serious economic problems.

This writing is out of control, but other parts of this same report are clear and readable. Here is a readable passage from the same study:

> No basing mode is likely to provide a substantial number of survivable MX missiles much before the end of this decade. While some basing modes would permit the first missiles to be operational as soon as 1986 or 1987, these missiles could not be considered more survivable than the existing Minuteman missiles until additional elements of the basing system were in place.

This is not beautiful, limpid prose, but it is readable. So is this:

> Nigeria is currently challenged by the need to adjust to a soft world oil market. Downward pressure on economic activity, which began in the second half of 1981, has persisted in the first half of 1982 and will likely continue until the world oil market improves. Because of its position as a major oil producer, however, Nigeria continues to offer signif-

icant opportunities for American business in direct sales, joint ventures, management contracts, and consultancy services across a broad spectrum of the economy.

Again, not beautiful, but clear and readable.

These two passages were not hard to find; much government and business prose is clear and readable.

Americans sometimes forget that writing problems are not new or unique. The problems are not restricted to government bureaucracies or even to bureaucracies. Old legal documents and tracts, old reports, even old newspapers are filled with their own jargon and formulaic sentence structures. We forget the junk written yesterday; we ignore the clear, readable prose written today.

When we stop comparing ourselves to the past, two things become obvious. First, there are enormous problems in business and government writing. We sometimes do sound illiterate; we sometimes do write gobbledygook. Second, much of the problem is that we are only now learning how to respond to the increased demand for very sophisticated literacy.

The 3 Cs

Clarity, conciseness, and coherence (the 3 Cs) are the criteria of effective business and government writing.

1. *Clear writing*. None of us wants to wade through unnecessary jargon and gobbledygook simply because someone was too lazy to revise a report or a letter.

2. *Concise writing*. This is not pleasure reading. We want information quickly so we can put it to use.

3. *Coherent writing*. The writer should put the argument together effectively so we can spend our time thinking about it, not trying to understand it.

It is hard to argue with the 3 Cs. Unfortunately, the 3 Cs have given rise to many absolute rules of style—rules about using passives and pronouns, for instance. Once formulated, most of these "rules" allow no exceptions.

Such absolute thinking is not helpful. In effective government and business writing, there are few absolute rules.

A Range of Styles

There is not *a* writing style that everyone in business and government should use all the time. Different places and different times call for different styles. In later chapters of this unit we show you some ways to take control of your style—the words and sentences that you write—to create the impact that you need. But first consider the flexibility of style.

> A thorough examination of the issues at hand reveals that decay has begun to manifest itself in the national consciousness of this Scandinavian country.

That is very different from the more conversational original:

> Something is rotten in the state of Denmark.

A major problem for many writers is choosing when each style is suitable. Style can be analyzed by many different schemes, but for our purposes, thinking of style as ranging from formal to informal works well.

Formal Writing

Formal writing is aloof. The tone suggests a gap between the writer and the reader. It is writing in fancy dress for a formal occasion. No contractions, no first- and second-person pronouns, no sentence fragments except as formal subheads (none like this one, for instance). The writing is grammatically correct in all respects, conservatively correct. The writer as a personality and a voice often disappears, being replaced simply by a disembodied force. Arguments are formally arranged.

At its extreme, formal style becomes ceremonial, the style of weddings and funerals, of proclamations, of legislation, and of legal briefs. It can be a language designed to keep the uninitiated or naive reader in the dark.

While formal style is often stuffy, it can be lively and forceful.

Just as tuxedos are worn less frequently now than they once were, so formal writing is seen less frequently. That is not necessarily bad, any more than wearing tuxedos less often is bad. It is a matter of style.

Official Style. Official style, the bureaucratic version of formal style, is filled with passive verbs, nouns, and prepositional phrases. No one ever does anything; things are always done to something. Everything is "considered" and "examined"; everything "appears to be" and "seems," but very little simply "is," unless of course, it "*is* a consideration."

Informal Writing

Informal writing is personal. It attempts to engage the reader, sometimes being chatty and intimate, pushing itself onto the reader. Lots of contractions, pronouns of all sorts, even slang at times. Fragments and perhaps even broken thoughts. While grammar is not ignored, possessives with gerunds, subjunctives, and distinctions between "who" and "whom" are generally lost.

This is the style of letters to good friends and of letters home for money. It is light and breezy, but it generally cannot carry weighty ideas and arguments, simply because readers do not expect them. Readers are put into a light frame of mind by the style; they come to expect jibes and jokes, not arguments.

General Writing

Between the formal and informal extremes comes the wide range of general writing, general in the sense of "all-purpose." It is the style we all usually write in, the style of this book, of most books, and of most published writing. It moves about in the enormous space between formal and informal, using the many tones and voices available. It allows some contractions and pronouns. It will use slang on occasion, but only for special effect. It engages the reader without being pushy; it recognizes the integrity of the reader, while inviting the reader to join with the writer in thought and experience.

General writing considers correctness in the traditional sense. But if a writer must choose between being "correct" and sounding natural, the writer chooses to sound natural or rewrites the sentences.

Compared to formal writing, general writing often sounds casual since it contains more pronouns, more active verbs, and fewer passive sentences. Still, general writing handles serious ideas and arguments well, and it can be more easily persuasive than formal writing because it engages the reader.

Most writing done in business and government should be in this middle range of styles. There is seldom the need for the formality that leads to the often stuffy, always aloof formal style. There is even less occasion for the colloquial informal style.

Style Illustrated

A World War II memo about blackouts illustrates the range of styles generally open to you. As told by John O'Hayre (*Gobbledygook Has Gotta Go,* U.S. Department of the Interior), Franklin Roosevelt received this memo:

> Such preparations shall be made as will completely obscure all Federal buildings and non-Federal buildings occupied by the Federal Government during an air raid for any period of time from visibility by reason of internal or external illumination. Such obscuration may be obtained by blackout construction or by termination of the illumination.

That is formal style at its worst—absolutely correct grammatically, but stuffy, and unreadable. There is no attempt to make contact with the reader; there is only the aloof, official, lifeless voice.

Roosevelt's reported response was direct:

> Tell them that in buildings where they have to keep the work going to put something over the windows; and, in buildings where they can stop work for a while, turn out the lights.

Roosevelt's *tell them* is direct, while the original, in the passive, leaves no one responsible for turning the lights off. Roosevelt's response, if it were put in memo form, would speak *to* the people addressed. The original talks *at* them.

But you are not the President. People do not hang on your words. If you were rewriting the memo, you would need to write the instructions more fully.

Here is a rewrite that is more obviously complete but still straightforward. Since it is addressed to all federal employees, we do not need to name them in the memo.

> Whether or not you work in a Federal building, you must observe all blackouts. You may either turn out all lights or place lightproof draperies or constructions in front of the windows. You must turn off all outside lights.

That's complete. It even specifies using something besides draperies to block the light and mentions the outside lights. Clear, concise, and coherent. The rewrite is significantly shorter than the original and much clearer. It also avoids the concocted *obscuration*.

But you may want the memo to sound more formal, relying on the tone to convey the importance of your message. That was no doubt the thinking that helped create the first memo. Starting from this clear version, we can make the tone more formal, without taking out the life, simply by taking out the *you*. Now you have something like this:

> All Federal employees, whether or not they work in Federal buildings, will observe all blackouts. They may either turn off all lights or put lightproof draperies or constructions in front of the windows. They must turn off all outside lights as well.

We have no *you*. Now we have an order, perhaps even an urgent one, underscored by the opening *all*.

The three rewrites are different, but one is not necessarily best. They have different tones and styles. The last is the most formal of the three, but not better or worse because of that. All are superior to the original.

Here's a more recent example. This form letter, from a lending agency, tells readers that the agreement they had for reduced payments has expired. They must now begin making full payments, submit a new request for reduced payments, or face eviction. Here is the final paragraph:

> No response from you before the next monthly payment becomes due will indicate to us that you can and will make the full payment or that you have no intentions of keeping the property, and we will begin to take the necessary actions to satisfy indebtedness.

People who called the office to find out what this letter meant were not illiterate; they were justifiably confused. The writer forgot about the reader.

Perhaps the writer is uncomfortable about the situation and would like to avoid unpleasantness, but the reader needs usable information:

> If you intend to keep your home, you must return the attached form to our office before your next payment is due or you must begin making full monthly payments.
>
> If you do not return the form or if you do not send in a full monthly payment, we must assume that you have decided to give up your house. The law requires us to begin foreclosing.
>
> Please call my office at 555-1234 if you have any questions.

Not a happy letter, but a straightforward one. This version makes contact with the reader. It clearly spells out the reader's responsibilities. If the reader calls, it will probably be to talk (or complain) about the situation. But the secretary will not have to spend five minutes explaining the letter. The less formal style makes this much more effective than the original.

Choosing Style

More styles are open to government and business writers than you may realize. By actively considering the full range of possibilities, by realizing that choosing whether or not to use a first-person pronoun is not a matter of correctness but of style, you can loosen up and reach out more effectively to your readers.

Good writers suit style to the occasion. They experiment with styles, sometimes trying out several tones for a single report or letter, and choosing the one that seems most likely to work with this subject on this audience at this time.

28
Being Correct

YOUR READER expects you to be correct.

Say whatever you wish about good communication and clear expression, your reader expects correctness as well. Correctness is a negative virtue: being correct, even being correct and elegant, is seldom noted. Failing to be correct is.

Failing to be correct detracts from your message. Make enough errors, or make them at the wrong time, and your writing becomes the butt of jokes; your thought, your message, your brilliant commentary, and your insightful analysis are lost.

This recently happened to a friend of ours who wrote complaining about some new testing procedures in his company. The one-page letter contained several misspellings, omitted several needed commas, and the climatic sentence, because of a confused pronoun reference, was nearly gibberish.

The letter got everyone's attention, but not the attention the writer wanted.

Failing to be correct can get your writing posted on bulletin boards. It happened to a major insurance company that sent a policy statement to all its field agents asking that they be certain that people hired in their offices were competent in "both grammer and spelling." The statement could have been worse; the writer might have misspelled *spelling*.

Any copy-editing error, any breach of proper style, any typographical error—no matter how trivial—undercuts your credibility. But it is just when everyone is overly self-conscious that someone is likely to goof. That's what happened with the insurance-company memo.

This chapter shows you how to find out about being correct. To do that, we must describe the many things that people mean by correctness; then we describe correctness in those areas; and finally we describe the tools you will use to help you answer specific questions.

Defining Correctness

Defining correctness in general involves us in some circular logic. Correctness is the standard of usage and language that people expect, the standard that people associate with being correct.

Correctness is not the province of one particular grammarian or of one grammar book or style guide. It is not even the exclusive domain of your office grammarian or of a language columnist in New York City.

At its least useful, correctness is an arbitrary standard found in one person's favorite rule book. At its most useful, correctness derives from the usage of well-educated writers in carefully edited publications.

Our language has an experimental laboratory: speech. Speech is where we try out new words and discard old ones; that's where we discover which grammatical distinctions are socially crucial and which are less important. The spoken language exerts a continuous pressure on the written language to change.

The written language, particularly the printed language, resists these changes. Words are not admitted until they have proven their usefulness or have become national fads. Sentence fragments are not allowed except under stringent conditions. Correctness—as found in rule books and classrooms, as used by professional editors, office grammarians, and businesses wanting to put forward a "professional" appearance—retards the acceptance of changes from the spoken language.

It is not that one is right and the other wrong; they are different. And for writers, the tension between the written and spoken language is more interesting than either language itself. The maverick spoken language constantly seeks to enliven and enrich the written language; the conservative forces prevent chaos in the written language and help maintain a stable language that people can use with precision.

The various tools we talk about in this chapter deal with usage and rules. They chronicle the tension between the written and the spoken language.

The Many Meanings of Correctness

When people talk about correct English, they may mean anything and everything from misspelling *separate* or *develop* to using the pronoun *you* in a report and to writing a sentence fragment or splitting an infinitive. They may even mean that someone did not follow the usual typing format for a letter or proposal. Some of these "errors" are more important than others; some are not errors at all. But you need to understand many of the meanings of correctness so that you know how to deal with each problem.

Breaking down correctness into the kinds of things people seem to be concerned with gives us four broad, not very neat categories:

1. *Traditional Grammar:* the parts of the sentence and how they relate to each other, including sentence fragments and run-on sentences, subject-verb agreement, pronoun use, and possessives.

2. *Style:* the choices we make about our language, including which word to use and whether or not to use a sentence fragment or passive verb. The individual small choices add up to the differences in writing styles.

3. *Mechanics:* the marks in the sentence that have little to do with the spoken language, including punctuation, capitalization, and spelling.

4. *Manuscript Style:* the physical arrangement of the letter, report, or proposal, including the appropriate formatting within a document, the handling of abbreviations, figures, and documentation.

Two other things are sometimes meant by correctness that we will not discuss in this chapter. First, people sometimes talk about logic and organization as a matter of correctness. Second, people sometimes talk about correctness instead of the real issue. The person complaining about your language may actually be disagreeing with the way you are handling an account or may be trying to "help you" find your place in the pecking order.

The Issues

If you are going to understand correctness and handle yourself in discussions of correctness, you need to know where to find information on each sort of problem you are likely to encounter. All books mentioned in this chapter are listed in the Bibliography. A few books that we mention several times we refer to with shortened names.

Chicago is:
The Chicago Manual of Style, 13th ed. Chicago: University of Chicago Press, 1982.

GPO is:
Style Manual, rev. ed. Washington, D.C.: U.S. Government Printing Office, 1973.

Harbrace is:
Hodges, John C., and Whitten, Mary. *Harbrace College Handbook,* 9th ed. New York: Harcourt Brace Jovanovich, 1982.

Hotline is:
Montgomery, Michael, and Stratton, John. *The Writer's Hotline Handbook.* New York: New American Library, 1981.

Writer's Guide is:
Ebbit, Wilma R., and Ebbit, David R. *Writer's Guide and Index to English,* 7th ed. Glenview, Ill.: Scott, Foresman, 1982.

Grammar

Matters of correctness in grammar are generally referred to rule books. These vary considerably in their usefulness. To use them, you need to be able to analyze grammatically the sentence or phrase you are working on, so you can relate the sentence to the offered rules. For a basic grammar review, a composition text or self-help book will do, such as *Harbrace* or *Writer's Guide*. *Hotline* reviews grammar to solve individual writing problems. An interesting basic self-help book that seems more accessible than many is Jane Walpole's *A Writer's Guide: Easy Ground Rules for Written English* (Englewood Cliffs, N.J.: Prentice-Hall, 1980).

Possessives seem to be the great conundrum these days. People omit apostrophes where they are called for and add them to plurals as if to bedevil those of us who think we know what a possessive is. Possessives are generally well explained in composition and self-help books, as are most standard grammar problems such as pronoun case and subject-verb agreement. Use a relatively recent book (from the past fifteen years or so) if you want to avoid hearing how *none* is always singular. (It's not; it often takes a plural verb.)

Specific questions about the number of a noun or pronoun can often be solved by a dictionary. You will often find usage notes or illustrative quotations at the entry for the word in question.

To study verbs, beyond the naming of the principal parts (found in a dictionary) and simple conjugation, you will need to use one of the fuller textbooks, *Harbrace* or *Writer's Guide*. *Hotline* has a good section on verbs and extended details on tense sequence and the subjunctive.

Other problems are not grammar problems but are matters of idiom—the way the language works—for instance, choosing the usual preposition to use with a specific verb. The best source of information about such things is a good dictionary (usually look under the verb in question, occasionally under the preposition).

Still other apparent grammar problems are matters of style or logic. Beginning a sentence with a conjunction, ending one with a preposition, and splitting an infinitive are actually matters of style, although we often talk of the ''rules'' of such things: check a good handbook or usage guide. Sentences have begun with conjunctions, ended with prepositions, and contained split infinitives for hundreds of years. The issue is the individual sentence, not the sanctity of a nonexistent rule. A sentence that doesn't sound right often contains a problem best resolved by rewriting.

Some excellent usage guides include H. W. Fowler's *Dictionary of Modern English Usage,* 2d ed. (New York: Oxford University Press, 1965) and Theodore Bernstein's *The Careful Writer* (New York: Atheneum, 1965). *Writer's Guide,* although a textbook, contains excellent usage notes. Also you may want to look at *Current American Usage* by Margaret Bryant (New York: Funk and Wagnalls, 1962), which contains useful discussions of usage during the fifties that are still relevant. Usage notes for individual words are included in some dictionaries, notably *The American Heritage Dictionary* (Boston: Houghton Mifflin, 1982); usage notes in the 1982 edition are more useful than those in the first edition. *Hotline* has relatively few usage notes but covers many of the most vexing problems.

Style

Even after removing both grammar and mechanics from this category—although both do often involve style choices—we are left with all those things that shape our writing without being associated with "hard and fast rules": whether to use first- or third-person pronouns (*I, we, us* or *he, she, one*); whether *you* is permitted, especially when referring to people generally; the use of passive sentences; the level of diction chosen, including the use of slang, and so on.

Style seldom involves clearly correct or incorrect choices. It is usually a matter of tone, as we discuss throughout this unit.

Studying writing that you believe to be successful and effective will often provide surprising insights into the practices of good writers and editors and the "rules" of style.

Many style guides are available. *Elements of Style,* 3d ed., by William Strunk and E. B. White (New York: Macmillan, 1979) is a standard perhaps because it is succinct and prescriptive, but it is too abstract and has too little discussion for us. *Revising Business Prose* by Richard Lanham (New York: Scribner's, 1981) and *Style, Ten Lessons in Clarity and Grace* by Joseph Williams (Glenview, Ill.: Scott, Foresman, 1981) are both excellent books about revising, by authors who understand writing on the job.

Mechanics

In considering correctness, punctuation, capitalization, and spelling must be treated individually.

Punctuation. Beyond the basic rules, punctuation receives scant treatment in most discussions of grammar and style. Grammarians want to talk about the structures of language; linguists want to talk about spoken language. The only people who seem to think much about punctuation are the people writing textbooks, and they seem to think more about each other's books than about actual practice.

These books try to reduce punctuation to a system of a few iron-clad rules. This leads to ludicrous office fights about whether a comma precedes the conjunction in a series like *red, white, and blue*. (We put it in; the editor, we trust, will leave it in, but if this were a newspaper or magazine, it would be out "for reasons of economy." Is that comma correct or not? It depends on where you are.)

Textbooks do seem to be right about basic guidelines, but there is more variation in practice than most American texts recognize. For instance, almost every book states as a rule that a comma should not precede the conjunction in a compound verb—for instance, no comma between *school* and *and* in the sentence "Every day Dick walked slowly to school and ran quickly home." No one is likely to put a comma before that conjunction. But there are many sentences with compound verbs, particularly those joined with *but*, that seem to ask for commas; "They gave up trying to drive through the snowstorm that night, but set out early the next morning." The books say No, but it has been done for many years. The usage is more complex than the rule.

Any composition handbook and numerous self-help books will outline the basic rules. If you want to examine rules and variety more thoroughly, then look at *Hotline, Chicago,* or an out-of-print book, *American Punctuation* by George Summey (New York: Ronald Press, 1949). These will give you enlightened rules. Summey deals with actual practice in well-edited prose. To gain more insight into punctuation and its possibilities, find effective writing of the type you are doing and examine the punctuation.

Again, the traditional rules are basically correct; generally what is lacking is an understanding of the exceptions.

Capitalization. "Practice varies"—that's what most honest books say about much capitalization. The rules of capitalization are clear; practice is not. In capitalization, consistency is probably more important than being "right." A dictionary will sometimes guide you, but dictionaries are overly conservative in dealing with capitalization. Find a style guide that deals with practice intelligently and follow it.

The most useful guides are those that give you hundreds of examples to compare your particular problem to. In general, we live in a time of few capitals, so unless you have a specific reason for capitalizing, don't.

For general use, *Hotline* and *Chicago* are the most useful, with *Chicago* including more categories and examples, but with *Hotline* providing much more discussion about solving your own problems.

If you work with the federal government, read over GPO's rules on capitalization. Basically, GPO capitalizes many common adjectives and nouns, when they refer to specific government agencies or personnel—*Federal* and *Army,* for instance.

Spelling. Spelling is probably the most rigidly fixed of all matters being discussed here. Generally acceptable alternative spellings exist for some words (*teenage, teenaged; enquire, inquire*). Most alternate spellings involve compound words (*day care, daycare*) and hyphenated words (*re-education, reeducation*). "Correctness" in these cases often depends on the particular dictionary you pick up.

Use standard spelling. When in the United States, use American, not British spelling (*color* not *colour; check* not *cheque*). Follow current reformed spellings only if your organization is participating in the crusade; otherwise write *light* not *lite* and *through* not *thru.*

GPO contains spelling for numerous compound words. Unfortunately, the present edition was issued in 1973 and lacks many currently troublesome words.

Manuscript Style

This is how the finished page looks, including conventions for formatting, documenting, and handling numbers, abbreviations, titles and names of things. These conventions are mechanical and routine, if you have a good source to check them in. Almost every style guide includes them.

Formatting. We have talked about two kinds of formats in this book, the formatting of individual ideas and series, and the formatting of large booklike projects. Your office, especially if it is a federal office, probably has a detailed correspondence manual that outlines letter and page formats. Otherwise use a good secretarial manual such as *Webster's Secretarial Handbook* (Springfield, Mass.: Merriam-Webster, 1976).

Documenting. Handling formal documentation is rigidly prescribed in most fields. If you do documented writing, we assume you have the correct style guide. Some major style guides are listed in the Bibliography. If your field does not have a style guide, use *Chicago* or Kate L. Turabian, *A Manual for Writers of Term Papers, Theses, and Dissertations,* 4th ed. (Chicago: Chicago University Press, 1973), which follows *Chicago* closely.

Numbers and Abbreviations. Handling numbers (whether to spell them out or use figures) and abbreviations is a matter of style. Pick a guide which seems complete and whose style makes sense to you and follow it. As with capitalization, consistency is important.

Titles and Names. The conventions of indicating the titles and names of things are fairly rigid. Your style guide will provide the major conventions. For minor details like the coined or descriptive titles of paintings or musical works, you will have to go to *Hotline* or *Chicago*. You can find a reasonable way of marking any title or name (or you can find out that it is not marked) by consulting a well-edited source that writes about it. Following the practices of a good encyclopedia works well.

Your Tools

To understand and deal with the many kinds of correctness, you may need to consult a good dictionary or two, a good style guide or two or three (because coverages are different), and even carefully edited writing of the type you are doing.

You cannot use these tools indiscriminately any more than you can follow indiscriminately the language rules someone gave you in the sixth grade. You need to understand what your specific dictionary and style guides cover.

Dictionaries

A good recent desk dictionary is a must. Desk dictionaries are generally more current than unabridged ones.

Does your dictionary include usage notes? If it doesn't, you will need to have a style guide that does.

Does your dictionary always spell out plurals or only irregular ones? How does it list the parts of verbs? Most dictionaries spell out irregular plurals and verbs and indicate widely acceptable alternate forms. But you will usually have to rely on a usage guide for useful information about choosing between *antennas, antennae* and *indexes, indices*.

The dictionary should help you check the level of diction of a word. If your dictionary does not tell you that a word is generally considered vulgar or slang, you will have to rely on other sources: on yourself, style guides, and perhaps the office grammarian.

Your dictionary should indicate spelling variants; some dictionaries list generally unacceptable although widely used variants (such as *alright*) without marking them clearly. Find out what your dictionary does.

Style Guides

A general style guide or usage guide should help you deal with the realities of contemporary written English. It should discuss language use, not merely prescribe its particular version of correctness. It should guide you in using punctuation, showing you the possibilities of the language as well as providing the usual explanations of punctuation marks.

A specialized style guide deals with documentation in your field. It may do little more than that. Examine it and find out what you need in a general style guide to supplement it. For instance, you may need rules and discussions of capitalization, hyphenation, and such matters as spelling out numbers, marking titles, and handling quotes within a text. If your specialized guide does not handle these matters, get a general style guide that does.

Beware of any style guide that has one rule for each situation and dismisses differing opinions. Most likely, you will find one or two style guides to rely on.

Other Writing

Examine successful work. Pick a report or letter that you think is good; find pieces of writing that have the tone you want; figure out how they work. Outline them; look at the facts they present; consider what was omitted. Look at sentence structures and word choices. Pull them apart and see how they hold together. Find useful *you*s and effective slang. Find a sentence fragment, a comma before the conjunction in a compound verb, sentences beginning with *and, but,* and *yet*. But don't let a few sentences beginning with *and* or *but* invite you to string sentences together with conjunctions like popcorn chains at Christmas. Don't throw out sentence punctuation or start adding commas to every compound verb.

Use your eye and your ear to discover the reasons for the exceptions. Examine and pay attention to practice, but be conservative. Let such exceptions add to your range of possibilities; do not let them make hash of your writing.

Office Grammarians

In every office lurks a frustrated grammarian, the office arbiter of the true, the good, the beautiful, and the correct—mostly the correct.

Confrontations with office grammarians, as wrong-headed and silly as the issues may seem at times, can increase your understanding of language and good writing, if you will let them. Whether the grammarian is right or wrong makes no difference if you use the confrontation to explore and understand language better.

29
Gender Language

FIFTEEN YEARS AGO, a writer could argue that the pronouns in the following sentence include both men and women:

> * Ask the plaintiff to explain his problem and to state what he seeks from the defendant.

We can no longer argue about this sentence. Many women feel excluded by it. The language has not changed, the history of pronouns has not changed, but we have changed.

Women feel the exclusion even more keenly when stereotypes are present, as in this sentence from a recent talk on international trade relations by a member of Congress:

> When hiring an executive, hire one who speaks the language of the country you are sending him to.

Discussions about sexism in language have sometimes been silly, and certainly people do not agree. But several points are clear, including the need to avoid sexual stereotyping in business and government writing as scrupulously as we avoid racial and ethnic stereotyping.

Stereotyping

The basic issue is stereotyping, fitting people into one category and excluding them from others on the basis of irrelevant criteria.

To help keep yourself from falling into sexist stereotypes as you write, remember that women fight in some armies, rule some countries, and shoveled coal in steel mills in this country at the turn of the century; and remember that men are nurses, work on PTA boards, and arrange flowers.

But much stereotyping is implied by our language. In this chapter we focus on eliminating stereotypes without concocting grammatically incorrect or silly-sounding sentences. We focus on three areas: narrative treatment, job titles and descriptions, and pronouns.

The list in figure 29-1 includes words illustrating most problems discussed in this chapter. It also suggests substitutions for some words not discussed in this chapter—*mankind* and *manpower*, for instance.

Salutations and signatures are discussed on pages 68–70.

FIGURE 29-I. SOME SEX-MARKED WORDS AND ALTERNATIVES

Sex-Marked Word	*Neutral Word or Substitution*
businessman	executive, professional, owner, manager
chairman	chair, convener, presider, chairperson
clergyman	minister
Congressman	member of Congress
Englishmen	the English
fireman	firefighter
fisherman	fisher
foreman	supervisor, boss, overseer
girl friday	clerk, secretary, assistant
laymen	laity, lay people, lay persons
lineman	line installer, line worker
maid	house cleaner, house worker
man (*as a collective noun, as in* the evolution of man)	people, men and women, human (human evolution)
man (*as a verb*)	staff, work
man-hours	work-hours, worker-hours, task-hours
man in the street	average citizen, consumer, neighbors
man-in-the-street interview	on-the-street interview, on-the-spot interview

---

FIGURE 29-1. SOME SEX-MARKED WORDS AND ALTERNATIVES (CONT.)

---

mankind	the human race, humans, people
manpower	worker, personnel, musclepower
newsman	reporter, newscaster
night watchman	guard, watcher
office boy	messenger, clerk, office helper
policeman	police officer
priestess	priest (*note that the ordained female clergy of the Episcopal Church are officially called* priests)
repairman	repairer
salesman	sales agent, sales representative, salesperson
spokesman	representative
statesman	diplomat, mediator, leader (*a more specific paraphrase may be the best solution here*)
weatherman	weathercaster, forecaster, meteorologist
workingman	worker, wage earner, laborer
workmanlike	skillful, conscientious, praiseworthy

Parallel Narrative Treatment

If you examine how we write about men and women, you will find interesting differences that suggest many things about our society's values. For instance, a press release about a woman becoming a corporate vice-president often includes the fact that she is the first woman to achieve that office. But it may also focus on her physical appearance (*attractive* or *blonde*) or family status (*recently divorced mother of seven*). These things are not in and of themselves evil, but they are issues that are introduced *because* the person is a woman.

Your guideline is simple. Do not raise an issue about a woman that you would not raise if you were writing about a man. Period.

Being attractive or not, being married or not are seldom legitimate issues at work. A man's meteoric rise in the company and the adversity he had to overcome—these things may be relevant in a feature or even in a press release about a new position. So might they be relevant to a woman. But be certain that the issues meet the test, that you are not raising the issue *because* the subject is a woman.

When you are writing about a man and a woman, refer to them by parallel names. If one has a full name on first reference, the other should also. If on second reference, you use only the last name for one, do so for the other. Don't write of the petitions that Harriet presented to Commissioner Smith. That makes an issue of the speaker's sex. Write of Commissioner Smith and Representative Tibbs, write of Smith and Tibbs; you would never write of Harriet and George. Finally, don't write of Mrs. Howard Tibbs; she is present in her own right.

Job Titles and Descriptions

Job titles and descriptions, both formal and informal, are changing in several ways. Suffixes designating women are being dropped. Old words that once applied exclusively to men are being revitalized as nonsexed words, although this happens seldom when the word contains *man*. And new words are being created, some useful and some silly.

American ingenuity coupled with our love of euphemisms will probably create some strange-looking titles in the near future. Some may be generally accepted, but we will probably create and discard many silly ones, too.

There is one caution here: Use nonsexed words consistently, not just when a woman is involved. Don't write *spokesman* when the speaker is male or unknown and *spokesperson* or *representative* when the speaker is female.

Suffixed Titles

In recent years both the suffixes designating a woman and the use of the word *woman* to modify a masculine job description have begun dying out. We no longer single out a woman poet (*poetess*) or pilot (*aviatrix*). The astronaut who happens to be a woman is simply an *astronaut*.

Some long-established words seem to be fading, at least as job titles. A pancake house now has the sign PLEASE WAIT FOR YOUR HOST HERE; that host may be a man or a woman, just as it was when the sign said "hostess." A recent lifesaving award ceremony honored a young hero (not a heroine), who happened to be a girl.

A few *-ess* words, like *actress*, seems so thoroughly entrenched that they will likely remain unchanged, and we use some specialized words so seldom that they will likely not change—*sorceress*, for instance.

Old Words

Besides *host* and *hero*, other traditional male words are apparently being adopted as general terms, even though useful substitutes exist. We have seen *salesman* used as a general term instead of *sales agent* or *representative*, and *fireman* instead of *firefighter*.

We don't know what will happen to some other common *man* words such as *businessman* and *chairman*. While *chairman* has often been taken as a general word, as in *Madam Chairman*, many people have tried to displace it with *chairwoman* or simply with *chair*. *Chair* is also replaced by *convenor*, *presider*, and similar words.

New Titles and Substitutions

You can create new words and rediscover some old ones by adding *-er* or *-worker* to many words. The *-er* suffix (originally spelled *-or*) has given us many words meaning "a person who does things": *driver, editor, fighter, hunter, lamplighter, photographer,* even *visitor* and *worker*. Now it can help us with words like *fisher* for *fisherman* and *launderer* for *laundress*.

Substituting *person* for *man*, to create words like *spokesperson, congressperson, chairperson,* and even *elder statesperson,* often leads to clumsy-sounding words. Perhaps we will get used to the sound or perhaps we will find more euphonious substitutes.

Substituting *woman* for *man* to create words like *spokeswoman* is even less satisfactory, for we are still left with the *man* word being generally used, the *woman* word being used only when the person is known to be a woman.

The Pronoun Problem

Discussions about sexism in language often focus on pronouns, probably because people have written silly sentences in response to the problem.

This sentence from a home health-care book written in the late 1960s well illustrates the problem. The authors are explaining how to do a pelvic exam.

> The person being examined should be lying comfortably on their back, preferably with a pillow under their head. Ask them to raise their knees. . . .

Since the person being examined must be a woman, why not use *woman* and *her?* When talking about actual people or about hypothetical people who can in fact be only one sex, use the appropriate pronouns.

Unfortunately, in hypothetical examples writers often use pronouns that reinforce stereotypes. Administrators are *he* and *him,* nurses *she* and *her,* as in this example:

> The conscientious hospital administrator insists that his staff members have numerous opportunities to improve themselves, and allows each to advance at her own pace.

Such a sentence is so easily changed that there is no excuse for its having been published. Here are five ways to handle the pronoun problem. One of these should solve any particular problem; often you have a choice of solutions.

1. *Eliminate the troublesome pronouns*. This is often the easiest way to handle problems. Certainly, not every *his* can be turned into an *a, an,* or *the,* but many can be. Others can be eliminated by repeating the noun. In the sentence above, the writer could have easily omitted the *his* in "his staff members." The pronouns can be eliminated in this sentence on child discipline:

> A parent who listens attentively helps convince his child that his ideas are valued and that he is respected.

becomes

> A parent who listens attentively helps convince the child that the child's ideas are valued and that the child is respected.

2. *Make the governing noun plural*. Usually you can do this with no loss of meaning or emphasis. The sentence

> At a hearing a parent will sometimes not let his child talk.

becomes

> At a hearing parents will sometimes not let their child talk.

(There is no need to make *child* plural; no pronouns refer to the child.)

And keeping the staff members of the hospital in the plural would lead to a strong sentence:

> The conscientious hospital administrator insists that staff members have numerous opportunities to improve themselves and allows them to advance at their own pace.

And making the listening parents and children plural would lead to a less cumbersome sentence:

> Parents who listen attentively help convince their children that their ideas are valued and that they are respected.

3. *Add the female pronoun with a slash or an* or. The example sentences become

> A parent who listens attentively helps convince his or her child that
> his/her ideas are valued and that he/she is respected.

and

> At a hearing a parent will sometimes not let his or her child talk.

This solution is, at best, inelegant. Once you establish the *he or she* pattern, you should carry it through. Dropping the alternatives calls more attention to the pronouns than simply using one or the other throughout. But carrying the paired pattern through often involves three or four sets of choices in one paragraph.

If you insist on carrying the alternative pattern through, try to reduce the number of pronouns in the passage. This is easily done in the first example:

> A parent who listens attentively helps convince the child that his or
> her ideas are valued and that he or she is respected.

(Once you begin using the pronouns, it is hard to omit them. Omissions must come first.)

4. *Introduce characters.* Particularly when creating hypothetical situations, make the the pronouns refer to "people." You will need to carefully avoid sexually stereotyping the roles these characters assume, just as you will try to avoid sexually stereotyping pronouns without names. Names must be introduced when the situation or character is first mentioned or the female pronouns will jar (we are, after all, conditioned to hearing the male pronouns; that's what this problem is all about).

> A parent who listens attentively helps convince Susie that her ideas
> are valued and that she is respected.

5. *Alternate pronouns.* You can alternate pronouns from one paragraph or one situation to the next. Be certain to change pronouns at the natural breaks between examples or anecdotes, not simply between sentences or paragraphs. Surprisingly, it is easy to fall into sex-role stereotyping as you alternate pronouns.

Using Their

Many people use *their* to solve their pronoun problems, as in these two sentences:

> Everyone is expected to have their presentations ready for the board meeting.

> An executive should make efficient use of their secretary's time.

Although some grammarians would condemn these two sentences equally for their use of *their,* the two sentences are very different. The first sentence is standard English, the second is not. Using *their* with a singular pronoun like *everyone* or *everybody* has a venerable history.

Everyone and *everybody* belong to a small group of words that seem both singular and plural at the same time. Although these words always take singular verbs (they do after all refer to individual people), for centuries fine stylists have used them with plural pronouns. The words do also refer to a group of people. Consider these sentences:

> Not everyone felt excluded by the ticket price, but many did.

> Everyone got to the picnic early and in good spirits; he brought plenty of food.

The first sentence is clear, the second is not. The *he* does not refer to the people at the picnic; it seems to refer to someone specific. But if *everyone* were only singular, the *he* would refer to *everyone.* It doesn't.

Because of the grammatical stigma often attached to using *their* with *everyone* and *everybody,* we suggest you work around the construction when convenient. Still, don't be afraid to use it if that seems best.

Two cautions are in order:
1. *Always* use a singular verb.
2. Do not use *their* to refer to a singular noun.
One example used above illustrates the problem:

> An executive should make efficient use of their secretary's time.

This sentence is so easily converted to idiomatic English that there is no excuse for it.

> An executive should make efficient use of a secretary's time.

or

> Executives should make efficient use of their secretaries' time (*or* of their secretarial time).

or

> Executives should make efficient use of secretaries and their time.

30
Rewriting and Style Guides

ELIMINATE JARGON, vary sentences, don't use passive verbs—these and dozens of other "rules" grow out of the belief that government and business writing should be clear, concise, and coherent and that you always achieve clarity, conciseness, and coherence in particular ways.

The realities are more complex. There may be times when you want to be unclear, verbose, and incoherent, although not obviously so. There are other times when a passive construction is exactly right, times when you want jargon, perhaps even times when you will load up with it, though such times are rare. We all know of experts whose reputations (and salaries) rely on their ability to produce the right-sounding jargon at the right time. There are times when it takes jargon to get people's attention.

The "rules," then, the dictates of clear business and government prose, are not absolute. They are best thought of as style guides to word choice and sentence patterns. Most contain some useful truth, but you will find that your own informed and insightful reading of a sentence or paragraph is often your most versatile and accurate guide.

Using style guides can be tricky. If you begin worrying about jargon and passives too early in the writing process, you may not get anything written; your worrying will interfere with the development of your ideas. If you don't worry about jargon and passives until the last minute, while you're checking spelling, looking for typos, and getting ready to turn your copy over to the typist, you will make only a few cosmetic changes.

Rewriting, revising, reenvisioning—whatever you want to call it —it is the often neglected step in the writing process. But it is rewriting that begins the process of turning rough, barely readable letters and reports into good business and government prose. Rewriting gets you ready to edit.

Whether you are rewriting a first draft or revising a position paper written several years ago, begin by reading as objectively as possible. Distance yourself. For the moment, become a member of your audience. Look for places that say something other than you intended. Look for gaps in the logic. Look for buried topic sentences that should be moved to the beginnings of paragraphs. Look for ideas that lack examples and for examples that are incomplete or unexplained.

Be sure that you have made contact with the reader, that the reader is involved. Early in the writing process, use *I* and *you* to remind yourself of the reader (you can edit out the pronouns later if you feel you must). Let this early audience be friendly, one that you do not need to impress with fine writing. Just be certain that you have said what you want to.

After this first reading, check your purpose statement (*see* pages 19–21) to be certain it coincides with your writing. Then check topic sentences to make sure that your paragraphs are organized and fit together logically. You may find, for instance, that you have halfway said something twice, and that you must cut one place and add a few words to another.

Try the next reading aloud, in a full voice, as if reading to someone across the aisle. As you read, you will find places where you stumble and other places where you only hesitate ("I guess that's all right," is the usual defense). Those are the places that need work (including the places that were "all right"). Your reader will stumble and hesitate more than you.

Fixing a place may involve changing a word or rewriting an entire paragraph. Sometimes, the place where you stumble is actually a sentence or two after the problem and your mind is registering a logic problem. Often you stumble over a too full sentence òr some needless jargon.

Somewhere in this process—shortly after you started fixing the places where you stumbled, probably—you will begin making fewer structural changes and more sentence and word changes. At this point you have moved from rewriting to editing.

Editing clarifies meanings and helps show relationships that you may have overlooked. As you edit, though you may continue to find structural problems, you are concentrating on word choices and sentence patterns.

Most individual editing decisions affect small units—words and sentences. But these seemingly small changes can add up to major differences in tone.

In this chapter, we focus on eight issues in style that can make the difference between barely readable and very readable writing. You may treat these as rules that you will occasionally violate or as guides. However, paying attention to these eight areas will give most writers greater control over their style. The first four guides deal with word choices, the second four with sentence structures.

Choosing Words

Follow these four style guides as you choose individual words:
1. Reduce the number of nouns made from verbs.
2. Use jargon and favorite buzz words only when necessary for meaning or (very cautiously) for effect.
3. Use loaded words deliberately and carefully.
4. Remove most excess words including intensifiers, redundancies, and compound prepositions.

Nouns from Verbs

By using suffixes we turn verbs into nouns; *affirm* becomes *affirmation*, *exploit* becomes *exploitation*, *deny* becomes *denial*, and *consider* becomes *consideration*.

Seldom is anything gained by *develop an appreciation* instead of simply *appreciate*, by *create a transformation* instead of *transform*, or by *do an examination* instead of *examine*. When you turn nouns back into verbs, you can often eliminate intensifiers and modifiers originally added to make your writing more forceful; they will now seem redundant.

The major suffices to watch out for include these:

-tion	*changes verbs to nouns,* commend *to* commendation
-ment	*changes verbs to nouns,* abridge *to* abridgement
-al	*changes verbs to nouns,* refuse *to* refusal
	also changes nouns to adjectives, instruction *to* instructional

This, from a technical bulletin on an endangered species of butterfly, illustrates the weakness of these noun forms.

> Existing habitat should be protected from further degradation, an objective that may involve habitat manipulation to prevent succession of the meadows to brushfields.

Eliminating a few nouns does not change the tone (or the passive verb) but makes the sentence more readable:

> Existing habitat should be protected from further decay; this may require taking action to stop the meadows from becoming brushfields.

You don't have to change entire sentences to dramatically increase their readability. Changing a *single* noun in this sentence will make the gobbledygook readable:

> The most important result of management by objectives is that it forces the administrator into the realization that there cannot be one single objective, notwithstanding the language of policy statements.

Change *realization* to *to realize* and you have a much clearer sentence:

> The most important result of management by objectives is that it forces the administrator to realize that there cannot be one single objective, notwithstanding the language of policy statements.

Jargon and Buzz Words

Jargon is technical or professional language that we use on the job. At its best, it is verbal shorthand. At its worst, it substitutes uncommon words for common ones simply to keep outsiders from understanding what is going on.

Jargon is necessary in many technical fields. Listen to some microcomputer hobbyists talk; their jargon names things and processes quickly and usefully, though to an outsider it sounds like a foreign tongue. When an expert tries to write about computers for people who know nothing about them, however, the jargon may get in the way, as it does in this sentence:

> Your printer must interface with your computer, through the I/O port using the appropriate serial or parallel interface.

The sentence is clear to a knowledgeable audience, though it could be more clearly written:

> Your printer will require either a serial or a parallel interface.

To the reader ignorant about computers, the rewritten sentence may sound more like English, but it still means nothing. Here is a well-written comprehensible version for the uninitiated reader:

> To plug your printer into your computer, you'll need an electrical gadget called an *interface*. Some printers need a *serial interface;* others need a *parallel interface*. Your printer must match your computer.

Buzz word is a jargon term referring to fad words. Buzz words often sound like technical terms, but have much less meaning. Individuals often have favorite buzz words that they sprinkle through their writing and talking. Words like *interpersonal* and *societal* sound more impressive than *personal* and *social* or *society's,* but they mean no more.

Buzz words can easily get out of control. If you are writing for a general audience, they can destroy the communication. In this example they smother the thought:

> This program is supported by voluntary giving, affordable program fees, and personal expenses of participants, the first being the limiting factor.

Removing the buzz words and developing the implied logic (money from three sources, voluntary giving the most important) gives us English:

While we receive money from program fees and participants, we rely on voluntary contributions to keep our program going and our fees low.

Figure 30-1 contains some current buzz words with possible translations.

FIGURE 30-1. BUZZ WORDS AND POSSIBLE SUBSTITUTES

Buzz Words	*Possible Substitutes*
ball-park	estimate, rough
behavioral	(*okay word, but being applied to everything*)
bottom line	cost, price
factor (*noun*)	influence, events, results, considerations, elements
factor (*verb*)	consider, separate
familial (*different from* filial)	family
gameplan	plan, approach
input	ideas, suggestions, comments
instrumental	important, crucial
interface (*noun*)	meeting, interaction (*okay as a computer component*)
interface (*verb*)	interact, cooperate, meet
interpersonal	personal, human
(the) nature (of)	*usually omit with a little rewriting*
operative	important, defining, determining
optimize	improve, enhance, increase
paradigm	pattern, model, outline, archetype
parameter	guideline, constraint, boundary (*okay in mathematics*)
phase	stage, part
process	(*okay word, but suddenly everything has become a* process)
(the) role (of)	*omit with some rewriting, sometimes rearranging sentence*
scenario	outline, possibility, estimate, contingency
societal	social, society's
syndrome	characteristics, symptoms

Loaded Words and Phrases

Loaded words are emotional words. Often they are persuasive words. These are the loaded words of advertising ("six lavishly illustrated volumes") and promotional writing of all kinds ("every attention to quality and value inherent in our aluminum extrusions extends to our brass shapes as well" and "this Medical Center is on the horizon of a new future, and the future has never looked brighter").

We expect loaded words in advertising and persuasive writing. We expect an instruction manual to tell us how easily the new bike can be assembled. The manual encourages us in the job ahead with its language.

But loaded language is often inappropriate. In reports it may create dismay, because the reader expects objective, neutral words presenting facts. In letters, loaded language can lead to disaster because it usually accuses and insinuates.

Controlling your tone is the issue more than the words themselves. We discuss tone in reports on pages 201–202; we discuss loaded language in letters on pages 65–66. We mention it here to remind you of its importance.

Words of Many Sorts

Excess words add length to your writing and dilute your meaning. We will discuss several redundancies to make you more aware of the problems. Some redundancies are straightforward:

> If and when Klopper Farms attempts to secure payment again, we can, if necessary, forestall further action through the same means we have used this time.

The writer is trying to sound like a lawyer (perhaps a lawyer is writing), trying to cover all the contingencies. But *if and when,* at least here, means *if. We can* and *if necessary* are not quite the same, but very close; the actual meaning is probably *we will, if necessary.*

Further is unnecessary, one can only forestall action that has not occurred.

> If Klopper Farms attempts to secure payment again, we can forestall them with the same means we used this time.

Eliminating excess words is seldom so straightforward. However, here are several types of redundancies to watch for.

Vague Intensifiers. Probably the easiest redundancies to eliminate are intensifiers. Words like *very, actually, relatively,* and *quite* have little force left in them. When you begin turning nouns back into verbs and following some of the other suggestions we make, you will not feel the need for so many intensifiers because your verbs will be stronger.

For the time being, eliminate all the intensifiers from your writing. Cut out every *very* and *comparatively*. Later, when you are comfortable without them, you may use one occasionally. You will miss the words when you begin cutting them, but not when you reread in a few days. Figure 30-2 lists some of the common intensifiers.

FIGURE 30-2. INTENSIFIERS TO CUT

absolutely	definitely	quite
actually	exceedingly	really
certainly	extremely	relatively
clearly	great	somewhat
comparatively	much	truly
completely	pretty (*meaning* very)	very

If your two favorite intensifiers aren't on this list, add them.

Compound Prepositions. Compound prepositions, such as *in order to, along the lines of,* and *by means of,* generally contribute to a heavy noun style. Figure 30-3 lists some of these prepositions and brief substitutes. Cutting compound prepositions can help you cut abstract nouns, since people often use compound prepositions to string these nouns together.

In light of the nature of the charges and in view of the delicacy of the situation, the prosecutor has requested a special prosecutor to conduct a Grand Jury probe along the lines of other select committees.

If you are rewriting this sentence, you may cut it and still sound official:

The serious charges coupled with the need for secrecy have led the prosecutor to request a special prosecutor and a full-scale grand-jury probe.

In addition to compound prepositions, figure 30-3 includes other stock phrases that you should think about cutting, such as *and/or* and *if and when*.

FIGURE 30-3. COMPOUND PREPOSITIONS AND WORDY PHRASES

Wordy Phrase	*Usual Substitute*
along the lines of	like
and/or	or; *sometimes* and
as of	*omit*
as to	*omit; sometimes* for, of
at that (point in) time	then
at this (point in) time	now
by means of	by
each and every	*usually either one*
if and when	when; *sometimes* if
in area (*or* in color, in depth, in height, in length, in size, in volume, in weight, in width)	*omit*
in excess of	more than
in light of (the fact that)	because
in order to (go, run, perform, etc.)	to (go, run, perform, etc.)
in terms of	*omit with rewriting*
in the event of	if *or sometimes* when
in view of	because of

many different (stages, levels, needs, etc.)	many (stages, levels, needs, etc.)
(the) nature of	*omit*
(in the) near future	soon
not un-	*usually rephrase sentence*
number of	some
one of the (things, reasons, motivations, etc.)	a (thing, reason, motivation, etc.)
per each	each
percentage of	some
pursuant to	under
relative to, in relation to	on *or* about
take issue with	disagree
with regard (*or* respect) to	*often omit;* regarding

Turning Clauses to Phrases. You can make some sentences more effective by reducing to a word or two what we might call a "filler" clause. Two brief examples will make the point:

> This unit is based on the premise that there is not a single style that everyone should write all the time.

becomes

> There is not a single style that everyone should write all the time.

And

> What is overlooked is the fact that the use of mathematical tools in the development of the physical sciences bears little resemblance to the use of statistics in psychology.

becomes

> But the use of mathematical tools in the development of the physical sciences little resembles the use of statistics in psychology.

Sentence Logic. Sometimes redundancy develops from the logic of the sentence more than it does from particular words or phrases.

Whether or not expansion of the ski area will have a serious detrimental effect on the species depends on the care taken to minimize such effects.

This sentence goes around in circles: The effect depends on the care taken to prevent effects. In a different sense it is not redundant, for it is saying that the agency can exert some control over what is going to happen. Unknotting the nearly circular construction gives this:

Whether expansion of the ski area will devastate the species depends on the care taken by the Forest Service.

Controlling Redundancy. Occasionally you may use redundancy to emphasize a point, but such occasions must be few and far between (to use a redundant cliché) if the redundancy is to be effective. Generally, redundant writing simply wastes everyone's time and energy. The writer of the Klopper Farms example above might argue for the redundancies because they make the statement sound more lawyerlike. Since the client paid a great deal for the letter, perhaps it should sound lawyerlike even at the expense of sense.

Shaping Sentences

Here are four guidelines, none of them inviolate, to shaping sentences. Understanding and using these guides will help you clear up much muddy writing.
1. Avoid passive sentences.
2. Avoid sentences that postpone logical subjects.
3. Break up sprawling sentences.
4. Write ordinary sentences.
These four points all imply the same thing: Be direct.

Passive Sentences

The sentence "The dog bit the man" is active. The subject of the sentence, *dog,* performs the action of the verb on the object, *man.* Likewise,

> The stockbroker bought futures on margin.

and

> People can use these tests to evaluate the political and cultural biases of books, newspapers, and even television shows.

Sometimes, however, we write sentences in which the doer of the action is thrown into the object position, as "The man was bitten by the dog." The doer in the sentence appears in a prepositional phrase, "by the dog," or is omitted entirely. "The man was bitten." The receiver of the action becomes the subject of the sentence. Likewise,

> Futures were bought on margin.

and

> These tests can be used to evaluate the political and cultural biases of books, newspapers, and even television shows.

Passive sentences drain energy and life from writing, but sometimes they are useful. Writing a memo to someone saying, "You have fouled up the recruiting for our new executive director" creates confrontation. Writing in the passive—"The recruiting for the new executive director has been fouled up"—*may* allow everyone to agree that a problem exists and to get to work on correcting the problem.

But even though *a* passive sentence may be useful sometimes, there is no cause for piling them up. The example below, from a technical bulletin, illustrates what can happen when writers pile up passive sentences. In this case, the passive verbs and the many nouns combine to blunt the writing. (The objectives mentioned all center on improving the habitat.)

> Once these objectives are achieved, reintroduction and establishment of additional populations on secure habitat can be explored. A major effort by all those involved in the recovery program, including the Fish and Wildlife Service, . . . and other participants, will be necessary to ensure consideration of this butterfly in resource planning for public lands. Although the long-term status of the species and its habitat on private lands is not well understood, these lands do hold promise as key butterfly habitat, and the cooperation of local private interests in development of management plans should be encouraged.

Adding a doer—we, the Fish and Wildlife Service, all those involved in the recovery program—to most of the sentences, allows us to dramatically reduce the nouns and passive sentences and make the passage readable. It still sounds official and technical.

> Once we finish improving the habitat, all agencies involved in this project can explore establishing additional populations in the secure habitat. All those involved in this effort, including the Fish and Wildlife Service, . . . will need to cooperate to ensure that the butterfly is considered in resource planning for public lands. Although the agency has not surveyed the habitat on private lands, these lands may hold the key to long-term survival. We need to encourage private local interests to develop management plans.

Buried Subjects

"A bird is in the tree" can be rewritten in many ways, including "There is a bird in the tree" and "It is a bird in the tree" (making that noise), and "It seems that there is a bird in the tree." Grammarians and linguists describe these constructions in various ways. However, all three constructions effectively bury the logical subject (the doer or actor) of the sentence. Likewise,

> There are many problems with the Ackroyd estimates.

> There may be difficulty documenting your claims against the estate.

It seems that we may have a problem limiting the damage to files and records once someone penetrates our computer system.

and

It is conceivable that a search could be performed using a technology that was able to detect the presence of a submarine whether or not it is snorkling.

Burying the subject softens the impact of the sentence, creating the written equivalent of a "mmmh, well . . ." Because of this, we often use such constructions for bad news. As a lawyer you want your client to know of a problem, but you don't want the client to despair. Instead of writing "You have a problem," you write "There is a problem."

Unfortunately, this sentence pattern has become habitual with many of us. We have apparently decided that the "mmmh, well . . ." makes us sound good, like an expert pausing to reflect before explaining the origins of the universe in three sentences.

Fortunately, if you are alert, these sentences are easily edited by identifying the logical doer or actor and making it the subject of the main clause of the sentence. In doing that, the *it* clause sometimes disappears and is sometimes reduced to a word or two; the *there* clause always disappears. In looking over the rewritten sentences, you may notice that the *it* sentences follow the pattern discussed earlier of reducing clauses to a word or two.

Many problems exist with the Ackroyd estimates.

or

The Ackroyd estimates have many problems.

Your claims against the estate are shaky.

or

Documenting your claims against the estate may be difficult.

We may have a problem limiting the damage to files and records once someone penetrates our computer system.

or

> Once someone penetrates our computer system, limiting damage to files and records will be a problem.

and

> Conceivably, a search could be performed using a technology able to detect a submarine whether snorkling or not.

Sentence Sprawl

There is absolutely nothing wrong with a long sentence that reads well.

> Our skilled people can precision-machine, finish, and assemble the extruded shapes you use in your products, whether they are intricately shaped rails for high-speed copiers or multisegmented housings for computer modems.

This one is longer and more complicated but still clear:

> Because major projects are often awarded on a turnkey basis, with major portions of the overall design, standards, and concepts left to the contractor, American firms, by becoming involved while a project is still in its early conceptual stages, may be able to influence a project's concept and goals, thereby strengthening the chances of obtaining the contract.

However, these sentences are the exception. Most writers get into trouble when a sentence is longer than twenty-five words. The average sentence should probably be no more than twenty words. But people with the long-sentence habit think it is impossible to cut sentences to twenty words. So, to begin, adopt a maximum sentence length of thirty words. While that is slightly long for business and government writing, it is a controllable length.

Any sentence over this length (or whatever shorter length you

want to give yourself) must be shortened. This is your maximum
length, not an average.

When you find a sentence over your maximum (even one word)
you must cut words out of the sentence or divide it into smaller
segments.

Long sentences often contain so many ideas or shift their focus
so frequently that they are hard to follow. Put two long sentences
together and you are going to tire out the reader:

> The social impact assessment literature clearly suggests that one of
> the instrumental factors in successful impact mitigation is the process of
> political negotiation with impacted communities to plan for social
> change, economic development, and growth management. In the case of
> MX/MPS [MX missile/Multiple Protective Shelters] the highly specula-
> tive nature of population distribution and impacts, together with the
> urgency of the time schedule for construction, would effectively pre-
> clude such planning to optimize the potential benefits or mitigate the
> adverse impacts of MX/MPS.

Most readers begin to skim such long sentences or skip them
entirely. Two sentences, the first thirty-six words long, the second
forty-one—that's too much.

To make the two sentences above more readable, first look at the
buzz words and jargon. We will need to eliminate phrases like *in-
strumental factors, impact mitigation,* and *speculative nature of
population distribution.* We won't be able to get rid of them all, but
we will scrutinize them all.

A few words are completely redundant: a *negotiation* is already
a *process; potential* benefits are the only kind you would seek *to
optimize,* and *adverse* impacts are the only ones you would seek *to
minimize.*

The final line, following *planning,* simply repeats the meaning of
successful impact mitigation. Perhaps if the definition had been
highlighted, the writer would not have felt the need for the close.

The strategy for rewriting emerges. Focus on the basic conflict:
we should plan, but we won't be able to. The reasons both for
planning and for not being able to will probably follow each point.

> According to social impact assessment literature, political negotiation
> between communities and the government is crucial if communities are

to plan for major social and economic changes. In this case, however, effective planning will be precluded by uncertainty about the population increase (including whether dependents will be present) and by the urgent construction schedule.

During actual rewriting, we found that the list of things to plan for (*social change, economic development,* and *growth management*) was a haphazard one and needed to be cut or developed. Cutting was appropriate here.

There are still only two sentences here (we had expected three as we began rewriting). The sentences are just below the thirty-word limit (twenty-five and twenty-seven words) and will not win many prizes. They are still bureaucratic and official, but they are readable.

Monstrous sentences often need to be hacked into small sentences. Observing the thirty-word sentence limit would have painlessly prevented this monstrosity:

> In an attempt to approach these issues, several major agencies at both the State and local levels are proposing the development of an integrated and well-coordinated system of long-term care, based on the fact that the needs of the elderly, handicapped, chronically ill, and disabled are both interrelated as well as multifaceted, and can be addressed only by recognizing that both similarities and differences in type and level of need exist.

This seventy-plus-word monster breaks into three thought units. The first unit ends at *long-term care;* the second begins with *based on the fact that* and ends with *multifaceted;* the third begins *and can be addressed.* When these units are isolated, many of the nouns and much of the repetition will take care of themselves as we rewrite.

> To approach these issues, several major State and local agencies propose developing an integrated and coordinated system of long-term care. This system will recognize that the elderly, handicapped, chronically ill, and disabled have many similar needs. It will also recognize that each group has unique needs, as does each individual within a group. Even individuals that require similar services may require very different levels of service.

You may not need the final sentence of the rewrite; it seems to get into another point. We left it in because the idea seems to be in the original sentence. The rewrite—still bureaucratic, still official, and still proposal-like—is four sentences long and contains fewer than seventy words, even though many words were added to fill out ideas. More important than sheer length, however, the rewritten sentences are much more readable.

Of the common writing problems, sprawl is one of the easiest to identify and to correct. Simply enforce the maximum word length and rewrite and edit everything over that.

Enforcing the arbitrary thirty-word limit should help you develop a feel for sentence length. Seldom does this lead to people writing a page of twenty-to-thirty-word sentences, but even if that happens, the writing will likely be more readable than it would have been. Still, you will want some short sentences, fewer than fifteen words, too.

Ordinary Sentences

Most of the advice in this chapter has been negative. Here is the positive counterpoint: Write ordinary sentences.

Write sentences that begin with subjects, have subjects next to verbs, have verbs next to objects and complements, and have modifiers next to the things they modify. Ordinary sentences are controlled; they begin with the idea of the preceding sentences and carry it forward a notch. They modify and explain one another.

The long sentence cited earlier is readable because it is ordinary:

> Our skilled people can precision-machine, finish, and assemble the extruded shapes you use in your products, whether they are intricately shaped rails for high-speed copiers or multisegmented housings for computer modems.

This sentence begins simply with a subject and verb. The complexity of the sentence (in this case a list) is in the object, where there is a clause. But the sentence has been well established by then, and the clause does not break the basic flow.

Thinking of ordinary sentences should encourage you to use effective parallelism—putting parallel ideas in parallel grammatical structures:

> The society was important for women since it provided certain benefits for members and their families. It conducted burials, provided death announcements, preserved family records, and gave legal and financial protection to widows and orphans.

Unfortunately, these sentences originally appeared this way:

> The society was important for women since it provided certain benefits for members and their families. Burials, announcements of death, preservation of family records, and protection for widows and orphans were among the benefits of membership.

Writing ordinary sentences helps prevent misplacing modifiers. This sentence from an otherwise clear economic report should not have escaped editing:

> American companies looking at Nigeria must be prepared to have their representatives make frequent visits and should seriously consider appointing an agent or stationing in Nigeria, a company representative to keep them abreast of current developments and to maintain contacts with government officials and the local business community.

Placing a comma between *stationing* and *in Nigeria* will clear up the problem, but a better solution is simply to move *in Nigeria* to its normal position.

> American companies looking at Nigeria must be prepared to have their representatives make frequent visits and should seriously consider appointing an agent or stationing a company representative in Nigeria to keep them abreast of current developments and to maintain contacts with government officials and the local business community.

By using ordinary sentences, you will write fewer passive sentences, with less jargon and fewer nouns. You will write more directly and clearly. You will rewrite out-of-control sentences and will write some short sentences. Indeed, your writing will be readable, the first necessary requirement for being effective.

Appendix

Practical Applications: Four Rewrites

RULES, EXCEPTIONS, and general discussions only make a difference if they lead to better writing. In these four examples we illustrate the rewriting process—the actual analyzing and thinking you will go through as you rewrite.

We discuss each of the rewrites in terms of the intended audience (*see* Chapter 1), the purpose (*see* Chapter 2), and the tone and style of the language (*see* Chapters 27 and 30).

When you do your own rewriting, you will find that you usually go through a piece two or three times. Each time you will cut and revise something more, focusing more effectively on the words, their meaning, and your audience. At times in this process you will stop and actually write out notes about your audience or reconsider your purpose statement.

Insurance Policy Jargon

A new version of an insurance policy arrived recently. It is attractively formatted and appears readable. The company says the policy has been rewritten in plain English. This is how it begins:

> We want you to be fully informed about your coverages as well as exclusions to and limitations of those coverages.
>
> If you have any questions about these coverages, exclusions, or limitations, we urge that you contact your Insurance Co. agent. . . .
>
> In case of loss under this policy, we cover only that part of the loss over the deductibles stated in the annual Extension Certificate.

In writing this, the writer created a strong sentence structure but got tangled in the jargon of the trade.

Audience

At first glance, most people see only the policyholder as audience. But two other audiences are crucial: 1) an executive who wants the policies in plain English and 2) the company, particularly the legal department.

There are three audiences, then, and as far as the writer is concerned, the policyholder may be the least important.

Purposes

Each audience has its own needs. The legal department needs an insurance policy that will hold up in court. The executive may have some precise ideas about sentence length and syllable counts. The policy holder would like to be able to understand the policy. These purposes should not be at odds with each other, but they may be.

Effectiveness

Since the policy was mailed, we can assume the writer met the requirements of the legal department and of the executive. The policyholder was left out either because the writer could not see past the jargon words, like *coverages, exclusions,* and *limitations,* or because the legal department insisted on keeping the words.

Rewriting

Once you identify the technical words as the problem, this part of the policy is easily rewritten:

> We want you to understand what your policy covers, what it does not cover, and the limits of your coverage.

If you have any questions about your policy, including what it does and does not cover and the amount of coverage you have, please contact your Insurance Co. agent.

If you have a loss, we will subtract the amount of your deductible from your settlement. The amount of your deductible is listed in your annual Extension Certificate. Your agent can also tell you the amount.

Looking for Substance

This story, from a monthly newsletter, announces a banquet speaker; it falls flat. Some people will show up for the meeting no matter what the program is going to be; they come for the social occasion. But others will choose to come or not because of the speaker. This announcement will not get them there. There is little information here and even that is not well used:

> Our October 11 meeting should prove to be exceptionally special for a number of reasons. The first reason is that Glenna J. Sammuelson, national program director for ABC, will be the main speaker. Her session title is "Where Do We Go from Here?" and she will share information with us on key forces and trends shaping the business communications field. She will explore some opportunities and avenues for development and pose some challenges facing the profession. It will be a thought-provoking session in which people can gain an understanding of the possibilities and parameters for business communications and explore some implications for their own career. Dr. Sammuelson feels that her program will be applicable for a variety of professionals in business communications and/or executives. It might even be a useful topic for members to invite their bosses to so they can see what the future state might be in business communications. Dr. Sammuelson is a partner . . .

This paragraph continues with Professor Sammuelson's background and credentials. The article concludes with other details that promote the meeting as "eventful."

In all fairness, the newsletter editor may have had nothing more to work with than the speaker's name, her topic, and a fast-approaching deadline. Sometimes you must fake it.

But some rewriting would make the story a more effective "fake." And, if there was time, a little research might have made a major difference.

Audience

The audience is a professional group, united by whatever caused them to join—keeping up in the field, having informal contact with other professionals, sharing ideas, or hunting jobs.

Purpose

This is a kind of news story; its purpose is not only to convey information about the speaker but also to entice people to the meeting. The story needs to be attractive; it needs to reflect some of the reasons people join professional societies.

Effectiveness

The story does convey the news, but the speaker and her title should be emphasized, not buried. The idea of having a speaker worthy of a boss' attention is strong, but the details in the story don't justify the invitation.

Rewriting

Two additions will help this story substantially. First, a grabber, something to get the audience's attention. If nothing else is available, the title of the talk will do.

Second, more information about the speaker—major publications, issues that concern her (based on publications and talks if nothing else), and perhaps something about the companies she is associated with (they are listed at the end of the story). One or two phone calls to professional contacts or simply to the person who invited her may produce enough information. Or the information may be available in directories and journals in the field.

Finally, the lead and the story need to focus on the speaker. The vague reference to other items (the meeting "should prove to be exceptionally special for a number of reasons") needs to be cut from the opening. The other items can be dropped from the story (and given their own stories elsewhere in the newsletter), or they can be buried at the end of this story without announcing them in the beginning. Dropping them from the lead and giving them their own stories works best.

Making these changes (including dropping the other stories) leads to something like this:

"Where Do We Go From Here?" That's the question Glenna J. Sammuelson, ABC program director, will help us answer at our regular meeting October 11.

We have heard for years about what electronics would one day do to our offices. Suddenly that day is here. We have kept up with our offices, and we have initiated some of the changes, but we do not always have the big picture.

Dr. Sammuelson will help us see and understand that big picture. She will help us sort out choices and possibilities, helping us look at our options as professionals in our field as well as exploring new individual possibilities.

Dr. Sammuelson is uniquely qualified to make this presentation. Her Los Angeles consulting firm has built its reputation by creating efficient and practical office communications systems that fit both the companies and the employees. As a program director for ABC she has seen hundreds of systems; she understands the real possibilities and potentials as well as the real problems.

The program committee hopes members will invite their bosses. This is an excellent chance to let the boss find out what electronics is doing to business communications and to get some ideas of how electronics might further enhance the office.

To entice you to bring your boss, tickets for bosses will be half-price. That's a bargain!

This rewrite still contains plenty of puffing and little solid information. But the come-on has been developed. The reader has a reason (in addition to the social occasion) for attending the event. The invitation to the boss makes a good close.

Official Nouns and Passives

Sometimes wanting to sound official and knowledgeable gets in the way of being readable. This paragraph from a government report introduces a list of tests to use in evaluating textbook bias:

> This section lists instruments that can be used for evaluating textbooks and instructional materials for bias. These instruments vary considerably in their focus (i.e., group/grade level/subject area), as indicated by the codes. Some variability was also observed in terms of the assumptions that underlie the instruments' formulations and concepetualizations. Moreover, extensive variation was noted with regard to the instruments' comprehensiveness and level of specificity or generality. Finally, only a few of the instruments provided any methodological or statistical basis for establishing their validity and/or reliability. As indicated in the introduction, the inclusion of these instruments should not be interpreted as an endorsement. With these caveats in mind, the textbook evaluation instruments can be used by parents, students, educators, librarians, textbook selection committees, researchers, state and local administrators, and others who are concerned with textbook biases. Familiarity and practice with these tools can result in a greater understanding of the issues and a more informed basis for decisions regarding textbook selection and adoption.

This is Official Style—words for the sake of words, passive verbs, verbs turned into nouns, and prepositional phrases strung together like beads on a string. Here is the voice of a bureaucrat, and pity the poor reader who doesn't already understand what is being said.

Audience

The paragraph says that the list can be used by students as well as professional educators, which implies that the audience for the report includes the general public (if not students). However, the writer is obviously more concerned with sounding expert than with being understood by the general public.

Any rewrite will still need to sound expert and official if the writer is to be satisfied.

Purpose

The purpose of the paragraph is straightforward: to define this section of the report and to suggest, in general terms, the usefulness and the limitations of the tests.

Effectiveness

This paragraph effectively covers the material. In fact, part of its problem is that it tries to include all possibilities. The main failing is the tone. The overt message may be that anyone can read the report and use the tests, but the message of the tone is different: only experts—those versed in the language—need read on.

Rewriting

Surprisingly, this is a straightforward rewriting task. The logic and structure of the piece are solid. Rewriting individual sentences in three ways (discussed in Chapter 30) shortens sentences and makes them more readable.

1. Turn nouns into verbs and participles (*evaluation* into *evaluating* and *variability* into *vary,* for instance).

2. Reduce or eliminate strings of prepositional phrases (*in terms of the assumptions* into *on assumptions*, and *with regard to* into *in,* for instance).

3. Eliminate some passive verbs (*was also observed* and *was noted,* for instance) and simplify verb phrases (*can be used* into *to use* and *should not be interpreted* to *is not,* for instance); doing this helps eliminate more prepositional phrases.

In addition, look skeptically at long lists to see whether they are useful. Reducing the long list near the end of the paragraph—as concrete and specific as it may be—to *anyone* makes the point much stronger, the paragraph shorter, and the reading easier.

While there are no logic problems, as you break the example into natural paragraphs, you find that the disclaimer sentence ("the inclusion of these instruments should not be interpreted as an endorsement") belongs near the beginning.

And as you turn the last (and least readable) part of this into English, you find that the final sentence adds little.

After working through the paragraph several times, you will get something like this:

> This section lists tests that can be used in evaluating textbooks and other materials for bias. As stated in the introduction, including a specific test in this list is not a recommendation.
>
> These tests cover materials for many grades, groups, and subjects; codes indicate the specific coverage of each test. The tests are built on different assumptions and concepts, and they vary greatly in comprehensiveness. Few tests provided any methodological or statistical basis for establishing their validity or reliability. With these reservations in mind, the tests can be used by anyone concerned with textbook bias.
>
> Using these tests should help individuals understand textbook adoption procedures better and should help them make more informed selections.

The rewrite is clearer and shorter, but still official, still expert.

Writing to the Audience

You must not only analyze your audience, you must use the insights you develop. Here is a case where the writers know what the audience needs because they work with them daily, but they failed to use this understanding when they wrote.

The Victim/Witness Assistance Unit, part of the prosecuting attorney's office, helps crime victims and potential witnesses assert their rights. It helps provide counseling and sometimes protection. The first contact many victims have with this unit is through this form letter, on Office of the Prosecutor stationery.

TO: _____

RE: _____

    STATUTE: _____

The Prosecuting Attorney, __th Judicial District, has requested that we (Victim/Witness Assistance Unit) make contact with you due to the recent crime of which you were a victim.

The primary function of the Unit is to aid and support those who are victimized through crimes of violence. We offer a wide variety of services, free of charge, including court preparation, support counseling, referral services, and citizen informational needs. It is NOT MANDATORY that you prosecute for Unit utilization.

Please call us at 555-1212 or 555-1234 if:

1. You would like additional information on services available.
2. You plan to prosecute and would like to know what to expect in court.
3. You have questions regarding law enforcement and the judicial system.
4. You desire to prosecute but aren't sure of the procedure.
5. You are prosecuting and would like a victim advocate to give support counseling and prepare you for court.

If you desire to prosecute but fear repercussions, contact this office immediately. INTERFERENCE WITH A VICTIM/WITNESS by threats or acts of revenge is a serious crime to which police, the Prosecutor, and the courts give particular attention. Your safety and well-being is the #1 priority of the Prosecutor. This Unit was developed to help you and others who are victimized. If we can be of service, please do not hesitate to call.

Sincerely,

In this letter the official voice, the government voice, has overwhelmed the helping voice.

Audience

Even though this is a form letter, the primary audience is limited to one person: a specific victim or witness. But there are other important audiences, including the victim's family and friends. These people may be the ones who will contact or convince the victim to contact the office.

Other audiences are less important—the bosses and the funding agencies. Their response to the letter as an appropriate way to make contact with victims is important, of course, but if the letter is effective, then most negative responses can be handled with "that's the way we need to write it to get people to come in."

Since this is a form letter, the potential audience has the same makeup as the community. Black, white, rich, poor, employed, unemployed, old, young—all are potential crime victims and witnesses. The letter must respond to the feelings that these victims are likely to have within the first few days of the crime—fear, anxiety, and anger.

Purpose

Although the letter explains the services, this is not a good-news or courtesy letter. This is a persuasive letter and as such has only one goal: to get the reader to call the office. The message is not simply that there is help available; the message is "call this office."

Other information is here to help persuade the reader to call. The writer wants people to know about the unit, but if the unit is going to do what it is designed to do, people must phone.

Effectiveness

From first to last, the original letter is much too official. Certainly, the writer wants to project a firm feeling, and so using a letterhead, for instance, is proper. But listing the statute relating to the crime is simply confusing.

To be effective, the writer of this letter must tread a thin line between being too official and too informal. Too official a letter may frighten the anxious victim; too informal a letter may seem to say that the writer is not strong enough to provide the promised services and protection.

Rewriting

The original letter buries the comfort that needs to be offered to the victim. Even if the victim is afraid of the prosecutor's office or afraid of reprisals, this comfort will create a way of making contact with the reader.

Beyond trying to increase the offered comfort, rewriting involves cutting down to essential information, making sentences more conversational, and involving the reader more actively in the letter.

The original format is confusing. The Re and Statute lines, particularly, are for the office—for filing and perhaps for a counselor's information—not for the victim. A coded, inconspicuous notation in the top or bottom margin would serve as well.

The letter needs to be only one page. And even though it is a printed form letter, it needs to look typed.

The rewritten letter (*see* figure A-1) is still official, but now it sells the services in much simpler language. It invites and reinvites the victim to call. It does everything short of picking up the phone and dialing the number.

FIGURE A-I. REWRITTEN LETTER

Office of the Prosecuting Attorney
Victim/Witness Assistance Unit

June 18, 198–

Dear Mr. Perry Jones,

The Prosecuting Attorney's office tells us that you were recently the victim of a crime. Most victims are afraid, confused, and anxious for a long time after the crime. You may feel lonely and frightened; you may feel no one cares or understands. We understand your feelings, and we can help.

We are the Victim/Witness Assistance Unit, and we help people like you get their lives back together as much as possible.
We will help you whether or not you prosecute.
We can get someone for you and your family to talk to.
All of our services are free.

As you think about going to court, you may feel confused or anxious. Many victims are nervous about police and court procedures.
We will explain police procedures to you.
We can help you decide whether you want to prosecute.
We will tell you what happens in court.
We will help you get ready for court.

Sometimes people want to prosecute but they are afraid something bad will happen to them if they do. We will help protect you.

IF YOU HAVE BEEN THREATENED OR IF YOU FEEL YOU ARE IN DANGER, CONTACT OUR OFFICE NOW.
Threatening you or any victim or witness is a serious crime; the police, the prosecutor, and the courts take such threats very seriously.

Your well-being is very important to us. If we can help you, or if you just want to know more about us, call us at 555-1212 or 555-1234.

Sincerely yours,

Simone Battres, Director
Victim/Witness Assistance

Reference: C-32/ 1-84-Jones

Selected Bibliography

This bibliography is not exhaustive, but it does contain titles that readers of *Writing on the Job* may find useful. It contains titles mentioned in the text as well as supplementary ones.

Books are listed only once, although some contain material on several subjects. Supplementary information on Part One, "Writing in Organizations," is contained in many of the books listed here; a separate listing has not been provided. The entries for Part Three, "The Writer's Self Help," are divided into "Dictionaries and Word Lists" and "Style and Usage Guides" instead of individual units.

UNIT II: Job Applications

Bolles, Richard N. *What Color Is Your Parachute?* Berkeley, Calif.: Ten Speed Press, 1976.

College Placement Annual. Bethlehem, Pa.: College Placement Council, annual.

Lewis, Adele. *How To Write Better Résumés.* Woodbury, N.Y.: Barron's Educational Series, 1977.

UNIT III: Correspondence

Explanatory and Persuasive Letter Writing. Washington, D.C.: U.S. Government Printing Office, 1977.

Wilkinson, C. W., Clarke, Peter, and Wilkinson, Dorothy C. *Communicating through Letters and Reports,* 8th ed. Homewood, Ill.: R. D. Irwin, 1983.

UNIT IV: Proposals

Corbett, Edward P. J. *Classical Rhetoric for the Modern Student.* New York: Oxford University Press, 1971.

Holtz, Herman, and Schmidt, Terry. *The Winning Proposal*. New York: McGraw-Hill, 1981.

Jordan, Stello, ed. *Handbook of Technical Writing Practices*. New York: Wiley-Interscience, 1971.

Smith, Craig, and Skjei, Eric W. *Getting Grants*. New York: Harper Colophon Books, 1981.

UNIT V: Reports

Houp, Kenneth W., and Pearsall, Thomas E. *Reporting Technical Information*, 5th ed. Encino, Calif.: Glencoe Publishing, 1984.

Lesikar, Raymond. *Business Communication: Theory and Application*, 4th ed. Homewood, Ill.: Richard D. Irwin, 1980.

Mathes, J. C., and Stevenson, Dwight W. *Designing Technical Reports*. Indianapolis, Ind.: Bobbs-Merrill, 1976.

Murphy, Herta, and Hildebrandt, Herbert. *Effective Business Communications*, 4th ed. New York: McGraw-Hill, 1984.

UNIT VI: Other Formats

Document Drafting Handbook. Washington, D.C.: Office of the Federal Register, 1980.

Editor and Publisher International Yearbook. New York: Editor and Publisher, annual.

Standard Periodical Directory. New York: Oxbridge Communications, biennial.

Ulrich's International Periodicals Directory. New York: R. R. Bowker, annual.

Webb, Kenneth, and Hatry, Harry P. *Obtaining Citizen Feedback: The Application of Citizen Surveys to Local Governments*. Washington, D.C.: Urban Institute, 1973.

Wilhoit, G. Cleveland, and Weaver, David H. *Newsroom Guide to Polls and Surveys*. Washington, D.C.: American Newspaper Publishers Association.

Part III: The Writer's Self-Help

UNITS VII and VIII

Dictionaries and Word Lists

American Heritage Dictionary, 2nd ed. Boston: Houghton Mifflin, 1982.

Louis, A. Leslie. *20,000 Words,* 7th ed. New York: McGraw-Hill, 1977.

The Random House College Dictonary, rev. ed. New York: Random House, 1980.

Webster's Instant Word Guide. Springfield, Mass.: Merriam-Webster, 1980.

Webster's Legal Speller. Springfield, Mass.: Merriam-Webster, 1978.

Webster's Medical Speller. Springfield, Mass.: Merriam-Webster, 1975.

Webster's Ninth New Collegiate Dictionary. Springfield, Mass.: Merriam-Webster, 1983.

Webster's New World Speller-Divider Book, rev. ed. New York: Collins, 1971.

Style and Usage Guides

Bernstein, Theodore. *The Careful Writer: A Modern Guide to English Usage.* New York: Atheneum, 1965.

Bryant, Margaret M. *Current American Usage: How Americans Say It and Write It.* New York: Funk and Wagnalls, 1962.

The Chicago Manual of Style, 13th ed. Chicago: The University of Chicago Press, 1982.

Ebbit, Wilma R., and Ebbit, David R. *Writer's Guide and Index to English,* 7th ed. Glenview, Ill.: Scott, Foresman, 1982.

Ewing, David W. *Writing for Results in Business, Government, the Sciences, and the Professions.* New York: John Wiley & Sons, 1979.

Fowler, H. W. *A Dictionary of Modern English Usage,* 2nd ed. New York: Oxford University Press, 1965.

Hodges, John C., and Whitten, Mary. *Harbrace College Handbook,* 9th ed. New York: Harcourt Brace Jovanovich, 1982.

Lanham, Richard. *Revising Business Prose.* New York: Charles Scribner's Sons, 1981.

Miller, Casey, and Swift, Kate. *The Handbook of Nonsexist Writing: For Writers, Editors, and Speakers.* New York: Barnes and Noble, 1980.

Montgomery, Michael, and Stratton, John. *The Writer's Hotline Handbook.* New York: New American Library, 1981.

Nicholson, Margaret. *A Practical Guide for Authors and Editors.* New York: Holt, Rinehart and Winston, 1965.

O'Hayre, John. *Gobbledygook Has Gotta Go*. Washington, D.C.: U.S. Department of the Interior, Bureau of Land Management, 1966.

Strunk, William, and White, E. B. *The Elements of Style,* 3rd ed. New York: Macmillan, 1979.

Style Manual, rev. ed. Washington, D.C.: U.S. Government Printing Office, 1973.

Summey, George. *American Punctuation*. New York: Ronald Press, 1949.

Turabian, Kate L. *A Manual for Writers of Term Papers, Theses, and Dissertations,* 4th ed. Chicago: Chicago University Press, 1973.

Walpole, Jane. *A Writer's Guide: Easy Ground Rules for Successful Written English*. Englewood Cliffs, N.J.: Prentice-Hall, 1980.

Webster's Secretarial Handbook. Springfield, Mass.: Merriam-Webster, 1976.

Williams, Joseph. *Style: Ten Lessons in Clarity and Grace*. Glenview, Ill.: Scott, Foresman, 1981.

Miscellaneous
Smith, Peggy. *Simplified Proofreading*. Arlington, Va.: National Composition Association, 1980.

Index